Networks Rising

Thinking Together in a Connected World

Christopher Burns

Networks Rising
Thinking Together in a
Connected World

GAUDIUM

Gaudium Publishing

Las Vegas ◊ Chicago ◊ Palm Beach

Published in the United States of America by
Histria Books, a division of Histria LLC
7181 N. Hualapai Way, Ste. 130-86
Las Vegas, NV 89166 U.S.A.
HistriaBooks.com

Gaudium Publishing is an imprint of Histria Books. Titles published under the imprints of Histria Books are distributed worldwide.

Library of Congress Control Number: 2022937059

ISBN 978-1-59211-165-7 (hardcover)
ISBN 978-1-59211-216-6 (eBook)

Contents

Chapter 1
Discovering Fire

For the second time in human history, we are on the verge of a great leap forward in health, personal freedom, and productivity, and networks are the reason. Not because the technology is amazing — which it is — but because the networks are changing organizations based on layers of power, replacing them with flatter communities based on collective intelligence and an open exchange of real-time experience. We are talking directly to each other in a connected world.

Twenty-five thousand years ago cavemen suddenly began living longer, healthier, and more productive lives. With the help of a new generation of elders, families learned to see themselves as part of a larger community. They began to raise food together, hunt in packs, and trust each other in good times and bad. After two million years of failed variations, Homo sapiens became the new model of modern man. Today, networks are similarly connecting us in larger, flatter information collectives, and research now suggests that those are smarter, more competitive, and more articulate than the old hierarchical models.

Networks are shifting power from a bureaucracy of the few to a noisy community of the many. Mandates and executive decisions are out; committees, marches, swarms, strikes, and insurrections are in, and authority is the weakest form of authority. Groups are bringing more diverse resources to the task, keeping in mind more aspects of the problem, and better engaging the imagination, loyalty, and enthusiasm of the participants. And they are making better decisions than individuals. Everyone knows what anyone knows, flash mobs storm the town square, and new ways to live and work together are rising all around us.

Networks are also changing the nature of the information we share. On social media, forums, blogs, and guerrilla television, we are sending and receiving faster, more accurate, and more emotional messages. We are no longer preserving scientific and religious "truth" on illuminated pages, treasured for a thousand years. We are no longer exchanging chunks of established, authoritative "knowledge," footnoted to the printed text. We are much more likely to be sharing experiences in real time. We are starting to think together. But without moderators to fact check and authenticate the dialogue, these new channels get polluted with false information and propaganda. Participants are manipulated and private information is exploited. In a freer, more caring, more interesting world, it is harder to tell who we are and where we belong. For some this is a feeling of freedom, for others it is a feeling of being lost.

We are at the beginning of a great transformation.

This idea that a worldwide network might one day lead to a new global consciousness was first suggested a hundred years ago by a young priest serving as a stretcher-bearer on the Western Front, and the language of his notebook entry was indistinguishable from madness:

> From day to day the human mass is... building itself up; it is weaving around the globe a network of organizations, of communication, and of thought... Through us, the earth is engaged in adding to its lithosphere, its atmosphere, its biosphere, and its other layers one more envelope — the last and most remarkable of all. This is the thinking zone, the 'Noösphere.' Is the world not in the process of becoming more vast, more close, more dazzling than Jehovah? Will it not burst our religion asunder, and eclipse our God?[1] — *Pierre Teilhard de Chardin, The Phenomenon of Man (written in 1915 and published after his death in 1955)*

Pierre Teilhard de Chardin [1881-1955]

August 1915: The Bosche artillery had started booming again as it did every night, sending shells whistling toward Allied positions that zigzagged from Dunkirk on the English Channel south into the Belgian countryside. Night after night, the men of the 8th Moroccan Regiment climbed out of the muddy trenches and threw their bodies against the wire, dying in the crossfire of the new German machine guns massed against them in the fog. Then, with the enemy on three sides, firing down on them from an elevated position, they saw a green cloud of chlorine gas rolling slowly toward them across the killing field.

Later, in the pre-dawn silence, a young man stepped around the blackened bodies of the dead waiting to be trucked back to the rear, names pinned to their crusty tunics, the watery, rose-red mix of heaved-up blood and spittle still drying around the mouth and nose. He was a French Jesuit priest serving as a stretcher-bearer, a scientist by training, and a mystic at heart, known to the Muslim soldiers of his regiment as *Sidi Marabout*, the holy man, the magician who held them in their agony and whispered them down into death. And he was strange. After a battle, it was his habit to sit alone in the low wind and the stink of blood and gunpowder, writing in his journal thoughts so heretical that the Church forbade their publication during his lifetime.

Pierre Teilhard de Chardin was not thinking about a worldwide network. He was thinking about a worldwide consciousness. He imagined that if we could share our thoughts and prayers with each other we might understand each other better, dream together, and together be capable of ideas that could change the future of our species.

Teilhard was the son of a scientist father and a deeply religious mother, and he spent his life trying to resolve the conflict between those two worlds. A Jesuit trained in paleontology, he was moved by the experience of war to think about man's relationship with the eternal and, as all soldiers do, about the deep communion that forms among men at the edge of death.

He had grown up collecting insects and rock samples with his father, and everywhere he looked he saw the beauty of the natural world. He came to believe that evolution must be a testament to some Divine plan, "a consciousness gradually waking by way of countless fumblings." Man's miraculous rise from the primordial swamp, he thought, would continue. Evolution was not just the past, it was also the future, and he set out to see where that might lead.

In the years that followed the war, he rose to become a world expert on the primitive origins of man and, as a religious thinker continuing to write in his journal, he became one of the important philosophical voices of the century. But the Church opposed his ideas on evolution and he was in trouble all his life. In 1923, after repeatedly offending the ultraconservatives in Rome, he was censored, relieved of his teaching post, and sent to China for the next twenty years to study bones.

But he kept on. Again and again, he crossed the boundaries set by the Church until he was finally forbidden to teach or publish anything, settling into obedient silence. But supported and encouraged by close friends and colleagues, he continued secretly to develop the great idea of his life:

Man is evolving toward a new state of being in which we will all share our lives through love and become superhumans, joined in a single worldwide network he called the noösphere, "stretched like a film over the lustrous surface of the star which holds us."[2]

He saw that the network might enable men to one day share not only their knowledge but their thoughts, exchanging their opinions, their questions, and the selfless fragments of experience that lead to science. Later, living in exile at the edge of the Gobi Desert and corresponding with his old friends through letters, notes, and unpublished essays, Teilhard imagined that someday we would all be able to commune with each other around the world in the same way — beyond the physical limitations of our fragile selves, with love and respect, mind to mind. And he thought the glow of knowledge and fellowship would someday rise around the world, a divine aura that embraced each in all, all in each.

In 1929, he was part of a small expedition to a cave system near Beijing. There, in the last days of their scheduled work, they found the first of several human skulls which Teilhard was able to date to approximately 700,000 years ago. Homo erectus, or Peking Man as the discovery became known, was clear evidence of man's first direct ancestor, and Teilhard was there at the beginning, a key part of the understanding and reconstruction of man's earliest origins. As much as any scientist of his day, he helped prove Darwin's theory that man had evolved from an earlier ape-like species.

Peking Man's predecessor, Homo habilis, had been a small chimpanzee-like creature living in Africa, able to make and employ stone tools but unable to speak or plan. Then about two million years ago a new species, Homo erectus, rose on two legs and, with an enlarged brain capable of speech, became the first creature to use fire, the first to hunt in groups and care for the weak, the first to leave Africa and migrate across the Eurasian steppes. The evolution of man had not come about through gradual changes in physical capability. It had always advanced with the unheralded emergence of a new model, a few individuals at a time, competing with the old and then driving the old into extinction. And so it was between H. habilis and H. erectus. Habilis co-existed, struggled, and finally failed, and for the next million years, H. erectus was man's most successful ancestor. Then H. erectus, in turn, gave way to the emerging Neanderthals who were stronger, had better eyesight, were able to bring down larger prey, cook their food, and murder each other. Then the Neanderthals gave way to Homo sapiens.

A New Species

The most provocative aspect of Teilhard's vision was his idea that this evolution was not just the past, it was also the future. He thought society was evolving toward a level of worldwide communication that, like the appearance of abstract thinking among the Neanderthals, would redefine the behavior of our society. A network might give birth to a model of man so new it deserved to be thought of as a different species.

This evolution offered Teilhard a way to resolve the conflict between science and religion. He wrote that the process of moving from simple to complex organisms was not random mutation and selection of the fittest, but some kind of internal attraction among the molecules of the world by which men would be drawn instinctively to accept one another in a "joyful unity." As we rise along the evolutionary ladder, he wrote, we will converge. As we communicate across the noösphere, as we see each other truly and accept our differences in science and religious thought, then will human beings evolve again.

Teilhard wrote that man was on the verge of a new species — let's call him Homo colloquium — characterized by shared consciousness and drawn together by a deeper understanding of each other in the same way that atoms are drawn together to create molecules. Homo sapiens had triumphed over the Neanderthals through a capacity for abstract thought, and Teilhard believed that the next species would triumph over ours by employing collective intelligence, sharing information, and caring for each other to the point where communities begin to think and act as one.

The downside of writing alone for twenty years is that you don't get the questions, the criticisms, and the challenges to your thinking that are so helpful in the happy fever of writing them down. Teilhard would have benefitted greatly from that. One idea blurs into another; theories shift across his books making it more difficult for us to know which variation comes closest to expressing his true belief. His irrational optimism and religious zeal twist his line of thinking, making it harder for the non-religious reader to hang on to the core idea. But from this great distance, we can see that he brought our hopes for the human race into a new light.

He was not predicting technology. He was recognizing that the long history of man had taken him beyond tool making, speech, hunting with his friends, and feeding his family. Man was now moving into a world where information had become the primary plane of existence. Discovery, imagination, and understanding each other better were now the essential human activities. In the future, he wrote, we will not only live together, we will think together.

A Mystical Vision

It is perhaps ironic that a man torn from his native country, isolated and silenced by his own church, and destined by his profession to live among the bones of his ancestors in the empty caves and deserts of the world, should give us the boldest vision ever of men living together in such an intimate new community. Ironic that a man so steeped in the dusty past should see so clearly into the future.

In the years between the discovery of Peking Man and the onset of the Second World War, Teilhard traveled, participating in many of the important developments in his field. He went on expeditions in Africa, India, Burma, and Java, toured the United States, and made occasional visits back to France where he spoke about his research to small groups. He was honored as a scientist but held under continued restriction by the Church. None of his new books or essays could be published, and those that had come out before the ruling were now banned from all Catholic libraries and bookstores. When Boston College invited him to accept an honorary degree, he arrived to find the Church had ordered the Jesuit school to rescind the honor. And as the Second World War broke out across Europe, he returned to China at the age of 60, to his little lab, and to his writing.

In 1950, Teilhard de Chardin was named to the French Academy of Science, the highest accolade his country could offer, and yet the Church refused to permit him to attend the International Congress of Paleontology, the ultimate gathering of friends and colleagues who had brought love and meaning to his life. In his last years, he moved into the residence of the Jesuit Church of St. Ignatius Loyola in New York, and there he died of a heart attack in 1955 at the age of 74, never knowing whether his thoughts would be shared with others.

Connection: More than anyone, Teilhard gave us a vision of man connected in real time with others around the world, sharing ideas and experiences in a way that would draw us together and make us more powerful as a species. In 1915, when only one in five households in the developed world even had a telephone, he could not have imagined the technology that would make this possible. Nor was the evolution of that network clear to others at any point. As we shall see, it just grew.

Community: Neither could he have foreseen how this network would shift the organization of groups from hierarchies to collectives, from the primitive ziggurats of emperors and warlords and priests where the organization held ultimate power, to a flatter world where individuals were free to share their lives directly with each other, up, down, and everywhere in private. In Teilhard's day, information was passed up the chain of command where it was gathered, selected, adjusted, and then redistributed back down to the people. Decisions followed the information, power followed the decisions, and wealth followed power. But a hundred years later, with information flying out in all directions, all that is up for grabs.

Most of all, he could not have imagined how a worldwide noösphere would change the way individuals think about their own identity, about membership in a tribe, a community, or a nation, and about the balance between individual freedom and social order.

Today's world is being shaped by networks. In the realm of war, non-state actors coordinate their forces online to strike from the shadows anywhere they wish. In the last fifty years the most efficient and destructive armies have not been top-down hierarchies but loosely coordinated coalitions operating in peer-to-peer networks that cannot be decapitated. Without uniforms or flags, without conventional supply lines, and with very low administrative overhead, they slip undetected back and forth across old borders, faster, smarter, and more lethal than the armies of the twentieth century still marching around in the dust.

More ominously, the events surrounding Russia's invasion of Ukraine in 2022 demonstrate that coordinated non-military attacks by a network of banks, governments, airlines, energy companies, technology suppliers, and even sports teams can now isolate and destroy the economies of even the largest nations, effectively expelling them from the international community. The first great blow struck against Russia was not to charge across their border or bomb them from the air but to throw them off a network (SWIFT). The age of traditional armies may be drawing to a close.

In the realm of business, global corporations with superior networks have become the new empires, as powerful as any government. They roam the world, dodging the taxes and regulations of unfriendly administrations. The ideas of citizenship and patriotism have been shaken as national borders fade into irrelevance.

Living together in a worldwide network, individuals are now free to join or leave their native group, to raise or topple governments, change the culture, brush religious beliefs aside, form new knowledge communities, and strike out into the world with new languages, new values, and new gods.

Consciousness: But of all the futures Teilhard could imagine, squatting there in the blood and smoke of war, the vision that most captured his imagination was a worldwide network that would bring people of all nations together, sharing information and "spirits." He saw a world connected into a single consciousness, even though he couldn't imagine how it would be done. He thought that when all men had equal access to information there might arise a different, less violent model of society, more like the small collegial world of scientists in which he lived. And he hoped that such a network would allow scientists the freedom to explore new ideas, even those in conflict with the institutions that ruled his life. There might be a new balance of power between social order and freedom of the individual.

After Teilhard had been banished to ecclesiastic oblivion, after his notebooks had been forgotten, after he died unnoticed in a New York retirement home and few if any could even remember what the old Frenchman was talking about, the idea that we might all be connected somehow in a future community of thought seemed to stumble forward in the writings of a few dreamers, each, like Teilhard, imagining a new world. Here is how we can build it. Here are some changes in our social behavior that could work. Here are some rules for thinking together that will help. They listened to each other, they traded ideas across time like old friends, and one by one they appeared among us, pointing the way. And then seventy years ago, in labs in Boston and San Francisco, funded by the Department of Defense of all people, the network Teilhard had been talking about started to wiggle up into view.

Chapter 2
The Network Comes to Life

At the outbreak of World War II, Grace Hopper was too skinny to enlist in the Navy and as a woman of 34, too old. But she appealed the ruling and after being commissioned in 1944, with her youth and marriage behind her, the brilliant young Vassar professor was assigned to a "math" project in Boston. There Howard Aiken was building the Mark I computer, the first sequence-controlled analytical calculator.

Grace Hopper [1906-1992]

The idea for a calculating machine was first proposed in 1642 by the child prodigy and mathematician Blaise Pascal. It was a simple odometer capable of adding numbers together, but the future was clear, he said. "The arithmetical machine produces effects which come closer to thought than anything."[4] In 1826, Charles Babbage and Ada Lovelace designed the first analytical engine, and in 1842 they drew up plans for an even more powerful machine. But the metalworkers of the time could not build such an intricate device, and the idea languished for another hundred years.

In 1939, inspired by Babbage and funded by IBM, then a typewriter company, Howard Aiken, a post-graduate student at Harvard, designed and built the first computer, and when America entered the war in 1941, he and his machine were quickly conscripted into the Navy. It worked, and faced with demands for more and more engineering calculations, Aiken needed someone to set the machine up for each problem it was to solve. But when Hopper joined the team she did far more than that. More than anyone in the history of computing, she and her computer took the first steps toward a man/machine relationship that over the next three decades would become the essential foundation for a worldwide network.

Hopper's skills with language were legendary. In order to finish her Ph.D. at Yale, she taught herself German from a bi-lingual math book, and she could later write on the blackboard in German with her left hand then switch and continue writing with her right hand in French. In her first meeting with Aiken, he pointed to the machine — the first of its kind in existence — and told her to learn how to program it and develop the interpolation coefficients for the arctangent series by next week. She later called her early days with the Mark I "great fun."[5]

As the principal programmer of the new machine, Hopper's job was to break down a given mathematical problem into a series of finite steps, set those functions up in the switches and dials of the computer, and supervise a small team of Navy mathematicians who operated and maintained the complicated mechanism. It could do three things: add two numbers, subtract one number from the other, and determine whether one number was higher or lower than the other. Pick up data from one location, apply one of those three processes, store the result in another location, and go to the next step. Hopper ran the operations, organized the input data, supervised the coders, and directed the operators. In a surviving one-page description of the work breakdown for a typical problem, she described who was to do what and when, ending with the notation: "Computed, designed, coded, babied, nursed, pleaded with, and mothered by LT(jg) Grace Murray Hopper, USNR."[6]

From 1944 to 1949, the work flowing through the Harvard Computation Lab involved most of the advanced technologies of the war, including calculations for guided missiles, radar, experimental aircraft, and a secret project going on in the desert out in Los Alamos, New Mexico. Building a fire control table for a new five-inch gun, for example, took sixty hours of uninterrupted Mark I machine time. Harvard folklore says that the vacuum tubes in early versions of the Mark I created so much heat that while it was running the operators had to keep all the windows open and work in their shorts. It was normal for Hopper and her crew to be on the job for two or three days in a row, catching naps at their desks. Aiken seemed never to leave the building at all except each day, promptly at noon, when he walked a few blocks home to have lunch and two martinis with his mother.

The challenge from the beginning was to find a way for fumble-fingered and impetuous humans who were good at conceptual thinking and semantic expression to communicate with a very precise and complicated machine —

the apotheosis of spinning shafts, electric relays, vacuum tubes, and thousands of dials and switches. But while Hopper's staff struggled to master the functions of the Mark I, Aiken was adding higher and more complex capabilities, tweaking the system and calling for new computing strategies. It was obvious that with the instruction set changing all the time, her staff could never catch up. They could never acquire the kind of deep competence that would be necessary if the full power of the computer was ever to be realized.

As a person who naturally thought in multiple languages, she saw that an intermediate communications method was required, allowing mathematicians to state the task in human terms and specify the calculations using commands that did not change with every technical improvement. Then each successive generation of machines could interpret those commands according to its own new and more powerful capabilities. She called this a "programming language" and over the next few years, she developed Flowmatic, later known as COBOL, the forerunner of all programming languages today.

Hopper's language worked, and programming computers became a crucial part of a suddenly emerging industry. Like a true Navy captain speaking of his ship, Hopper had a habit of referring to the Mark I as "she," and may have been the first to see a glimmer of something spiritual in the machine. In time, she developed ever more powerful and efficient ways to deliver its instructions. With her Navy colleagues and a generation of programmers trained by her, she lifted the massive, stammering, and temperamental apparatus out of its cradle in the basement of the Harvard physics lab and raised it among humans.

Later, ascending slowly through the ranks of the postwar military, this still skinny, no-nonsense woman with blue eyes, thick glasses, and her bobbed hair tucked behind her ears, took charge of all programming for the Navy and led the way for the other services as well. A heavy smoker (Lucky Strikes) and always a heavy drinker (Manhattans), she was an administrator, an inventor, a teacher, and an evangelist, and in 1976 she began to entertain a very different idea about how large-scale computing might be done.

And here was her second and most extraordinary insight: she was naturally averse to authoritarian hierarchies and suspected that if people could talk directly to each other, they might be more productive. Then she applied that insight to machines. As recalled by computer pioneer Russell McGee:

While all of this was going on, we began to hear stories out of the Pentagon about an approach to data processing and computing being fostered by my old acquaintance Grace Hopper. Large computers were going to be replaced by networks of small ones capable of communicating with one another and with common databases that might be hosted on computers of any size. Any user at any node could then communicate with any other user at any other node, provided he or she had the proper clearance and permission to do so.[7]
— *My Adventures with Dwarfs (2003)*

In a world where computers were designed as top-down processors, each step dictated by the actions of a higher entity, her vision was of a broad, egalitarian connection of processors, working together peer-to-peer, and sometimes acting on their own. It was a dream of the world to come. She thought it should be called a "network."

Hopper continued to develop revolutionary programming strategies and techniques, and to set the standards for all the computer languages used by the Department of Defense in the '60s, '70s, and '80s, as one of the most highly respected leaders in a rapidly changing industry. She received the Defense Service Medal, the National Medal of Technology, and many other honors, including having an Arleigh Burke-class guided-missile destroyer named after her, and later a college at Yale. She was not just a pioneer in computer technology, she was a world-class groundbreaker for women in the military, an honor she bore with great humor. "I see that there aren't many women here," she often told her audience, "but I'll go slow, and hopefully you will be able to keep up."[8]

Hopper served in the Navy for a total of thirty-four years. She accepted mandatory retirement at the age of sixty in 1966, was called back to active duty in 1967, was retired again in 1971, was called back again in 1972, and after several special Acts of Congress was finally retired involuntarily in 1985 with the rank of Rear Admiral. She was 79. The retirement ceremony was held on the deck of the *USS Constitution*, the oldest and most precious ship in the Navy, anchored three miles from where the Mark I had first gone operational 40 years before. Admiral Hopper appeared wearing white gloves and carrying her beloved Navy-issue black handbag.

Within a few years, the whole idea of what could be done with computers began to change.

Douglas Engelbart [1925-2013]

A thousand people filed into the main ballroom at the Fall Joint Computer Conference in San Francisco. It was December 1968, and computer systems in those years meant punched-card batch processing and mainly numerical or scientific calculations. A big topic on the program was the potential for time-sharing, allowing multiple users to run programs on the same computer at the same time. Other papers announced new programming languages, better memory technology, and the latest scientific applications. But the title for this session stood out for its sheer otherworldliness and audacity: "A Research Center for Augmenting Human Intellect." On the stage was a neat, middle-aged man in a short-sleeved white shirt and tie, sitting at a table facing a standard video terminal and a strange keyboard. Behind him rose a projection screen twenty-two feet high. In what would later be called "the Mother of All Demos," he nodded awkwardly toward the audience and without introduction began a ninety-minute presentation that changed the computer world.[9]

Doug Engelbart grew up poor in rural Oregon, and while a young Navy radar technician in the Philippines, read Vannevar Bush's 1945 article "As We May Think," which described the Memex, a hypothetical online electromechanical library of all knowledge.[10] Engelbart never forgot it.

Ten years later, he was an electrical engineer at the Stanford Research Institute in California, quietly diverting funds from other government-sponsored projects to bootstrap the development of this Memex idea. He wrote papers about a man/machine interface that would allow multiple users to tell the computer what to do and see the results in real time, and in 1961 he created his own lab to pursue what he called the "Augmentation Framework." He said computer networks could be used to exchange thoughts.

By 1967, Engelbart had accumulated enough Department of Defense funding to put his prototype up on a time-shared computer so others in the lab could access the Augment machine. But pushing the boundaries of human intelligence was a concept too abstract for people to support, and he decided he had to somehow make it real. Sneaking more money out of research and into the prototype, he bet everything on a demo to show the whole computer world what he was trying to do.

It was not at all clear at the time what the role of computer technology should be. Lewis Mumford, a widely respected culture critic, wrote that the computer was a threat to individual freedom. Like science fiction writers and other contemporary pundits, he feared that engineers intended to build a giant brain that would rule the masses. And he was partly right. Corporations were heralding automation as a way to control many traditionally labor-intensive office jobs and procedures, eliminate costly errors, and reduce the need for clerical employees. Computers were the new engines of authority, imposing order and discipline on famously errant and unpredictable humans. Punched cards were appearing everywhere in our lives with the warning: "Do not fold, spindle, or mutilate."

The Augmentation Project

But Engelbart saw a very different future. Beyond Grace Hopper's world of interconnected computers, he thought a more powerful network might enable the users to communicate directly with each other, share ideas, and expand the unique power of human intelligence into new realms. "My colleagues at SRI thought I was crazy," he said later.

> To them, hearing about people using computers to communicate through a network to collaborate was crazy talk. They laughed at me when I talked about word processing. Using computers for writing. Ha! Why would we need that? We have secretaries that do our typing for us.[11]

The idea of "word processing" was radical enough for its time, but Engelbart's demonstration that day went much, much further.

On the giant screen behind him, the audience saw the first graphical user interface. Instead of the usual green text blinking against a black background, here was black text moving around on a paper-white screen along with graphs, drawings, and even live video inserts showing his colleagues back at the lab. In his hand, he had a small block of wood connected to a wire, and when he moved it around on the table a "tracking spot," as he called it, moved around the screen, allowing him to hover over a word or a phrase and click on it to call up related information. He called the block of wood a "mouse."

He could select a word and edit it on the fly. He could type in messages and send them over a temporary microwave link back to his fellow researchers thirty miles away. He could click on an item and call up a new document linked to that item. As the audience watched, he searched for a memo in an online library of materials, edited it on the screen, and then saved the new version back in the library for later retrieval. He called up a video panel on the screen, side by side with the text, showing a colleague back at the lab as they chatted back and forth. None of this had ever been seen before.

The demo was made even more exciting by the addition of sound. Stewart Brand was then creating *The Whole Earth Catalog*, a hip compendium of new technology tools and resources that would become the bible of the computer revolution for the next decade. But Brand had taken time out to help his friend Engelbart jazz up the demo with the sound of keys tapping, motors whirring, and engineers breathing and muttering as they clicked and glided through each task. Of course, everything on the screen was being driven remotely by a dedicated mainframe computer back in the Stanford lab, and the ability to mix video and graphics was accomplished with established television techniques, not computer processing as we know it now. But Engelbart's vision, so magically presented, sent the imagination of a generation leaping ahead into the future.

When he was finished, the crowd rose in a standing ovation. Friends and fellow researchers rushed to the stage. The press hurried back to their typewriters and telephones, and for the rest of the conference, people talked of little else. One reporter said Engelbart was "dealing lightning with both hands." Another called it the "Fantastic World of Tomorrow's Computer." This was a world in which man was technology's master, not its servant, augmenting his intelligence with online access to an information library and collaborating in real time with colleagues miles away. It was a world of intellectual creativity and freedom, a world of people working in parallel with machines, thinking together.

Department of Defense grants were increased, military and corporate customers trooped to Palo Alto to see how this new magic could be put to a profitable purpose, but Engelbart started to have problems keeping his young team focused. At the time, Stanford University was a magnet for a generation of bright and ambitious computer engineers, and Engelbart's lab was a conspicuously crazy gathering place. Technicians, staffers, and barefoot hippies, including high school students Steve Jobs and Stephen Wozniak, were drifting unchecked in and out of the building day and night, camping out in the corridors, trying to catch available machine time. Hackers were smoking pot, sleeping under their desks, and naming their programs and projects after characters and places in Tolkien's *Lord of the Rings* saga. The Grateful Dead were the hometown band, and encounter groups, anti-war demonstrations, and LSD parties were regular weekend fare. Haight Ashbury, the capital of America's drug culture, was only thirty miles away in San Francisco, an hour up the coast by bus.[12]

If the information revolution had begun in any other American city, the outcome might have been different. But San Francisco was, down to the bone, a city settled by risk-taking individuals who had tossed convention aside in their hunt for gold, by immigrants from Chile, China, and elsewhere who were coming out to the new frontier and betting everything they had on their ability to innovate and survive. If there was ever an American city that valued individual freedom over social order, this was it. And in this soil the new network technology took root.

While his corporate and government sponsors wanted more powerful computers to automate our lives, the young people building the technology were going in the opposite direction, seeking more personal freedom and less social integration. Their goal was to discover and promote the greatest fulfillment of the individual, not the community. According to John Markoff, whose book *What the Dormouse Said* chronicled Engelbart and his times, personal empowerment, not community solidarity, became the central theme of the information technology revolution from the '60s on.

Engelbart's father-knows-best, white-shirt-and-tie world was in danger of disintegrating into an undisciplined techno free-for-all, a bootstrap project simultaneously giving birth to a hundred more bootstrap projects. It wasn't clear who was in charge, or what the program goals really were, and Engelbart began to worry. With his whole program at stake, he sent the team off to a commune in the mountains north of Taos, New Mexico, but he — older than the others, a loner, shy, fiercely committed to his own vision — stayed home. Without a leader, the problems with the organization metastasized.

When Xerox started the Palo Alto Research Center (PARC), an office automation lab a few miles away, Engelbart's key people began to trickle out, and in 1971 the company offered to take over Engelbart's Augment project with him as chief scientist, bringing it into the corporate fold. But Engelbart declined, unwilling to give up any control. He reorganized his project again, seeking still more ambitious ways to liberate the human intellect. He sank deeper into the human potential counterculture, became more committed to the movement, and imagined that his new network technology would change the world, one lab at a time. But a shiny new future was beckoning to his staff, and the great migration of people and money began.

In 1974, the Department of Defense cut off Engelbart's funding and he went back to Xerox, hoping to rekindle their interest in his lab. But by then they had all his best people, his innovative technology, and his ideas. He had nothing left to offer.

I visited PARC myself in the late seventies. As an information technology consultant, I was asked by Xerox to look at several of their office automation projects and offer a critique. In Dallas, a research team had assembled an electric typewriter with interchangeable fonts, a four-line display screen, and an eight-inch floppy disc where text could be stored. They thought it would be a competitive replacement for the then ubiquitous IBM Selectric typewriter.

At a skunkworks out near the Los Angeles airport, another team was struggling to improve the resolution of a small CRT display, hoping that they might soon be able to present proportional black type fonts against a white background. Elsewhere in a low-ceilinged conference room, a small group of engineers explained their idea for a cable connecting computers together with enough capacity to handle the transmission of document images. Ethernet, as they called it, could already send pages to laser printers stationed on each floor of the office, although it was impractical to consider sending the pages to a printer across the street. They wanted to know if such a network had the potential to become standard office technology.

At PARC I saw the Alto system, which then consisted of one or two graphical displays showing black monospaced text and images against a white background. The researchers had made major improvements on Engelbart's mouse, and the cursor now moved quickly and dependably across the digital page. A user could compose the document on the screen, edit it, and send it to a printer nearby. But further progress was blocked by the lack of computer power. Even the small Alto screen required a computer capable of refreshing 100,000 pixels fifteen times a second. (The current laptop displays more than a million pixels, refreshed 60 times a second.) Any increase in screen size or resolution was beyond the speed and processing power of the computers available to them. They could imagine maps, full-screen images, and even color, but the technology was not there, and a device like Alto for every office worker seemed out of the question.

IBM's Hursley Lab in England was by then privately demonstrating a computer prototype that could "sit on the desk." In the mid-seventies, they asked several technology consultants to suggest possible uses for such an extraordinary machine, and I am chagrined to report that as far as office applications were concerned, the best we could come up with was standard word processing functionality. We could not imagine a future of email, text messaging, spreadsheets, database access, music, interactive video, color graphics, slide presentations, and video conferencing. But of course, IBM could not imagine them either.

Few people at Xerox or IBM could foresee how these new tools would make much of a difference. Xerox saw itself as a document company. They thought office automation was about new devices for the traditional workplace, designed to speed up the preparation and exchange of paper so management could reduce unnecessary clerical labor. Engelbart's idea that technology might augment human intelligence and allow people to share ideas in real time had no attraction for the corporate world. They just didn't get it.

At the same time, the Homebrew Computer Club was meeting monthly in rooms they could schedule around Stanford, swapping hardware, software, and designs. After work, the Xerox PARC people were all having beers with the Stanford lab people and trading ideas, but Xerox management saw no future in "little computers," one to a worker. Good for games, maybe. After a while, the company walked away and left the opportunity to others.

Ten years later, the personal computer revolution was firmly established in both businesses and the home, launched by many of the people who grew up in Engelbart's lab. It was now clear that the power of computer technology would expand steadily into the future, and people like Alan Kay, who had moved from the Augmentation lab to Xerox PARC, confidently predicted the day when even young people would have their own computers to play games, listen to music, draw, write, and learn.

By then the Augmentation technology was owned by Tymeshare and MacDonald Douglas, and while they found Engelbart's ideas interesting, they declined to fund him any further. In 1986 at the age of sixty-one, he retired and started his own research institute, loosely affiliated with Stanford. Federal funds trickled in, but he was one old man trying to keep up with the dazzling whirligig of computer technology he had done so much to set in motion.

The Unfinished Revolution

On January 14, 2000, Engelbart, then seventy-five, was invited back to Stanford to give a lecture he called "The Unfinished Revolution." Jacques Vallée, a fellow researcher and longtime friend, wrote that there were forty-five people in the room.[13]

Engelbart thought, as Grace Hopper did, that databases attached to large computers could become the great repositories of scientific knowledge, and he had designed an index system that would help people navigate such a world. Some of this had already been done by others, and what had not been done was dismissed as blue-sky. He said that technology could boost mankind's collective capability for coping with complex problems, but then he observed, perversely, that networks cannot force agreement. They sometimes have the opposite effect, allowing people to challenge authority with raucous impunity.

He thought the technology would provoke people to restructure their information communities, allowing them to escape the constraints of traditional organizations and achieve a new openness where anyone could speak up, even if what the person said was wrong. Life on the network would be like a big encounter group, he thought, noisy, turbulent, and frank. He did not expect the smooth evolution toward consensus and rational problem solving that other futurists were promising. On the contrary, he thought there would be a much more disruptive shift toward anarchy and peer-to-peer debate with millions of voices bordering on chaos. But he thought such freedom might lead to an increase in the "collective IQ."

His next comment was the most interesting one, and it went right over the heads of his audience. He said that in this worldwide Memex of ever-changing knowledge, the way we find information was going to change.

In the early days of large information databases, Ted Nelson and others proposed that items be "hyperlinked" to related material so the user could follow an article to a biography of its author, to other articles by that author, to the source of data used in the article, and so on. These links were created when the document was entered into the knowledge base, and every item was linked to every other relevant item until all knowledge was deeply "intertwingled," as Nelson put it. But the problems were obvious. As the database grew, the latest documents to be added — the most valuable of all — would be the slowest to get linked. Older links would get out of date. A document might be moved to another file and the link would no longer work. The importance of index terms and relationships would change over time as new research and insights appeared. In 1993, the upstart World Wide Web was being indexed by hand. When this became impossible, an effort was made to automatically index documents by simple attributes like author, date, and title, but even this was hard.

Then serious search engines emerged. Programs scoured all known documents on the web and tried to capture the keywords into a general index. Later all the words in the document were indexed, allowing a search command to find a document based on the appearance of words, word strings, or words within a distance of other words. The old hand-made hyperlinks were abandoned. The sovereignty of an index disappeared forever, and now the user could search the world's content in real time for a document based on the words it contained, often getting millions of hits.

But Engelbart was talking about a still more powerful way to navigate knowledge. He understood that words are merely proxies for the idea the document presents, and he thought we should use artificial intelligence to "structure" knowledge, parsing its attributes and meanings so we could search even more deeply.

He thought that each sentence could be analyzed to reveal the verb, the object of the verb, the attributes of the event, and a record of previous associations between this document and others. The time of the event being described could be inferred and tagged, as well as the implied certainty of the verb: it happened, it might have happened, it will happen, it is in dispute. The location of the event, the time the event took place, and the source of the report would all be automatically detected and coded, along with other information about the event, including source, reputation, and places or personalities involved.

Each part of an argument can be coded with its own symbol to help the reader determine fact from opinion, research, analysis, etc. New symbols may be created to define parts of an argument such as research, premises, findings, opinions, hypotheses, or other categories.

Pointers would link the searcher to other documents that have questioned these results or made this version obsolete, all being updated all the time.

What if groups of people could access their collective knowledge quickly when faced with a decision, sorting through all other "noise," and keying in on the most relevant information? It would vastly improve our ability to deal with complex, urgent problems — to get the best possible understanding of the situation, including the best possible solutions.

He imagined that sensors on the body might pick up non-verbal signals, allowing us to communicate with gestures as well as words, with a twitch or a flick of the eyeball — the kind of expression that is visible face to face, but not in a digital channel. Handwriting and speech recognition would be too slow, he said, too limited to control the power of a machine. But in a less hierarchical organization, with people slipping in and out of roles, gesturing to each other beyond language, we could break through to a new level of knowledge. He said technology was being held back by our limitations as humans.

And whenever he described this idea, then and in other speeches, he would move his arms as if swimming or flying. He thought we could communicate our search request with gestures, less like this, more like that, flying through color-coded three-dimensional infospace by flapping our hands and pushing irrelevant data out of the way. We would be freed from the boundaries of clumsy wording and the static, two-dimensional plane of the printed page.

And then he would sigh and smile, fully aware that no one in the room understood what he was talking about.[14]

In 2007 Doug Engelbart was diagnosed with Alzheimer's and he died in 2013 at the age of 88. He often said that according to the Whorfian hypothesis the thoughts we can think are restricted by the vocabulary available to us. But with a greater technical and emotional vocabulary we might think greater thoughts.

Alan Kay, who later became an Apple evangelist for the personal computer, said

> Doug was like a biblical prophet... His talks were not for information, but to show a promised land that needed to be found and the seas and rivers we needed to cross to get there... He always had a powerful physical presence, and his demos with the projector reminded me of Moses, as played by Charlton Heston, parting the Red Sea in '*The Ten Commandments.*'[15]

Chapter 3
The Deep Network

Bob Kahn, one of the inventors of the internet, told me once that in the very early days of the network he kept a list of all the subscribers on an index card in his shirt pocket, and if he wanted to send a message he would take the card out and look up the network address. Today there are 4.5 billion users around the world, and any one of them can connect to any others on web in about three seconds. This changes how we think of knowledge, how we organize for work, and how we live together beyond the traditional boundaries of geography and kinship.

In 1966, the first commercial computer in general use filled a room. IBM had sold about 5,000 of these by then and had 20,000 more on order. The Model 360 central processor alone cost almost a million dollars, about $8 million in today's economy. For that, you got a machine that could store about sixteen thousand characters in memory (16 Kbytes), could access another ten million characters (10 Mbytes) on a removable disk pack the size of a small washing machine, and was sequestered behind glass in a large, air-conditioned room with raised flooring, separate power, and several full-time operators. Fifty years later a high-end laptop costs about $1,500, offers a trillion bytes of storage, runs all day on a single rechargeable battery, and can be operated with two fingers.

Today, for less than $100, you can buy a processor or neural stick like the Raspberry PI, the size of a stick of gum, able to be squeezed into any household object. With four billion bytes of memory, a USB port, Bluetooth, and Wi-Fi capability, it can drive a display screen, support a mouse, control security cameras, drones, and robots, and manage industrial-strength process control devices.[16] These are still in the hands of hobbyists, but they already show how much processing power is moving into the smallest corners of the network.

In 2030, if the price/performance of computers continues to improve at the current rate, forecasters tell us a machine with the functionality of today's laptop will be about the size of a silver dollar, cost as much to manufacture, and run on sunlight. More specialized computers will be the size of a shirt button or a gelcap. And beyond that, the continued advance of nanotechnology means that in a few more years we can have processors the width of a human hair. From research reports and patent filings by Sony, Samsung, Google, and several startup companies we can see the development of smart contact lenses ten to fifteen years from now that might take a snapshot or transmit a video of what you are seeing, focus more closely on a small object, help you see in the dark, or display the prompts, alerts, and reports we now expect from our smart watches.[17] [18]

And these processors will be fast. Grace Hopper's Mark I computer took 3.3 seconds to complete a typical multiplication function. The new "Exascale" computers expected to come on line in a few years will be capable of five billion such calculations in the same 3.3 seconds, and they will be connected over a network 500 times faster than the one we use today.[19] Facebook, now known as Meta, has announced the development of an even larger computer intended for natural language analysis and boasting five billion billion operations per second.[20] At that speed, the computer can crack any twelve-character alphanumeric password in a second.

But none of this matters anymore. Computers as Grace Hopper understood them will have disappeared in ten years, becoming mere synapses in a vast new humming, blinking network of humans and machines thinking autonomously, closer to Teilhard's vision than her own. Any who wish can have a supercomputer at their fingertips as long as there is a good access device, a fast data link to the network, applications to bring this new power to bear on our daily lives, and membership in a community that provides data and computing services. Most personal and business data will be kept in the network, not on our own machines, and the only thing we will need to manage is our identity.

Talking Among Themselves

Our forecasts of technology and applications understandably tend to emphasize activities that involve people, but the greatest impact of new technology by far will come from a non-people development: a deep network of machines, following their own instructions, and talking directly to each other. These devices, operating in a network of their own, will make decisions with little or no human intervention, following algorithms and rules which in turn reflect the values of the application's original creators. Hidden goals like profit, data harvesting, channels of preferential transfer, cross-promotion of related products and services, and political propaganda are already a part of today's network of sponsored applications and media, and will certainly grow in scope and ambition.

Some of these sensors will be in our clothes and the furniture we use every day. Jackets, tattoos, makeup, stickers, and other objects in daily use will incorporate sensors. Wristwatches will track our vital signs, detecting signs of a fever, an irregular pulse, or the level of glucose in the blood.[21] Pills we swallow at night will measure metabolism and radio the results to our watch or phone. Mattresses will monitor our sleep, adjust to our position, and report the data to a health monitoring service.[22] Google and Levi have developed "interactive denim," weaving conductive threads into the material and turning sleeves into touch-sensitive panels for controlling electronic devices.[23] Some processors will be incorporated into the dolls our children play with.[24]

New specialized sensors will monitor health, household security, and any deviation from normal daily patterns. Sensors around the house will be on the lookout for temperature changes and water flows above or below the normal range. Sensors in the cupboard will watch for everyday supplies running low, and remind us to take our medications. Communicating processors attached to the animal's ear will allow the farmer to track and manage the herd.[25]

And these aren't your normal temperature and motion detectors. Thanks to leading-edge science, they can measure changes in time to the trillionth of a second, and measure mass to such an extent that these systems can tell the difference between gravity's pull in the cellar of the house and gravity's pull in the attic. (Time speeds up the higher you go from sea level.)[26] They can predict a volcano by measuring shifts in mass a mile below the surface of the earth. They can identify all the cars traveling at high speed down a four-lane highway.

Some sensors will be attached to the offspring of migrating herds, even small birds and insects. Other sensors will be robots disguised as birds, butterflies, roaches, and small animals, watching, listening, and reporting on activities within their prescribed view. They can be mass manufactured and deployed individually or in swarms to visually record movement, sense body heat, recognize faces in a crowd, and report the results not to humans but to other systems whose management and purpose may not be apparent to the user.

A team of researchers in conjunction with the US Air Force Office of Scientific Research is developing what they are calling a micro aerial vehicle (MAV) that will undertake various espionage tasks. The robotic insect can effortlessly infiltrate urban areas while being controlled from a long distance, and it is equipped with a camera and a built-in microphone.[27] — *Robotics Tomorrow (2017)*

Zeynep Temel at Carnegie Mellon University has developed a variety of "bug robots," as she calls them, that swarm and communicate together like ants or bees — no hierarchies here — to survey dangerous situations where even normal-sized robots might be in jeopardy.[28]

Most of this data will be processed by very high-performance supercomputers in windowless bunkers located near rushing rivers, deep in the desert surrounded by solar panels, or wherever cheap electric power can be found.[29] This is where the sensors will send their data; this is where all the world's little daily decisions will be made.

Supercomputers there will do parallel processing faster than the speed of thought, and be able to instantly compare an individual observation to millions of other individual and household records being updated all the time, looking particularly at similarities among demographic groups, communities, and lifestyles. Then the data center will send information, recommendations, and adjustments back to the user's device or appliance, often without involving the user at all. Have your processor call my processor.

In 2017 there were twenty-seven billion intelligent devices already online, and experts expect this to rise in ten years to 125 billion, or about fifty intelligent devices for every household on the planet,[30] separately identified and addressable, updating each other all the time, reporting observations, and receiving adjustments or instruction. They will be in the yard, on the street, in elevators, cars, trains, and planes, at home and work, day and night, detecting toxins in the environment, tracking storm movements across the planet, following every shopper around the supermarket, and measuring the humidity in the back yard.

All this data will travel over a vastly expanded worldwide network. The current thinking is that an intricate mantilla of high-altitude balloons or low-orbiting cross-linked satellites will form a mesh network that can be accessed from a portable modem at any point on the globe, able to pass data from origin to destination without transiting a ground station. Among other benefits, this will further reduce the power of any local government to monitor and control the information its people can access. About 3,000 such satellites now ring the planet, some the size of a shoebox. In ten years, that number is expected to rise to 100,000.[31] Contact with the nearest overhead node will connect you to any other node in the world, and thereby down to any user or device. Cell towers will disappear and Wi-Fi as we know it will give way to interlocking regional networks, wrapping around the globe.[32]

Social Technology

Things have begun to think. A network of innocent devices will soon be watching, listening, examining our choices, and telling our personal systems how to respond. Devices will be prompted to send and receive data from nearby devices on command. Let's exchange contact information, compare calendars, or swap photos and music? Bump. Pay a bill, check into a hotel, or pass through a security screen? Bump. Wave your phone and all your information is transferred.

At another level, devices will exchange information because they have come within the "exchange aura" of other devices, without the user's permission, and sometimes without the user's knowledge. Devices set to "disclose" will broadcast your identity and other required information to all devices within listening range as you move through the company's office, through a public building, or on planes, trains, and subways.

Perhaps the most common and most valuable information exchanges will come as a byproduct of normal device-assisted transactions. Personal preferences will be mined and recorded by the message systems we use, the forums we visit, the e-commerce systems we buy from, and the whole world of devices we come in contact with every day. Banks and insurance companies will watch our activities on the lookout for behavior that might alter their expected risk. Health information services will monitor our daily routine and alert us to troubling trends. All without interrupting us with questions or even telling us what they are working on.

Thus, over time we will each leave a personal trail of likes and dislikes, as well as patterns of behavior that can be used by others to predict and even control our future actions. In the process of living this bionic, device-assisted life, we will be creating a new layer of knowledge, sharing the minutiae of our lives like bees leaving pheromone trails back from a fruitful source of pollen. As intelligent devices track and communicate our actions and decisions, we will unwittingly become the data field hands, organizing previously unpredictable behavior into useful patterns. The emerging network draws us all into a kind of reverse entropy as, through the random business of daily life, we create new knowledge of value to others. In ways we cannot see or manage, life becomes naturally more organized, more predictable, and more controlled.

Spoiler Alert: It is popular to think that the burgeoning technology we call "Artificial Intelligence" will manifest itself as machines that speak and understand our language. But this is hubris. The deeper and more pervasive manifestation of AI is likely to be algorithms embedded in the routines of everyday living, talking to each other at high speed in a language all their own, just getting stuff done. We will be on the periphery, trying to understand. And if the devices do choose to talk to us at all, it is likely to be in a curt, condescending tone.

Surveillance

Since 2018, when Amazon bought Ring, the video doorbell company, it has begun sharing those videos with over 1,800 local law enforcement agencies who can now access the largest corporate-owned, civilian-installed neighborhood surveillance network in the country, without a warrant, and without the owner's awareness or permission. Millions of doorbell cameras are now installed.[33]

Bluetooth beacons are now being installed in large stores to track the movement of customers' cell phones as they move up and down the aisle. Able to follow movements precisely up to 150 feet, these sensors send the traffic data to subscribing stores and suppliers in order to better understand and influence the decisions shoppers make. Combined with other information available from the shopper's phone and elsewhere, companies can develop a useful profile of the individual without the shopper's awareness or permission.[34]

The NSO Group, a software company backed by the Israeli government, now sells its Pegasus software to companies and governments who wish to spy on the activities of its friends and rivals. Once installed on the smart phone, the app can read anything the user can see, steal photos, locations, passwords, and social media posts, as well as activate cameras and microphones for real-time surveillance. The consortium of news organizations that broke this story reports that 50,000 phones are known to have been infected, including those of reporters, heads of state, senior business executives, politicians, members of the Saudi royal family, officials of the US State Department, and six leaders of the Palestinian human rights organization.[35] NSO claims it gathers no information itself, so it is innocent of any breach of privacy.[36] In late 2021, the company was blacklisted by the US government, saying it knowingly supplied spyware that has been used by foreign governments to "maliciously target" the phones of dissidents, human rights activists, journalists, and others.[37]

Less powerful versions of "stalkerware," as it is called, are now available as apps for most smart phones. Like their more powerful cousins, there are dozens of programs now on the market, used mostly by families tracing the travels of demented grandpas, or couples concerned about each other's activities. They track locations, collect data about phone calls and messages, and in the most extreme cases, turn on the camera and microphone of the person being tracked.[38]

Innocent travel around the neighborhood can be tracked and used by police to round up suspects. In 2019, Zachary McCoy, 30, was notified by Google that they had captured his bike trips from an exercise app he was using, placing him in the vicinity of an unsolved robbery. The police had come to the company with a "geofence warrant" for all location data it had from users who were in the neighborhood at the time, and the company was about to disclose McCoy's identity. Young, white, and computer literate, McCoy appealed to the court, and after ten months of legal wrangling succeeded in protecting his privacy.

Will we become resistant to this constant surveillance? Hal Varian, chief economist at Google thinks not:

> These digital assistants will be so useful that everyone will want one... Everyone will expect to be tracked and monitored, since the advantages in terms of convenience, safety, and services, will be so great. Continuous monitoring will be the norm.[40]

In the process, we are creating a new class of economic players, infomediaries who exist entirely to gather information about our behavior, integrate it with demographic and psychographic data, and sell the profiles to advertisers, vendors, political entities, and others who wish to predict and control the choices we make. Like financial service companies that profit from detailed information about the market activity they facilitate, infomediaries are in the business of what Shoshana Zuboff calls "surveillance capitalism."

And we don't always know our behavior patterns are being harvested. In her comprehensive study of this information-gathering activity,[41] Zuboff cites an analysis of sixty-five diabetes apps that offer to help users keep track of their blood sugar levels, but which also upload personal information and sell it to others without the user's knowledge. More than half of the smartphone apps tested capture the user's identity, 27 percent track the user's location, 12 percent record the user's wi-fi information, 11 percent access the user's photo and video files, and 4-6 percent upload the user's contact list. 86 percent place tracking cookies on the user's system so subsequent internet activity can be recorded, and 76 percent of the apps shared the information they gathered with third parties. None of them inform the user of this activity.[42]

Forbrukerrådet, the consumer protection organization in Norway, studied the degree to which Facebook, Google, and Microsoft use default settings, dark patterns, misleading instructions, take-it-or-leave-it choices, and interface design to get users to disclose personal behavior.

> The privacy settings from Facebook, Google, and Windows 10 provide users with granular choices regarding the collection and use of personal data. At

the same time, we find that the service providers employ numerous tactics in order to nudge or push consumers toward sharing as much data as possible... Choices are worded to compel users to make certain choices, while key information is omitted or downplayed.[43]

The same organization reported that Grindr, a popular dating app for LGBTQ people, shares its users' names, tracking codes, precise locations, and online activity with at least a dozen other companies, effectively disclosing the individual's sexual orientation and personal history. And those companies report the data to 180 other companies with whom they have information-sharing relationships.[44]

Amazon now offers smartphone users a free program called Amazon Shopping (Version 17.21) which helps them browse and buy products from their online catalog. But it discloses, as now required by Apple, that in using the app, the owner of the phone gives the company permission to collect information from the user's phone and share it with associated companies, organizations, and business partners, specifically including the user's search history, purchases, location, health and fitness information, financial and payment information, the names, phone numbers, addresses and email addresses of all contacts, photos, video and audio data, user "content" — presumably any data that can be found in the phone — user identifiers and passwords, usage data, diagnostics, "sensitive information," and "other."

One of the biggest buyers of cell phone location data is the U. S. government. In 2018, the Supreme Court denied the government access to a wireless carrier's database of physical location information, calling it an invasion of privacy.[45] But now the government skips around this prohibition by simply buying the data from resellers, and using it to track the movements of millions of immigrants and others suspected of illegally crossing the border."[46]

Facebook and others are experimenting with large-scale manipulation of opinion, buying behavior, and voting patterns by placing information on the screen that will nudge consumers toward actions and beliefs that serve their own interests. As Zuboff puts it: "Facebook sharply increases the predictability of consumer actions, now, soon, and later, effectively, automatically, and therefore economically".[47] She quotes a senior Facebook executive: "The fundamental purpose of most people at Facebook working on data is to influence and alter people's moods and behavior... Everyone does this, and everyone knows that everyone does this."[48]

Games, video players, news services, and social network apps offered by Google Play and others, are also infiltrated by fraudulent software that takes up permanent but invisible residence on the user's phone. Once downloaded, these free apps then begin operating in the background to click on ads throughout the network, running up the number of "visitors" for which those sites can charge advertising fees. The result is that advertisers are charged billions for customer exposures that never happened. The infected apps also secretly enroll the user in subscriptions, data sharing agreements, and other financial transactions without the user being aware of what happened until the charge shows up on their credit card. The number of these apps has doubled in the last year, while platforms that offer these apps make no effort to remove them from their catalog.[49]

The Evolution of the World Wide Web

From its beginning in 1991, Web 1.0 was a simple one-to-many digital publishing system allowing users to visit a site and view or download the content there. The bigger platforms acted as aggregators and resellers of products (Amazon), and as directories of other websites (Google), selling advertising on their pages and trying to keep count of the users who visited.

Beginning in 2000 or so, Web 2.0 emerged, allowing users to send information back to the publisher over the same web link. It was now one-to-many and many-to-one. Social media businesses like Facebook and Twitter emerged, enabling users to send comments, messages, and content to each other through the central intermediary. In addition to collecting a percentage of sales and advertising revenue, the major platforms (Amazon, Facebook, Google, Twitter, Microsoft) began to exploit the user's transaction history to modify the content and ads the user might see, increasing the precision of the advertising and manipulating the user's experience without assuming responsibility for the information or sharing the revenue with the content providers. For the big platforms, it was a bonanza.

Today these platforms provide four basic services: (a) a searchable directory of products, places, and people, (b) a shopping platform for those goods and services, (c) order fulfillment, and (d) financial collection and adjustment. In this process, the platform keeps a record for each user — the user account — including individual identity, characteristics, transaction history, and behaviors, as well as additional information gleaned, often surreptitiously, from the user's activity elsewhere on the internet. Then the platform mines those user records and sells advertising opportunities and access to others. While it is presented as a service to the user, the user account is actually a proprietary record owned by the platform, serving as the basis for virtually all of the platform's revenue. The more comprehensive and detailed the user account, the higher the value of the platform. User accounts are everything.

But Web 3.0, now evolving, is imagined as a many-to-many system in which the user account may be disbursed. The seller or content provider may continue to list his products and services in an aggregate directory or on its own site. Third-party companies like Amazon may be contracted to handle browsing, purchasing, and fulfillment as before. But in this scenario sellers, content providers, and users could begin communicating with each other peer to peer as the power of the big platforms is significantly diminished. In a new distributed web architecture, information about the user could be closely held, allowing greater control over how that information is shared. Blockchain technology allows this information to be embedded in the eyes-only transaction rather than stored in a database that can be hacked or exploited. The privacy of the participants is protected while creating the possibility that content providers can be held accountable for their products and gain greater control over the distribution of revenue. Like the decentralization of control in the larger political and social world, Web 3.0 promises to become a flattened community of buyers and sellers talking directly to each other.

How do we rebuild social media? It's done great good in the world, but the ad model is pretty broken, it creates strange incentives. Users of a platform are not owners of a platform... so, there's an inherently exploitive and rent-seeking model that's [intrinsic to] any sort of system built in that way... There was an old analogy that these social media companies were town squares — and they weren't. They're private, for-profit corporations that mine your data and use it to sell ads. Yes, they deliver value back to you in exchange for that, but if we really are talking about rebuilding the world, rebuilding social institutions to exist in these open spaces that can't be run by any corporation, that needs to be community-owned, that needs to be built as a giant digital co-op.[50] — *Austin Federa, Head of Communications at Solana Labs.*

Metaworlds

But we face yet another technology disruption in the future. Today we communicate over a network we didn't have ten years ago. In ten to twenty years out, a third network is likely to rise in which avatars meet and interact on our behalf in a simulated world, challenging many of the social, political, and even legal guidelines that govern our lives. Few examples of that new model exist at this point beyond the fantasy/game playing world, but from science fiction, enthusiastic startups, university labs, and the speculation of pundits and forecasters we can piece together a picture of what this future metaworld might be like:

Technology: We overestimate the importance of immersive technologies like helmets and special glasses that change the scene as you move your head. They are amazing, even in their primitive early-technology state. But much of the functionality of the new metaworld can be accomplished by wrap-around video screens, traditional laptop displays, or even hand-held devices and wearables. What is important about the new network is that it allows several participants to gather in a virtual software-assisted space — the user's own room, a hosted online metaverse, or a virtual reality experience — where they can collaborate on a project, share and manipulate digital objects and documents, be entertained, join in activities, and conduct commercial transactions in a secure and orderly manner.

Virtual Rooms: Defined interaction spaces — let's call them rooms — are the basic building blocks of the new metaworld as we migrate away from web pages, smartphone apps, and social media. Deal rooms will be designed for the exchange, revision, and signing of documents. Meeting rooms will be built for lectures, conferences, trials, and even dating, where the discussion can be translated into multiple languages, recorded, and transcribed if necessary. Some rooms will be private where friends regularly meet, a permanent refuge in a busy world. Other family rooms will offer persistent collections of pictures, notes, and news. Magazines like *Vogue*, *Sports Illustrated*, or *Martha Stewart Living* might morph into interactive communities. Some rooms will let anyone enter, others will require the approval of the participants already there, and still others may allow unseen visitors to "lurk," watching the action without the ability to participate. Each room will have its own access rules.

Avatars: People may appear in these rooms as animated figures they have chosen to represent themselves, but the success of Wikipedia suggests that these worlds will work best when each participant has one and only one persistent identity in any given metaworld, with any avatar's reputation available for review by any other participant. The identity and privacy of the real-world individual behind the avatar must be secure.

Objects: Avatars will be able to present, examine, and manipulate virtual objects as big as a house for sale, or as small as a sore finger. All the world's goods will be available for inspection and sale in public showrooms or private booths, and full e-commerce functionality will be available. In training classes, the object can be rotated, dismantled, reassembled, and modified. In doctors' virtual offices, the patient and the doctor can share x-rays of the finger or even microscopic details of the nerve at that point. Psychotherapy and telemedicine have already begun this migration.

Activities: In some rooms equipped with supporting software and run by expert hosts, participants can return to a multi-player fantasy game in progress, do their taxes, or book a flight to Boise. Recording studios will be available for rental with helpful engineers on hand, and betting parlors will abound.

Studios: Some places on the new network will be presentation spaces: movie theaters, art galleries, jazz joints, or basketball arenas where your avatar can go alone or with friends and always score courtside seats. Thousands of avatars can sit in the same chair and each participant will have the experience of being the only occupant. You can drop into the CNN newsroom for a quick briefing, catch a lecture on the paintings of Winslow Homer, or create a studio of your own to read your poem or present your latest demo.

Crime: Some actions taken by avatars may have consequences in the real world. The laws of contracts, libel, defamation, fraud, obscenity, privacy, and conspiracy are likely to still obtain, though it will take years of courtroom wrangling before the full legal profile of this new world is established. In the meantime, early users of shared virtual worlds already recount instances of bad behavior, hate speech, harassment, and even groping. It is rarely possible to identify the real person behind the offending avatar, or even to report the incident to a moderator.

Andrew Bosworth, chief technology officer for Facebook's new Meta initiative, says moderating what people say and how they act in the metaverse "at any meaningful scale is practically impossible." And he argues that whatever harm such toxic behavior may cause is more than offset by the benefit the new technology brings to Facebook and its new "Metaverse" incarnation:

> So we connect more people. That can be bad if they make it negative. Maybe it costs someone a life by exposing someone to bullies. Maybe someone dies in a terrorist attack coordinated on our tools. And still we connect people. The ugly truth is that we believe in connecting people so deeply that anything that allows us to connect more people more often is *de facto* good.[51]

Governance: In China, Russia, Saudi Arabia, and other authoritarian regimes, the metaworlds are likely to be run by the government itself, strictly controlling what can be said or done. Other metaworlds may operate like the dark web or an underground bazaar where anything goes, with regulations existing only to protect basic system functions. Rules of acceptable behavior will evolve particular to each world, as they do now in communities. Certain actions will be permitted or proscribed and members can be voted in or out, celebrated or condemned. As we shall see, Wikipedia presents a model of a current metaworld run by a thin hierarchy of editors, super-editors, and stewards elected to their positions by a majority of the active contributors. Most important, metaworlds and their rooms will become the new offices and communities with most of the characteristics of fellowship, leadership, innovation, collaboration, and mutual care that we have seen in the real world.

Monetizing the metaworld: The world of avatars living alternate lives in virtual rooms is clearly a trillion-dollar opportunity, likely to subsume the digital gaming industry, online retail, social media, fantasy sports, podcasts, zooming, and the gambling business. Metaworld membership fees, cover charges and admission fees for entrance into the rooms, product placement and advertising, avatar and object development, service fees, and sales commissions have the potential to deeply divert the real world's existing information revenue flow.

Danger: The most difficult aspect of metaworlds as they evolve is the extent to which the virtual "meta" life may be confused with real life. For a person who becomes immersed in a metaworld for hours every day, virtual values and truth systems may displace the values and truth systems of the real world. The stimulation, fellowship, joy, and pleasure of accomplishment that the metaworld is engineered to deliver may make the real world seem, when you tear off the mask, suddenly tawdry and uninteresting by comparison, with deeply dysfunctional results.

But metaworlds in some form are certain to appear among us over the next ten to twenty years. Much of the relevant technology is already available, and every major new media company — Facebook, Microsoft, Google, and Amazon among others — is already filing for patents and putting business development teams together. This is going to happen.

Grace Hopper looked at the task of connecting machines as a way to extend our control over the world around us. Computers were tools designed to do our bidding. And we still think, perhaps naively, that our future networks are intended to monitor and manipulate our environment at a more detailed and pervasive level. But now the devices we installed have become social. They are exchanging data all the time, guiding us to make decisions in accord with algorithms and instructions designed to deliver profit to others. Connecting us in a new world we can hardly see.

Chapter 4
Freedom and Social Order

New information technology changes how we live together, and the biggest change until now has certainly been Gutenberg's printing press. He did not develop movable type or printing on paper in 1493; that had been done centuries before by the Chinese. But in coming up with a low-cost way to publish books, he created a technology by which everything we knew about the world could be challenged. In his wake, control over information shifted from a robed hierarchy of priests and scholars to a new class of upstart publishers who had the machinery for selecting, editing, and distributing the written word. Strange new discoveries could be shared, even ones that contradicted experience. Old theories could be overturned and new ones offered in their place.

Before Gutenberg, "truth" was ordained by the Church, a thing gloriously illuminated by monks, unchanging and treasured for a thousand years. But after Gutenberg came a dynamic, contentious, and confusing new age when anyone with a printing press could produce competing visions, all in the same type, on the same kind of paper, and appearing to be as true and worthy as the holy texts. Gutenberg invented the raucous new world of "knowledge," not a thing but a process.

Presses broke free and raced ahead to keep up, setting in motion a century of scientific and political revolution. Within a hundred years, every young person with expectations was being taught to read. The Age of Enlightenment was born and with it the idea that individuals armed with new information could start thinking for themselves.

As printed broadsides and treatises flew back and forth across the continent, Europe began to leave the tranquil comity of village life and the simplifying rule of empire. With access to knowledge, openly shared, natural philosophers full of new thoughts began to suggest that men might be capable of making decisions on their own.

It was an idea that took time to catch hold. Three hundred years after Gutenberg, Immanuel Kant suggested that every person had an innate understanding of space and time, true and false, right and wrong, that was more reliable than the ideas being offered by the Church and State. That may seem like an obvious idea to us now, but it was revolutionary in his day.

And dangerous. Global shipping and the industrial age opened the world to commercial activity that was no longer beholden to any government. An enterprise like the Hansa League in Europe or the Silk Road in Asia might be powerful beyond the control of the empires it served. Skilled craftsmen began to leave the protection of an established shop and set out on their own. So how was all this to go forward in an orderly fashion?

On the European continent, Voltaire and Rousseau argued back and forth about whether a government run by a few aristocrats should manage education and commerce for the benefit of all, or whether individuals, impetuous, irreverent, and inventive, should be free to scramble off in new directions. A new arrangement might be required.

And then a hundred years later, Nietzsche and Sartre took it all to the next level: forget conventional government and the rules of society. They have failed us. God is dead, society is deeply dysfunctional, government is corrupt and addicted to violence, and the customs and morality of our everyday world are little more than the unexamined relics of older days, themselves the stale remnants of even earlier failed cultures. Nietzsche said the courageous individual must shake off the constraints of tradition and remake the world. Sartre said we are all on our own, "condemned to be free." Empires had collapsed under the weight of their own excesses; pointless wars had destroyed our faith in government.

The social stage was being cleared of old furniture and props, the lights were coming up, and now, like actors in a Samuel Becket play, people were struggling to find a new social order in an absurd world where no one had authority over anyone else and everyone was whispering at once. In the background, the sound of strange new machinery was clicking and whirring in the wings.

Immanuel Kant [1724-1804]

Kant is the one who started it. In 1781, he was teaching natural science and metaphysics at the University of Konigsberg, on the Baltic Coast of Russia, and he had published only a few papers on astronomy and anthropology. A little man who stood less than five feet tall, he was thought of as punctual, unassuming, and certainly not a provocative thinker. He had rarely traveled more than twenty miles beyond the university and lived alone in rented rooms all his adult life. According to his contemporaries, he was a teacher of great affection and wit, though he managed to suppress both gifts completely in his writings.

Watching the exuberant bloom of natural science, Kant had followed the writing of Scottish skeptic David Hume, who said that what appears to be real is not always so. It was the first step into the matrix. Our senses fool us, Hume argued, and on important issues we cannot trust the nature of anything outside of our mind. Even the morality of the Church and State are just social ideas. But Kant had a problem with this. He believed there was some "natural" sense of order that enabled us to organize our experience and tell truth from lies. A natural impulse to faith, a love of freedom, and a sense of time and space all helped us make sense out of day-to-day events. And yet these rules were not taught by the schools, they were not obvious in nature, and they were no longer whispered to us by oracles. We reach conclusions based on thoughts that are sometimes contrary to our immediate well-being. Where could such ideas be coming from?

What if these organizing faculties are part of the way the mind works? What if they are the natural mechanisms of thought, a palimpsest of God's own mind, the faintly visible remains of an older script lying beneath our knowledge and offering clues to a deeper order of things? They are not rational judgments, he suggested. They are an instinctive framework used by our species in managing the flow of information. The "laws" of nature are not in nature, but in the way the mind experiences nature.

Kant concluded that we all have a sense of what is true or not true, and we should trust our hearts, not be enslaved by philosophical tricks or the dictums of Church and State. He argued that in a new world of natural philosophy, man should think for himself.

Now the little professor was in trouble. He had peered into the roiling darkness of human behavior and backed away, seeing where his reasoning led. It was one thing to say that God exists only in men's minds, but to suggest that right and wrong are merely "social ideas" was to challenge the fundamental order of the State. His persistent questioning of the official moral code had been permitted to continue because even Kant's enemies had to admit that few people could read him, and even fewer could figure out what he was saying. But by 1794, a spirit of rebellion was in the air. With the French overthrowing their king and Americans in Philadelphia inventing democracy, his dangerous ideas about individual morality caught the attention of the royal court, and he was called to present an "exact account" of his impertinence. In the future, he was told, his work must be more supportive of the King and Church on pain of "unpleasant consequences."

The old man capitulated and took upon himself a vow of silence, leaving it to braver souls to follow his thinking to the next stage. His radical dreams were already stealing across Europe.

Les Philosophes: Voltaire and Rousseau

In the mid-1700s, with thousands of printing presses pumping out new scientific discoveries, political tracts, poetry, and plays, the Age of Enlightenment was dawning over Europe. Information and opinions were now shared freely across the continent, focusing on one dangerous issue above all others: individual freedom vs. social order. Should people be ruled by the traditional hierarchy of kings, lords, and bureaucrats, or should they be free to think for themselves? Two voices were particularly clear in this debate. Opposed in thought and style, each personified the major philosophy of an age. And just as a dancer is permitted by the strength of his partner to test grander and more elaborate embellishments of his own, each man was taunted by the other to search for more extreme forms of his belief. They lived in mutual hatred, died within weeks of each other, and may have come in time to be buried like lovers in the same grave.

Voltaire was born in 1694 into Paris aristocracy; Jean-Jacques Rousseau was born poor in Geneva in 1712. Voltaire had a brilliant career as a playwright, essayist, and professional cynic. He attacked the Church with witty invention, arguing that men should strive for a better life through science and the arts, not settle for blessings after death. While making great fun of the clergy, patriots, and philosophers around him, he nonetheless believed that the few should lead the many. He had considered the possibility that a community of men might think for themselves but dismissed it sarcastically: "When the people undertake to reason, all is lost."[52]

Rousseau was a self-educated music copyist and teacher. In 1745 he moved to Paris, took as his lover Thérèse Levasseur, a dull but devoted chambermaid, and was at one point hired by a friend to revise a minor opera on which Voltaire had collaborated. The two corresponded but never met. A pretty man, Rousseau was a romancer as well as a romantic. But his poverty and lack of education blocked him again and again from ascending to the society he admired, and by the time he was 37, he was frustrated and afraid. Then in 1750, walking to visit a friend in prison, he read that the Academy of Dijon was running an essay contest on the topic "Has the restoration of the sciences and the arts contributed to corrupt or to purify morals?" He was struck by the question and, in a quarrelsome mood, saw the potential of a radical answer: science and the arts have corrupted us. "Man is by nature good, and only our institutions have made him bad."[53]

One of the first to blow the whistle on ten thousand years of top-down bureaucracy, he wrote that in a new world where information was shared and individuals were free to think for themselves — in a network, for example — a monarchy was at best merely an expensive apparatus the people invented for handling the day-to-day business of the community. Among people who are truly free to talk among themselves, he argued, there would arise a "general will," a body of knowledge, values, and aspirations emerging spontaneously as ordinary people debate the issues every day. And this general will, bubbling up from the people, should have precedence over the dictates of empire, religion, or aristocracy.

His essay won first prize and became the battle cry for romanticism. Rousseau proposed that society, sciences, and sophistry had gone too far.

Philosophers (by which he meant the elite) "sap the foundations of our faith, and destroy virtue":

> They smile contemptuously at such old words as patriotism and religion, and consecrate their talents... to the destruction and defamation of all that men hold most sacred... Let men learn for once that nature would have preserved them from science as a mother snatches a dangerous weapon from the hands of her child![54] — Jean-Jacques Rousseau, *Discourse on the Arts and Sciences (1750)*

He wrote that free people, pure and strong in their primitive "state of nature," are drawn through friendly debate and family love into communities and clans, which in turn evolve into a "civil state" of equality and mutual support. No government should be permitted to distort that natural progression or to enslave its people when they themselves are determined to be free. "Let us then admit that might does not create right and that we are obliged to obey only legitimate powers." Rousseau's rousing cry found immediate sympathy among the rabble of Paris, restless and oppressed under the bungling rule of Louis XV and his pastel parliament of nobles. His essay was widely debated and Rousseau became famous.

Voltaire was a brilliant child of the powder-and-silk aristocracy who lived like a rock star with his much younger mistress, Mme du Châtelet. In 1749, when she died giving birth to a child fathered by another man, Voltaire was at her side and, according to legend, the writer who had risen to fame by ridiculing sentimentality now returned to the house they shared and wandered all night through the darkened rooms, calling her name.

He was a skinny man who drank coffee constantly, firing off insulting letters in all directions, and in time the world turned against him. He moved to Berlin, to Potsdam, and to Geneva, hounded in every city by lawsuits and criticism. His plays were banned. His books were refused by booksellers, and he retreated to Ferney on the Swiss border, where he gathered his talents around him for a long and remarkable rebuttal. He said that a few men of wit and reason (like himself, no doubt) must do the thinking for the rest.

As Rousseau rose in fame, he too became bolder, more inflammatory, and harder to have around. And in the course of this writing, he attacked Voltaire.

In 1764, Voltaire responded with a pamphlet, "The Feelings of the Citizens," in which he ridiculed Rousseau as a hypocrite and a madman. At least he had the facts on his side. Rousseau, who grew rapturous on the natural beauty of children, had abandoned five of his own to foundling homes, reasoning coolly that they would burden his career. The man who gave so eloquent a voice to natural passion, when caught stealing a ribbon, placed the blame on his girlfriend. And he was crazy. In his last years, he grew deeply paranoid and antisocial, fleeing from town to town under assumed names, floating alone in his flat-bottom boat in the middle of a lake, writing the extraordinary *Reveries* that epitomized romanticism.[55]

The Social Contract

In his writings, Rousseau acknowledged that even in the most liberal communities people might be required to give up certain individual freedoms in order to gain a larger goal that benefited everyone.[56] And to illustrate this point he created a little parable that has since become a famous logic problem called "The Stag Hunt."

As Rousseau tells it, the men in a village set out to hunt down a great stag that has been seen abroad in the forest, but since none of them can capture the elusive beast alone, they decide that each will stand guard in a corner of the forest and when the stag appears, block his escape and chase him toward the others. If they all do their duty, the stag will be caught and the whole village will share a magnificent feast. As Rousseau points out, any one of the men might be tempted to leave his post and chase a rabbit in the hope of feeding his own family. But if any of them abandon their position, the stag will escape across the unguarded boundary, and though it may never be known who betrayed the agreement, the whole village will lose. How do you balance the opportunity of one against the welfare of all?

If none of the men were in communication with each other, any one of them might feel free to run off unseen. The power of a cooperative attack would never be realized, and no one would know who broke the covenant. Alternatively, if the members of the group communicated with each other through a trustworthy leader, someone aware of what each man was doing and capable of inspiring them to greater unity, then the men might be more willing to hold their positions out of loyalty. That sometimes happens. But imagine that each man could know what the others were doing in real time, if they were connected as Teilhard envisioned, then the threat of shame and the promise of their greater collective power would keep each man at his post. The members of the village would know together, learn to trust each other, and outperform any collection of uncommunicating, untrusting, uninspired, and poorly led opponents. That is the impact of a knowledge-sharing network.

If people have a natural sense of right and wrong, Rousseau believed they should be free to follow their own ideas, nudged back to the center from time to time by others in their community. If we are not sinful by nature, as St. Augustine claimed, then the Church has no intrinsic power to "save" us. If men are not instinctively malicious and predatory, then Voltaire's pampered bureaucracy was at best an accessory to power, tolerated by the people to manage the day-to-day business of education, security, and order. The true source of war, depravity, and injustice, Rousseau reasoned, was thus not the people but the institutions that had risen in their midst. And from time to time those institutions may need to be modified or overthrown.

If people are free to speak openly and truthfully among themselves, Rousseau thought they might indeed ascend to a new age of peace and productivity. But then he raised a more difficult issue: without an aristocracy to manage such communications, how do we avoid being swept away in a cacophony of unreasonable opinions and harebrained theories? If the community is weakened by leadership loyal only to its own interests, or by a government twisting the system with fraud, lies, and corruption, then we may all become just another mob chasing the tumbrels down the streets and alleys of Paris.

Voltaire died in 1778 and was buried secretly lest the Catholic Church deny him a place in any cemetery. Rousseau died four weeks later. In 1791, the remains of Voltaire were removed in honor to the Pantheon in Paris, and there the bones of the two men rested for a few years in nearby graves. But their journey together was not over.

Voltaire left the world a few great works of literature — *Candide*, a short satire on optimism; *Zaire*, a tragedy in verse about a young slave girl destroyed in the savage politics of race and religion; and a praiseful history of Louis XIV.

Rousseau left behind one idea, deeply relevant to the question of how networks should be governed today.

Rousseau advanced the argument that in every community there is a "general will," independent of government, a collective intent that emerges spontaneously among people talking together all the time. In a network, perhaps. But when government drifts out of alignment, a captive of alien interests, the people must act to bring it back into obedience. The law is not an unreasonable constraint on freedom, it is an expression of the community's "luminous will," an organizing model of behavior by which men raise themselves up from their primitive state of nature to a more productive and civil society.

But he warned that if the process is to work, everyone in the community must have an equal voice. And on that issue, he was two hundred years ahead of his time. Legal slavery continued in pockets around the world until the mid-twentieth century, with Africa, ironically, the last practitioner. The idea that women should vote was not seriously considered anywhere in the modern world until 1900 and was not made law in the US until 1920. Rousseau wrote that only freedom from slavery and a system of universal human rights would ensure the sense of brotherhood and loyalty essential to a peaceful self-governing community. Only a free people could govern themselves.

> ...Nothing is more gentle than man in his primitive state, as he is placed by nature at an equal distance from the stupidity of brutes, and the fatal ingenuity of civilized man.[57] — *On the Origin of the Inequality of Mankind (1754)*

The challenge of honoring individual freedom while preserving the social order was very much on the minds of Enlightenment politicians and philosophers at the end of the eighteenth century. In America, the founding fathers struggled with the design of a new government, and crucial to them, according to historian Thomas Ricks,[58] was their belief in "virtue," respect for the public good, and a sense of the common weal, the bedrock of Rousseau's philosophy. In Ricks' study of how classical Roman and Greek ideas influenced the thinking of Madison, Jefferson, Adams, Hamilton, and the other drafters of the constitution, he notes that the word "virtue" appears more frequently in their writing than "republic," or "democracy." They thought the success of a diverse, flattened, considerate, and, yes, noisy, polity would depend upon a pervasive commitment to the welfare of the community, and was more likely to succeed over the long term, even when imperfect men might from time to time seize the levers of power.

But the spirit of aristocracy was still abroad in the halls. Alexander Hamilton resisted the "tumult and disorder" of a popular election and proposed the creation of an electoral college to mitigate the danger of runaway suffrage. A specially chosen collective of Voltaire's white male property owners, he said, would stand between the popular vote and the final election, lending their education, perspective, and political sophistication to ensure a more stable outcome.[59]

It all depends on whether you think man is basically good or not. Thomas Hobbes [1588-1679] had argued that government is necessary because people are naturally selfish, venal, and short-sighted. Left to make their own laws, they would fall into an endless "war of all against all." Only the "terror of some [greater] power," Hobbs wrote, would keep men in line.

John Locke [1632-1704] was more sympathetic. Like Kant, he thought people in their natural state were inspired by the "Law of Nature" to act morally and not harm each other. But they needed the government to serve as a "neutral judge," offering tranquility and protection for their lives, liberty, and property. Hobbes and Locke both agreed that people should give up some of their personal liberties to the government, in return for the social order and protection government can provide.

And so a compromise was struck: kings and emperors lost dominion over the lives of their subjects, but bureaucrats would remain and form a government, with the understanding that citizens had the right to overthrow that government should it abandon its obligations and "become destructive" of the social order. And so the revolution began. On a vote by Parliament, Charles I was beheaded in 1649. Louis XVI and Marie Antoinette were guillotined in 1793. Abraham Lincoln was assassinated in 1865. Tsar Nicholas II and his family were murdered in 1918. In Bulgaria, China, France, Hungary, Iran, Iraq, Italy, Japan, Norway, Pakistan, Romania, and Turkey, the governments of the people have executed their presidents or prime ministers at least once in the last century.

The apparatus of Church and State, however, remained safely in place, the only bureaucracies with the information systems necessary to govern effectively. Neither Rousseau nor Locke could figure out how to change that.

Interment

The fates of Rousseau and Voltaire, so deeply entwined in life, may have continued together after death. Based on a contemporary eyewitness account, James Parton in his *Life of Voltaire* (1881) claimed their bones were later disinterred and buried together like lovers in an unmarked grave.[60]

In 1815, with the failed Bonaparte now exiled on the island of Elba, the brothers of the executed Louis XVI were restored to the French throne as a fever of retribution and realignment swept the ravaged nation. The old aristocracy returned, recaptured the lands that had been taken from them during the revolution, and began to ferret out those who had acted against the interests of the royal family, particularly intellectuals like Voltaire and Rousseau. According to De Puymorin, Director of the Mint who told this story years later, the idea of those two men resting honorably in their graves at the Church of Sainte Genevieve was an insult not to be borne, and after several conferences on the matter it was decided that their remains should be removed, in secret lest the action revive the dying embers of the fiery past.

So it was that on a night in May of that year the bones of Voltaire and Rousseau were taken from their lead-lined coffins and tumbled together into a sack, thrown into a hackney coach waiting at the rear of the church, and driven out of town, accompanied, De Puymorin tells us, by five or six persons who walked ahead of the coach to wave away anyone whose curiosity might be aroused by this nocturnal outing. The coach rode slowly down the back roads to an old field beyond the city limits, public property but not in use. There they met a small party of fellow conspirators who had dug a deep hole in advance and now waited for their moment in history. The sack containing the remains of the two philosophers was thrown into the hole and covered with lime. The hole was filled with earth, all traces of the burial were removed, and the men went their separate ways into the nameless night.[61]

Chapter 5
Souls of Gold

Now the great truth of modern life begins to emerge: a network is not just a system for exchanging data, as Grace Hopper said, or sharing thoughts, as Douglas Engelbart tried to explain, or even disclosing the deepest details of our personal lives, as the new technology now promises. A network is also a community. Each person's participation in the network changes that network, and in important ways, the network we belong to changes each of us.

Looking back across man's long evolutionary rise, Teilhard said that the earliest people had lived in primitive tribal groups, loyal to each other, following the decisions of whoever among them had the most power. In time these collectives evolved into a second phase he called "societies of mind," not just families or clans but communities defined by geography, language, religion, and ethnicity. He thought we were on the verge of a third phase he called the "conscience collective," a global mind in which many decisions would be made spontaneously by the members themselves, thinking together in a network of shared information. "This is a mental entity that [will be] as real, distinct, and 'living' as the mind of an individual person... diffuse in every reach of society."[62]

In one important way, the transition to this next stage has already begun. Geography once largely defined the rights and obligations of citizens. The town, the state, or the country we lived in long determined our economic, political, and cultural allegiance. But we live increasingly on a stateless planet, freed by the worldwide network to choose the community we belong to, and able to switch our membership with a few keystrokes. Multi-national corporations, industry collectives, global charities, and even terrorist groups move about the networked world, electing which taxes to pay this year, which laws to follow, and which political agenda is most useful to them at the moment.

As individuals, we are no longer likely to see our lives reflected in a local newspaper or even a regional TV station and more likely to follow a cable channel or social network designed to serve our demographic, lifestyle, or political preferences. The idea of community has slowly diverged from the idea of village. What does community mean? How does a community think together? In the late nineteenth century, the French educator Émile Durkheim began to ask these questions for the first time, exploring the benefits members should expect from such communities and, ominously in his case, what sacrifices might be required of them in return.

Émile Durkheim [1858-1917]

Durkheim was an oddball, a short, birdlike, sepulchral man in pence-nez glasses with a pointy beard. And for one whose life and works focused on the dynamics of social groups, he was a perennial outsider, detached from most of the communities to which he might have naturally belonged. The son and grandson of rabbis, he left the church behind him in his youth and thought of religion not as the fruit of Divine revelation, which is how most of his colleagues viewed it at the time, but as something invented by its believers to hold themselves closer together. "It is necessary to regard religion as the product of a delirious imagination."[63]

He was a scientist at a time when most academics were literary, and he approached everything from social behavior to suicide through the eyes of a statistician. He was a fierce patriot and a cultural Jew when all about him were internationalists and anti-Semites. But his uncontested brilliance in many academic fields won him important positions in the French world of education, even as his own rectitude kept him from enjoying the kinds of friendships he wrote about.

Early in his career as a teacher, he received the following performance review:

M. Durkheim has a very serious and somewhat cold appearance. He is conscientious, hardworking, well-informed, and very clever, though perhaps his mind is more rigorous than penetrating and more capable of assimilation than invention. Nonetheless, his teaching is very exact, very precise, very concise, and very clear, though the clarity is, it is true, of a scientific rather than a popular nature.[64] — *quoted in Steven Lukes, Émile Durkheim: His Life and Work*

His lectures and articles on the nature of society gained him a national reputation from which he was able to promote his key ideas and launch a new scientific discipline he called "Sociology."

Durkheim thought a community was the natural condition of man and that individuals join collectives like the social networks of today not just to exchange information but to experience the nourishment of shared experiences, memories, values, and mutual support of others like themselves. Others have come to the same conclusion. For years, Billy Graham, the mid-century American evangelist, surveyed his new followers at the end of each mission to find out what convinced them to join his crusade. The second most popular answer was always "fellowship." It wasn't the word of God that drew them. They joined his movement because they wanted to be with others like themselves.[65]

Over a lifetime of research and writing, Durkheim focused on four aspects of a community that are fundamental to understanding the evolution of today's networks. (a) The members of any successful group naturally break up to cover different fields of interest in more detail — he called that "division of labor." (b) Networks engender in their members a sense of solidarity and kinship so vital to their sense of identity that when that solidarity weakens the member falls into "anomie" — a feeling of profound alienation and despair that Durkheim says often leads to suicide. (c) In time, a network community grows to provide inspiration, fellowship, and a dramatic literature of heroes and villains to entertain its members, especially those of lesser wealth and resources, giving them the feeling that they are living in a larger story. A network has a soul. (d) A network can play such a strong role in the lives of its members that it becomes a source of morality, a code of conduct, bringing identity and meaning to the lives of its members, and demanding obedience and sacrifice in return.

A Conscious Collective

The network thrives on our differences. Beginning with primitive man, Durkheim said, members of a group profited most when they respected their differences. If each person specialized in one kind of work, one area of knowledge, or one style of thinking, he or she would be better positioned to contribute uniquely in a way that brought recognition and authority. A committee is formed, a team is assembled, the gang gets together, and each of us looks around and figures out how we can be uniquely helpful. We become the task champion, project cheerleader, information gatherer, or the joker, depending on our nature and the mix of others in the group. An individual can even have different roles in the different groups to which he or she may belong, a leader in one collective, and a lowly information gatherer in another. A diversity of minds emerges to make the collective more successful; Durkheim called it the "fundamental basis for social order."[66]

The network shows us our similarities. The network also allows the members to celebrate some attributes they have in common. Individuals with a weak or fragile sense of identity can find comfort and reinforcement from their community, whether it is a pub, a club, a political movement, or a church. And membership in a network is often taken by others as evidence of character. In that sense, the network is a reflector of our daily life, and a guide for our actions, alone and together. And we, in turn, shape the network. The collective is our selfie. To some extent, in a network, we are each other.

Durkheim was deeply concerned that in moving people from fields and villages to a world of faceless cities and factories the industrial revolution disconnected them from the identity their old communities provided. They got confused about who they really were. While industrialization made society more productive, he thought there was a need for something to replace the natural moral code and sense of belonging the agrarian village had always offered. A network helps members understand themselves, and see their value in the eyes of others. When individuals are removed from that network, or when they see it becoming corrupted or conflicted, he thought it was harder for those individuals to orient themselves in the world. They begin to feel their life has no meaning. And the consequences, he said, are grave.

When an individual loses his identity within a group — within a family, a band of fellow workers, a community of political friends, or a nation — he suffers what Durkheim called "anomie," a hopeless alienation from the fellowship of the group that once sustained him. Durkheim saw this happening all around him, and statistics supported his thesis. As traditional village, craft, and cultural networks began to weaken in the nineteenth century, the rate of suicide rose sharply across industrial Europe.

Suicides have also increased in America over the last twenty years, particularly among middle-aged white males living in rural areas, even as the rate has declined in every other major country in the western world.[67] According to the latest report from the Center for Disease Control and Prevention, the rate of suicides among Americans 16-64 years of age has increased 40 percent from 2000 to 2017, and among young people ages 10-34, suicide is now the second leading cause of death in the United States.[68] [69] Even as physical networks expand and become integral to our lives, our feeling of belonging to a community has grown weaker.

Analysts attribute this rise to anxieties tied to the issues of the economy and demography. Working-class wages have failed to keep up with economic growth, and people conclude that their lives have somehow lost value. There is a sense that ethnic minorities have gained jobs and political influence that once belonged to "middle America." And there is a loss of faith in the power of government to achieve income fairness and opportunity for all people. Whether the collective is the tribe, the company you work for, or the nation you live in, alienation, as Durkheim observed, leads to deep despair, and a sense that life is no longer worth living.

The network acquires a spirit. All communities develop a unique style and spirit, a set of exceptional characteristics and eccentricities that distinguish them from others. They have a history of struggle and achievement, an unwritten code of behavior, and habits that rise to the level of ritual. Durkheim thought that as the power of kings and priests declined, the power and social significance of this community spirit seemed to rise.

But then he hinted at something far more radical. Without calling down upon himself the wrath of the entire intellectual establishment, Durkheim asked a provocative question. If religion, patriotism, and social order are just man-made constructs binding us together into closer communities, if they are just schemes we made up along the way to comfort ourselves in times of trial and adversity, then where did the idea of God come from? If God, too, is just a social construct, a big imaginary friend, then is it possible for a collective to invent its own god?

Buried in Durkheim's discussion of religion is a reference to the work of Edward Burnett Tylor, Durkheim's near-contemporary at Oxford and founder of the new field of cultural anthropology. Here was the science Durkheim needed to support his dangerous inquiry. Working from field notes written about the customs of primitive peoples in Australia, New Zealand, Africa, pre-Columbian America, and elsewhere, Tylor had proposed what he called a theory of souls that attempted to explain the origins of God.

According to Tylor, primitive peoples puzzled by the experience of dreams came to believe that the voices and visions appearing to them in the night were evidence of a second self, a soul that lived within them. Greenlanders believed something quits the body during sleep and goes out into the misty world. Dreams are fragmentary messages back from the dance. Indians of North America believed the souls could leave the body and ride off in search of adventure. New Zealanders thought the souls could even visit the land of the dead and converse with old friends. Dreams might be the soul communicating with the self. Some dreams might be messages from beyond, warnings from the soul of an enemy, or whispers from the soul of a beloved.[71] In time, the disposition of the soul after death became an essential part of the religious cosmology. It might wander forever. It might return to occupy another body. It might burn in Hell. People in nearly all the world's religions began to make decisions in their daily lives for the benefit of their imaginary post-mortem "soul."

Tylor's next step is the interesting one. In scouring the field notes of explorers and anthropologists, he found that primitive peoples believed that a family can have a soul that is distinct from the souls of its members, providing guidance, inspiration, and identity to the group. A clan could have a soul that lives on through successive generations, embodied in the totem or iconic image that decorated their sacred and ceremonial equipment. It might have several souls representing different aspects of the clan's life like the bear, the eagle, or the snake.

And as clans and tribes combined to form larger political entities — nations among North American Indians, for example — their souls, too, were merged. They joined a pantheon of gods, including one who was greater than the others. Thus, out of the nocturnal churnings of lonely individuals was born the soul. The soul begat the spirit of the clan and, according to Tylor, the clan spirits begat God.

Does a gaggle of teenagers texting each other all the time develop a dialect, a body of customary practices, a tradition of fears, biases, and jokes that continue even if this or that teenager leaves the group? Does a news or entertainment channel or a forum for software engineers or a private network for radical activists develop characteristic acronyms and protocols, adopted by all its members as a sign of their qualification and belonging? Does the online forum come to have a style of decision-making, a set of unique values, and a distinct personality? What Durkheim was trying to understand is whether the members of any group, like the clans in Tylor's research, can come to believe in a guiding spirit that exists beyond the lives of its members. In reflecting the behavior of its members, can the network be a platform for celebration in victory, and solace in times of loneliness and loss? Can a network include the very spiritual dimension that Teilhard imagined for the noösphere? Can a network have a soul?

The network offers fellowship and calls for sacrifice. It is liberating to find yourself in a group that talks like you, laughs at the same jokes, and thinks about the future the same way. Whether the network is an extended family, a sports team, a political or religious sect, or another closely-linked social group, members often mark the boundaries of their kinship through an insignia such as a baseball cap, lapel pin, ribbon, or a style of speaking that declares who is and is not a member. Being with others like ourselves expands our vision in a common direction, and the shared knowledge and vocabulary of the group, in turn, empowers us to discover new thoughts that are consistent with the group's beliefs. Recognizing clearly who is not one of us is just as important in erecting strong community bonds.

Collectives also alter the nature and quality of the information they share.[72] When information is passed from person to person within an organization, ambiguity and uncertainty get removed. Unpleasant warnings are unconsciously demoted or ignored, and data inconsistent with the group's beliefs is discredited, deleted, or suppressed in favor of the prevailing view.[73] Elements that are ambiguous, contrary to accepted fact, or disturbing to consider are set aside, not respected as a contribution, or conveniently forgotten.

Given the same set of facts, different networks enforce different assumptions, different sensitivities, and different knowledge. One group may have neither the language nor the experience for dealing with the new information, and it is reframed in a way that distorts or negates its meaning. Another group, trained to listen for dissent and practiced in the protocol of honest messaging, will see in the same information an important new opportunity. The same unexpected warnings will be heeded by some groups and ignored by others who view the larger world through the lens of selected data, biased media reports, social networks, and lies, wrapping themselves in a cloak of virtual truth, comfortable, internally consistent, broadly accepted by friends and colleagues, and sometimes dangerously wrong.

But other groups, thinking together, can find their way to revolutionary insights that might have been impossible for an individual. They develop their own language, political values, inside jokes, customs, and legendary characters. Weak contributors fall out and disappear while strong contributors thrive, get respect, and gain influence over others.

The computer geeks who gathered in the Homebrew Computer Club in 1970s San Francisco willingly shared hardware, software, and ideas, allowing their colleagues to exploit those gifts, each according to their talent and opportunity. Impressionist painters in nineteenth-century France saw new ways to capture light, leaving behind the old beaux-arts tradition of realism. Monet, Renoir, Cassat, Manet, Cézanne, and others formed their own school, painted together en plein air, competed for inclusion in the annual salons, and taught each other the power of coarse brushstrokes and a wild palette. At the University of Göttingen, a rebel group of theoretical physicists, along with their extended network of friends and alumni (Max Born, Werner Heisenberg, Max Plank, Niels Bohr, Enrico Fermi, Edward Teller, Albert Einstein, and others) wrote back and forth in a language no else understood, competing against each other as they invented an astonishing new world. In Chicago in the 70s, the

Second City comedy troupe — John Belushi, Gilda Radner, John Candy, Dan Aykroyd, Catherine O'Hara, Eugene Levy, Harold Ramis, and Bill Murray — riffed off each other, revolutionized the form, and provided the nucleus for *Saturday Night Live*.

We no longer "know" alone. Networks form naturally to give individuals a way to share information, divide the work, confirm their mutual support, and gain a sense of fellowship and usefulness. The more coherent and trustworthy the network is, the more effectively the group competes against other groups, in families, in communities, in business, and in war.

Durkheim wrote that a crucial ligament holding a society or a network together was the shared image of "civil man," reflected in the person of the group leader, who must embody the will and aspirations of its diverse members. He or she must become the "interpreter of the great moral ideas of his time and country,"[74] strengthening in the members their shared "sentiments of discipline, equilibrium, and moral order."[75] This is the element of leadership that was missing from Rousseau's stag hunt model.

The community offers fellowship. Most of all, Durkheim said, a community gives us the assurance that we are not alone and that others are ready to help. Like any religion, a network can offer solace, a code of ethics, and inspiration to its members.

> Every society is [therefore] a moral society... Because the individual is not sufficient unto himself, it is from society [the network] that he receives everything necessary to him... He becomes accustomed to... regarding himself as part of the whole.[76] — *Durkheim, Division of Labor (1893)*

But — and on the matter of individual freedom and social order this was his crucial contribution — he said the individual must pledge his loyalty and support to the community, even to others he may never know. A strong collective will call upon members to make great sacrifices. And when the time comes, the member must step up.

A Sacrifice Is Called For

In the middle of all this, war flared up across Europe and Durkheim's research was interrupted. From the summer of 1914 on, his life was consumed in a new nationalist campaign, and as a patriot — as the most eloquent philosopher of patriotism in his time — he was forced to make a decision.

There comes a time, he had written, when every member must renounce his personal identity and devote his life to the group — and now that time was upon him as well. At fifty-six, he was too old to fight and increasingly burdened by ill health. Instead, he set aside his work as an educator and became a tireless writer and speaker in the cause of his country. By the fall of 1914, before England entered the war, Durkheim was devoting all his waking hours to the effort, committed to meeting the grim demands of a nation rising to battle. He chaired committees, he drafted resolutions, he argued the cause of national defense. The translation of war pamphlets into seven languages was taking over his life. In Rousseau's parable of the stag hunt, Durkheim stood fast in his corner of the forest, and put all personal dreams and aspirations out of his mind. "I do not think I have worked so hard for twenty years."[77]

But an even greater sacrifice would be required. So many of Durkheim's students were going off to fight for France, and now his own son, André, a brilliant linguist and his protégé was being sent to the Bulgarian front. In January 1916, with France and Germany locked in a bloody battle of attrition, word came back that André was missing in action. Durkheim waited anxiously for more news, watching the days fall into weeks, slowly untying the blessed little ribbons that bind us to the ones we love and must at long last learn to lose. He wrote to his friend that he was "haunted by this image of an exhausted child, alone at the side of the road in the midst of night and fog... that seizes me by the throat." His worst fears were confirmed in April.

Durkheim kept on, alone in his thoughts, running hard from grief. His life's work sat half-finished on the sideboard as he turned his talents to writing the propaganda he thought his country needed. He refused to let his friends talk about the tragedy or even mention his son's name in his presence. He disciplined himself to keep working, but as he was leaving a meeting of one of his many wartime committees, Durkheim suffered a stroke. America entered the war a few months later in 1917, and Durkheim, on his sickbed, was optimistic that Germany might be defeated at last.

A hundred years later, the outcome of the war is known to us in all its pointless horror, and the value of Durkheim's contribution to our understanding of social networks is almost universally recognized. But in those last weeks, Émile Durkheim was thinking about his beloved France. He had another stroke in November and died at the age of fifty-nine with his research unfinished.

H. G. Wells [1866-1946]

At the same time, as the fever of anarchy began to threaten the stability of Europe's great empires, the aristocrats of the world rose to reassert their influence. Fine, people have more information than they used to, and that's good. But communities are still best led by an intelligent few. Let us shift the basis of government from military power to reason, they said. If intelligent, well-educated leaders are allowed to take the wheel, they can steer us peacefully into the next millennium. Those of us who have the privilege of education and moral training can create a world government that might guide others. Here was Durkheim's idea of moral leadership in action.

All through history, there has been a cadre of leaders guiding the affairs of men. In the fourth century BC, Plato advocated government by an aristocracy of educated men with "souls of gold" trained to recognize and enforce the absolute good. A second caste of soldiers regulated the behavior of the third caste, the people. For a thousand years, the Mandarins of China were scholar-bureaucrats rigorously trained in law, poetry, history, and politics, constituting a cadre of officials. It was a civil service from the most exalted courtiers and diplomats down to the tax collectors in every village, making the day-to-day decisions for the empire. In the Middle East, a religious bureaucracy of rabbis and mullahs administered a world of tiny congregations, interpreting the wisdom of the holy text. In medieval Europe, barons and sheriffs enforced the law and collected the taxes, while a wealthy brotherhood of priests counseled the souls of the people. Aristocracy was an idea hallowed in history, and now in the decadent glory of the Edwardian Age, it was strutting back into fashion, offering its services in a silk top hat.

In 1895, at the age of twenty-nine, H. G. Wells was on a tear. His first novel, *The Time Machine*, was being serialized in the *New Review* and he was well along with his second, ominously titled *War of the Worlds*. Raised in humble circumstances in Bromley, a rural London suburb, he had been apprenticed first to a draper and then to a chemist while struggling to educate himself on borrowed books. He won a position as a science teacher, got into the Royal College of Science where he studied biology under T. H. Huxley, the great proponent of evolution, and after getting a degree in zoology from the University of London extension program, began writing ha'penny humor and hundreds of book reviews for the local journals. Now he had broken into national print, and the earliest reviews were very encouraging. It was a new world.

The railroads had doubled their passenger traffic in the last twenty years, and regularly scheduled trains now criss-crossed the country at speeds of up to seventy miles per hour. Ocean-going steamships, widely adopted by England, made Britain the greatest trading nation in the world. Electricity was already available in most major English cities, promising to banish darkness forever from the earth. X-rays had just been discovered, revealing the human body in unimaginable new ways, and Freud had exploited hypnotism to light the guarded caverns of the mind as well. Several London companies offered telephone service to businesses and wealthy households, and it was possible to envision the peoples of the world someday chatting with each other like neighbors over wires strung around the globe. And now, in D. H. Lawrence, James Joyce, and the prurient pages of the *Yellow Book*, everyone was whispering about sex.

In 1898, *The War of the Worlds* started appearing as a serial in London, New York, and Boston, and young Wells became famous. In the next decade, he published ten more novels, including *The Island of Dr. Moreau, The Invisible Man, The First Men in the Moon, Tono-Bungay*, and *When the Sleeper Wakes*, creating a world of science fiction that one critic claimed would become part of the mythology of our species. As a science-trained futurist with a gift for imaginative detail, he predicted flying machines and war from the air, television, and wireless communications, the atomic bomb, a man on the moon, laser weapons, organ transplants, and genetic engineering.

His friends included Arthur Conan Doyle, George Bernard Shaw, Maxim Gorky, Teddy Roosevelt, Henry Ford, Charlie Chaplin, and Winston Churchill. And by the time he reached the age of fifty, *The Nation* called him "the most influential writer in English of our day." In 1921, he was nominated for the Nobel Prize in Literature.[78]

But what brings him to our attention was his dream of a world brain. By the middle of the nineteenth century, England was in the throes of a religious upheaval. As scholars challenged with facts things that had for centuries been taken on faith, farmers, miners, and working people of England flocked to the songs and solace of revivals. While the oldest stories of the Bible were questioned by linguists and archeologists returning from the desert, religious leaders convened, argued, and went off in different directions, scrambling to catch up with their followers. Thousands of new Anglican churches were being built or rebuilt. In the Church of England, the number of clergymen doubled in thirty years.[79] Faced with a confusing onslaught of new science and industry, people were seeking reassurance that man was still the gleaming pinnacle of God's work. And still at the center of man's world lay England's green and pleasant land.

Then came Darwin.

The traditional understanding at the end of the Victorian Age was that God had created the universe in seven days. He rolled up the sun and hurled it into the sky; he brushed the waters aside and scattered the dry land with flowers, called the birds and animals up out of nothingness, and then, from a bit of mud at his feet, molded man and woman in his own image and gave them dominion over the new world. But in 1859, Charles Darwin [1809-1882], a Cambridge naturalist, wrote that as a young man on a voyage in the Galapagos Islands he had found among the tortoises and mockingbirds systematic variations that seemed linked to their location. In the twenty years since, he had expanded his research to examine similar differences among humans, and now, pressured to publish by similar findings of others, he presented his theory: through a process of random mutation and survival of the fittest, he declared, the living creatures of the world had evolved over millions of years from the smallest single-cell organisms to the impossible complexity of man. He said we were descended from apes.

On top of the scientific, economic, and spiritual tumult of the times, Darwin's idea challenged our very sense of self. If God was the creator of the universe, then the Bible was true, the Church in all its variations was secure, and two thousand years of inspiration and moral guidance still had judicial relevance. But if God was not the creator — if he was merely a force for order and beauty in the universe — then man was out in the world on his own, riding the random winds.

Darwin's theory of nature "red in tooth and claw," as Tennyson put it, could not have been better fitted to his times. It was survival of the fittest in society as well. In his youth, Wells had seen the rise of mechanized looms and steam technology calling workers in from the villages to run the great rumbling mills twelve hours a day. The wealthy escaped the city in summer and rested in Italy or Spain, but for everyone else it was a hard life. London was overcrowded and plagued with homelessness, drug abuse, and poverty. The air was black with soot and the alleys crawled with bludgers and dollymops, with the destitute and dying. While the rapidly rising middle class sipped tea in comfortable drawing rooms, typhoid fever and cholera swept over the East End. Tons of raw sewage were being dumped daily into the stinking Thames, the city's main source of drinking water, while parliament debated how to reform the morals of the masses. In 1861, Prince Albert, the queen's beloved consort, died from what was believed to be typhoid fever,[80] and still nothing was done.

Darwin said this was natural. But for H. G. Wells, it was a troubling sign of things to come. He had made his reputation by imagining tomorrow, and for him the importance of Darwin's theory lay not in how it explained the past but in what it predicted for the future. Darwin was saying that evolution would continue to favor not the hardest working or best educated, not the well-born or the just, not those who pray or follow the teachings of the Church, not even necessarily the strong. Everyone was in the scramble, believers and non-believers alike, and the prize — the future of our species — would go to the fittest. Darwin was saying that struggle as we might, the future of our species would be shaped by chance.

War of the Worlds

For the rest of his life, Wells searched for a better answer. Over the course of more than a hundred novels, non-fiction works, and political pamphlets, he moved from science fiction to social commentary. He began as a cheerful advocate of the human race and ended in 1946 fearful that the latest war had been a warning of worlds to come. And in all these years he struggled with the question of how a few privileged and intelligent people could best lead the masses.

In *The Island of Doctor Moreau (1896)*, a brilliant scientist is attempting to take evolution into his own hands, operating live on animals and humans to create a new creature, free from the torture of human desire and strong in the ways of the wild. But as the novel unfolds it is clear that after a decade of gruesome experiments, the doctor has failed. The island is inhabited by his botched efforts, and the "Beast Folk," the half-man, half-animal creatures he created, finally rise out of their agony, revert to their more primitive nature, and kill him.

Wells appeared to believe that the most intelligent and creative of our species should be permitted broader moral range, meting "unequal laws unto a savage race/ That hoard, and sleep, and feed, and know not me."[81] But his ideas were not well received. In its review, *The Times* wrote: "[*The Island of Doctor Moreau*] should be kept out of the way of young people, and avoided by all who have good taste, good feeling, and feeble nerves."[82]

The War of the Worlds (1897), begins:

Yet across the gulf of space, minds that are to our minds as ours are to those of the beasts that perish, intellects vast and cool and unsympathetic, regarded this earth with envious eyes, and slowly and surely drew their plans against us.

The Martians have landed in Woking, and as the local army rallies to attack their spaceship, the aliens incinerate them with "heat rays" and poisonous black smoke. All-out war follows, the people run for their lives, and the visitors from a superior species stride out through the ashes to harvest the remaining population for food and genetic revitalization. But just when it seems the Earth is lost, we see that the creatures have begun to die inside their spaceships, overcome by a simple earthly virus to which they have no immunity. In an essay published around the same time,[83] Wells speculated that life on Mars would have evolved beyond our own and, like the English aristocracy perhaps, might be a wealthy, indolent, passionless race, starved for primitive stimulation and fresh genetic material.

In many ways, the novel reflected the author's obsession with class. At some level, he thought a superior species had the power and thus the obligation to lead the lower classes to a less miserable, more productive life. But he worried about the price the upper class might pay. The benefits of a ruling aristocracy were obvious to him, as they had been to Voltaire, but the people were wonderfully primitive in their urges, rebellious in spirit, strangely powerful, and more likely to win the evolution lottery. This was not going to end well.

In *Anticipations (1901)*, Wells presented an extraordinarily prescient view of the world in a hundred years, prominently featuring among his speculations the potential of eugenics to shape the evolution of the species. He imagined a "World State" that would control human activity in order to "favor the procreation of what is fine and efficient and beautiful in humanity." While the least promising half of the population in each generation would be "restrained from or tempted to evade reproduction," the other half of the population would be freed from the fetters of conventional sexual morality. The "nation that most resolutely picks over, educates, sterilizes, or poisons" its less promising members, Wells wrote, would be the one destined to rise. For the masses "born of unrestrained lusts... and multiplying through sheer incontinence and stupidity," death would mean merely "the end of the bitterness of failure."

The reaction to these views was highly critical, and Wells beat a hasty retreat. In *A Modern Utopia (1905)*, he argued that "Idiots, drunkards, criminals, lunatics, congenital invalids, and the diseased" would "spoil the world for others," but admitted that eugenics might be too extreme a solution. Instead, he suggested that people below a set income and intelligence level should be prevented from reproducing. Social "failures" should be relocated to an island, leaving the Samurai, as he called the upper classes, to live in a world that might, as a consequence, be more peaceful and more free. "People of exceptional quality must be ascendant. The better sort of people, so far as they can be distinguished, must have the fullest freedom of public service."

Wells was by no means alone in his view that the prospects for the human race would be greatly improved by sterilizing the lower classes. Virginia Woolf, T.S. Eliot, D.H. Lawrence, Julian Huxley, and Marie Stopes — all prominent intellectuals at the time — were proponents of eugenics in one form or another. Winston Churchill was vice-president of the first International Eugenics Conference in London in 1912. Scientists, ethicists, and politicians on both sides of the Atlantic, and conspicuously in Germany, were pushing for a government policy that would block "mentally feeble" and "morally defective" individuals from having children. In the United States, the Mental Deficiency Act of 1913 set out to separate them from the rest of society.[84] If the world was run by those with "souls of gold," then the odds of evolution might be shifted in favor of a "better sort."

In *A Modern Utopia,* Wells imagined four classes of future citizenry. The creative were the Poetics; the skilled but unimaginative were Kinetics. The Dull were dull, and the Base, as he called them, wallowed in small-minded egotism and moral squalor. Machines had taken over all physical labor not pursued for its creative or recreational value. No one ate meat because their refined sensitivities could no longer tolerate the slaughter involved. And everyone was required by the World State to spend one week a year hiking in the woods.

The privileged young, as in all his books, would lead lives of unbounded academic, social, and sexual freedom, an aspect of his vision that his younger readers found absolutely super. Vincent Brome who wrote the first major biography of Wells said the book was highly popular among university students and "released hundreds of young people into sexual adventure."[85]

This was a philosophy he heartily embraced in his own life. Wells was an enthusiastic and prodigious philanderer, having married three times and engaged in more than a dozen long-term extra-marital relationships including with Margaret Sanger, the American pioneer for women's rights, birth control, and family planning. Women threw themselves at him. In his biography of Wells, Michael Sherborne recounts an incident in 1923 when Hedy Gatternigg, a young Australian journalist and sometimes lover, stole into his London house, got past the butler and into his study, and arranged herself on the floor in front of the fire, naked but for stockings, shoes, and a raincoat. If Wells did not have sex with her there and then, she announced, she would kill herself, and brandishing a man's razor she began to slash her wrists. Wells, on his way to dinner with the Secretary of State for India, called for the porter. And as she was being taken away, she screamed "I love him. Just let me die."[86]

His magnum opus, the two-volume *Outline of History (1920)*, became the best-selling nonfiction book of the decade and stands as his most complete statement on the sort of society he hoped might emerge. And now we hear the beginnings of a "world mind." Echoing notes from Teilhard's own vision, Wells imagined a common heritage in which individual lives and experiences were joined in a "wider being," a shared identity that would carry the species to a new stage in its evolution.

> Man will breathe sweetness and generosity and use his mind and hands cleanly and exactly. He will feel better, will be better, think better, see, taste, and hear better than men do now. His undersoul will no longer be a mutinous cavern of ill-treated suppressions and of impulses repressed without understanding. — *H.G. Wells, Outline of History (1920)*

Throughout his writing, Wells was deeply angry about economic inequality and the tyranny of England's social classes, but scornful of the radical ideas of Karl Marx, of https://en.wikipedia.org/wiki/A_Modern_Utopia_-cite_note-32 business tycoons, and of politicians on both sides of the Atlantic. He believed that a world government could prevent aerial bombing by controlling the world's airspace. He thought it could provide "protection from private, sectarian, or national violence... protection of natural resources or the planet from national... or individual appropriation, and a world system of money and credit."[87] And all this would be brought about by universal access to a network of information.

All the World's Knowledge

As war approached for the second time in a generation, Wells focused on the hope that new technology might make it easier for people to learn the truth about current events, allowing them to avert a new wave of tragedy.

He scoffed at the possibility that universities might organize themselves to make this knowledge available, calling them "medieval organizations, bent on [their] own promotion and aggrandizement." They have "far less influence upon the conduct of human affairs, than, let us say, an intractable newspaper proprietor, an unscrupulous group of financiers, or the leader of a recalcitrant minority."

> I do not believe there is any emergence for mankind from this age of disorder, distress, and fear in which we are living, except by way of such a deliberate vast reorganization of our intellectual life, a consciously and deliberately organized brain for all mankind.[88] — *H. G. Wells, The Brain Organization of the Modern World (1937)*

From the pen of a man who could foresee atomic war, intergalactic travel, and a vast reorganization of society, we might have expected the nature of this new organized brain to be revolutionary and bold, but what Wells had in mind was a microfilm index of the world's best books.

> It seems possible that in the near future, we shall have microscopic libraries of record, in which a photograph of every important book and document in the world will be stowed away and made available for the inspection of the student.

In fact, in 1936, at the time of this writing, storing documents on microfilm was already a widespread practice in banks and libraries. Vannevar Bush, a well-known American academic, made a similar suggestion in his 1939 article describing the Memex, and expanded it later in his now canonical essay "As We May Think" (1945)[89], the article that later inspired Douglas Engelbart. But both men saw beyond the mere storage of information.

Bush imagined a mechanized method of retrieval, allowing the researcher to browse the contents of the library from a single screen. He also suggested that the fruits of one search might be saved for the benefit of others, tracing the exploration and comments made. Knowledge might thus not only be retrieved; it would also be linked to other relevant knowledge along the way.

Wells thought the key to making this work was a noble priesthood of supremely intelligent editors and librarians, a permanent team of experts building and maintaining the collection. "Copies of the library would be deposited and kept up to date in all the world's major universities. The library would be a "cerebral cortex where the universities are the ganglia, in direct touch with all the original thought and research in the world."

Looking deeper into the process of curating such a critical body of knowledge, Wells realized how important editorial independence would be.

An encyclopedia appealing to all mankind can admit no narrowing dogmas without at the same time admitting corrective criticism. It will have to be guarded editorially and with the utmost jealousy against the incessant invasion of narrowing propaganda... Visions and projects and theories [must be distinguished] from bed-rock fact.

Wells was a utopian, a stout-hearted and imaginative believer in the promise of science. But his faith in mankind was weakening as a second world conflict seemed ever more likely. And his kind of big-think had gone out of style. By 1940, intellectual fashions had swung away from the literate grace of Arthur Conan Doyle, George Bernard Shaw, Rudyard Kipling, and E. M. Forster, toward the frank realism of Faulkner, Steinbeck, and Hemingway. Wells had become increasingly irrelevant in a world slouching once again toward war.

Now comes a strange shift in his writing. In Russia, in Germany, in Spain, in Japan, and elsewhere the aristocrats in power were practicing eugenics with a vengeance, ruthlessly exterminating dissidents, minorities, and undesirables. Stalin murdered millions. Hitler's national socialist party promised the triumph of a superior race over the mongrels of the world. In Japan, the generals gained control over the government and began to militarize the country. In 1931, Aldous Huxley, grandson of Wells' biology professor, published *Brave New World*, in which he envisioned the masses being genetically manipulated, drugged, and brainwashed to provide slave labor for the upper classes. Huxley said Wells' earlier novels had been his inspiration.

As the prospect of war cast its shadow over the world for the second time in a generation, the question of how the freedom of individuals should be balanced against the need for social order returned to prominence, and Wells' life-long obsession with the primitive and unruly lower classes was somehow transformed into a concern for the freedom of people everywhere.

In 1940, he published *The Rights of Man*, in which he dreamed of "a profound reconstruction of the methods of human living." What are we fighting for, he asked, suggesting that at stake was nothing less than "a declaration of rights for the common welfare, a code of fundamental human rights which shall be made easily accessible to everyone."

One of the rights he was fighting for was this one:

Right to Knowledge: It is the duty of the community to equip every man with sufficient education to enable him to be as useful and interested a citizen as his capacity allows... Furthermore, it is the duty of the community to render all available to him and such special education as will give him equality of opportunity for the development of his distinctive gifts in the service of mankind. He shall have easy and prompt access to all information necessary for him to form a judgment upon current events and issues.[90] — *A Declaration of the Rights of Man (1940)*

Wells continued to travel the world, even in the war years when transatlantic crossings were very dangerous. In a lecture called "Two Hemispheres or One World," he argued for the emergence of a new world order, understandably dominated by Britain and North America.[91] But by then he was an old man with a squeaky voice. His suits no longer fit his shrinking frame, and he tired easily. He had given up telling stories about time travel and feats of fantastic science, and now he focused on a message of moral urgency. He pointed to a future when better medicine would heal us all, when all man's knowledge would be available to everyone in the world, when man could be free from the punishing prejudice of race and class. Like Teilhard de Chardin, he dreamed of a world "without tyranny," where men's minds were "brought together in something like a common interpretation of reality," a "unification of our race," a new "collective life."[92]

People walked out on him.

In 1943, the University of London awarded him a Ph.D. based on his thesis about the future of the species, struggling with secular sin and salvation through science.[93] In 1944, at the age of seventy-seven, he was diagnosed with liver cancer, and after that he stopped traveling. America's decision to drop an atomic bomb on Japan in 1945 reignited his darkest fears about the future of the human race, and in his last book, *Mind at the End of Its Tether (1945)*, he said he thought that humanity being replaced by another species might not be such a bad idea after all.

He devoted his final days to drafting the Sankey Declaration that became the basis for the UN's "Declaration of Human Rights," issued shortly after his death in 1946. In the draft that was finally published, Wells recited again the themes of his life: the danger of modern times, the promise of science, the tyranny of little laws, and the hope that the social classes might all be joined together someday in a "collective" world, under the enlightened control of a global aristocracy.

> We of the parliamentary democracies recognize the inevitability of world reconstruction upon collectivist lines, but, after our tradition, we couple with that recognition a DECLARATION OF RIGHTS, so that the profound changes now in progress shall produce not an attempted reconstruction of human affairs in the dark, but a rational reconstruction conceived and arrived at in the full light of day.[94]

In his last days, he seemed to renounce the superior interests of the few and he appealed instead to the good sense of the many. "Read me," he wrote. "Use all I have to give you. But please do not imagine that you are being invited to line up behind me. You have a backbone and a brain; your brain is as important as mine and probably better at most jobs."[95]

In Wells' late-life world, the people must prepare to revolt against the aristocracy, seizing as their primary weapon, the power of knowledge shared by all.

Chapter 6
Breaking Free

Those who came after Rousseau embraced his idea of the noble individual and carried it to its logical extreme. The individual should be free. With kings and emperors deposed, the thought began to circulate that the remaining bureaucracies should be overthrown as well. Two of philosophy's most important thinkers emerged to argue the case.

In 1882, Nietzsche said that individuals should ignore the regulations of Church and State and pipe their own tune, however wild. In 1945, in the ashes of World War II, Sartre went even further. He said that Church and State had manifestly failed to lead civilization wisely into the future. They were obsolete artifacts of the nineteenth century, and it was now every man for himself. But what at first sounds like a rising call for anarchy turns out to be, in his case, surprisingly the opposite.

Friedrich Nietzsche [1844-1900]

In 1869, twenty-four-year-old Friedrich Nietzsche arrived at the University of Basel to take up his duties as professor of classical literature, one of the youngest men ever appointed to such a prestigious post. Equal parts brilliant critic, ex-Prussian cavalry officer, and loony, Nietzsche began to teach and write about the power of the individual acting alone. He published *The Birth of Tragedy* in 1872, a still influential essay about the perpetual struggle between the organizer (Apollo) and the artist (Dionysos), between the orderly and the disruptive forces in literature and life. *All Too Human* (1878) was a book of aphorisms drawn from his lectures, including skeptical and sometimes sarcastic ideas that fell well short of a philosophy. But even as he launched his distinguished career as a literary critic, he was already suffering migraine headaches, loss of vision, and violent indigestion. Finally, in 1879, too ill to keep up with his teaching load, Nietzsche resigned his position and at the age of thirty-four left Basel on a small pension to begin a new life as an independent philosopher.

From 1880 to 1888 his health deteriorated further. Suffering from what is thought now to have been brain cancer, Nietzsche continued to experience vision problems and sleeplessness, treating himself with massive doses of opium and the sedative chloral hydrate. He sought relief in Italy during the winter months and in other European cities and spas when he could, alone and in misery, cared for intermittently by his mother, his sister, and a private secretary. His caustic attacks on God, the Church, and academics in general made it impossible for him to find another teaching position. He fired his publisher over what he perceived to be the man's anti-Semitic sentiments, and then he had trouble finding another. And during these years he wrote some of the most important philosophy of the last two centuries.

He said God is dead.

Have you not heard of that madman who lit a lantern in the bright morning hours, ran to the marketplace, and cried incessantly: 'I am looking for God! I am looking for God!' I shall tell you. We have killed him, you and I. We are his murderers... Do we not hear anything yet of the noise of the gravediggers who are burying God? Do we not smell anything yet of God's decomposition? Gods too decompose. God is dead... — *The Gay Science (1882)*

God is dead: Nietzsche was convinced that religion blocked us from seeing the world for what it really is. Reason from Descartes on had challenged the logic and usefulness of church doctrine. Science (Darwin) had just shown that many of our fundamental "truths" are wrong. Even democracy is a myth, Nietzsche said, calling it a corrupt process of propaganda and manipulation that tricks us into thinking we are in control of our world.

Reality has lost its value... and an "ideal" [imaginary] world has been fabricated to take its place.[96] — *Ecce Homo (1888)*

To cling to these outdated ideas instead of facing the world head-on, to choose fables over fact, to indulge ourselves in dreams of some future utopia in this life or the next, all this was the behavior of slaves. He wrote that he would shatter these dangerous falsehoods and do everything within his power to set us free.

Beyond good and evil: Nietzsche didn't just kill God. He murdered God's family, burned his house down, and held a Bierfest in the ashes. All our rules, he wrote, depend on values inherited from previous regimes which have come from even earlier unexamined decrees. So saying an action is "good" or "evil" merely applies a set of out-of-date standards. There are no "facts," he said. There are only interpretations of experience based on previous interpretations of experience. All rules must therefore be discarded as corrupt. Every man must make his own world.

In some ways, this is a philosophy for three-year-olds. I don't believe in your authority so I don't have to follow any of your rules. (Stamping feet.) I want to do what I want to do. But abandoning the rules of Church and State left Nietzsche with a big problem. Without the guidance of thousands of years of culture and social mores, without the inspiration of religious art and myth, without the fellowship of the church, what guidance was there to help him in confronting the real world day to day?

And there was a second problem as well which Nietzsche may have implicitly recognized. The mind uses learned ideas and concepts to organize, remember, and apply experience. True or false, these concepts are an important part of our mechanism of knowing, and if we strip them all away to deal directly with the details of experience we often find ourselves confused. There are limits to the amount of raw reality any one person can manage.

To these problems Nietzsche offered the answer that made him famous. If God was dead, and good and evil were merely illusions resting on centuries of myth and pretense, then man was truly alone with nothing to guide him. Man was free.

The will to power: If God was dead and the traditional rules were no longer in force, then the burden was on man to bring order to the void. Nietzsche was not afraid of nothingness. Let the order of the world be shaped by the strong and imaginative among us, those with an appetite for danger. He said the will to power was present in everyone, and that even cruelty may be understood as a natural part of the pleasure of exerting power.

There is will to power where there is life, and even the strongest living things will risk their lives for more power. This suggests that the will to power is stronger than the will to survive.[97] — *Thus Spake Zarathustra (1883)*

Often driven from pain, the desire for power over one's environment creates a heightened state of consciousness in an intelligent man, raising him to the level of an artist shaping a godless world. And to this already rich drama, Nietzsche added a touch of the tragic: the world would thus be saved by the suffering hero, the one besieged on all sides by idiots and adversity, alone, brilliant, beyond the law, and awesome in his creative power.

The individual has always had to struggle to keep from being overwhelmed by the tribe. If you try it, you will be lonely often, and sometimes frightened. But no price is too high to pay for the privilege of owning yourself.[98] — *Attributed*

One must still have chaos in oneself to be able to give birth to a dancing star.[99] — *Zarathustra*

The man of power, the artist giving order to the universe, must face life bravely on his own terms, without the guidance of the Church or State. And in his most brilliant insight, Nietzsche says that we should not fear to live each day as we would wish to live, over and over, every day for the rest of our lives, accepting that no one else is to blame for what we are or what we do.

It is hard for us to imagine how miserable his own every day must have been. A man of great intelligence, sympathetic to the predicament of the world, he had cut himself off from the love and loyalty of others and now struggled with the pain and loneliness of freedom. In 1888, in the last stages of his illness, the gaunt, hollow-eyed Nietzsche wrote, rewrote, and republished many of the major works on which his reputation now rests. Ignored by other philosophers and reviled by the academic and Christian worlds, he continued to suffer the migraines, nausea, and loss of vision that were closing him up in a prison of pain.

In the winter of 1889, according to those who were there, Nietzsche, then forty-four, was walking through Turin when he saw a carter cruelly beating his horse. Spurred perhaps by his life-long affection for horses, Nietzsche rushed to save the creature, throwing his arms around the horse's neck and pulling him to safety as a crowd gathered around him. Then he fell to the ground himself, unable to speak. His friends rushed him to a nearby hospital but his mother, seeing the deeper nature of his condition, moved him to an asylum. For a few days, he wrote incomprehensible notes to his friends, signing himself "Dionysos," the epitome of the tragic artist he had defined in his first important book. Then he fell into permanent silence. For ten years he lay in a sanatorium, subjected to various experimental treatments intended to shock him out of his declining state, but strokes in 1898 and 1899 left him immobilized, and a final stroke killed him in silence in 1900.

Jean-Paul Sartre [1905-1980]

Sometimes our understanding of the world moves ahead like an army in the field. Before the troops advance together in formation, individual soldiers like Teilhard and Nietzsche crawl forward under fire. And sometimes, as in the case of Jean-Paul Sartre, the soldier scouting out beyond the perimeter falls alone into an old shell hole and hugs himself, trying to come to grips with the danger he sees ahead.

In October 1945, the young playwright gave a lecture at the Club Maintenant entitled "Existentialism and Humanism" and more than anything else he wrote, it presents clearly his view of how to live in a godless world. It was scarcely a year since Paris had been liberated from Nazi rule. Germany had surrendered in April, the Japanese were bombed in August, and the final documents ending the war were then only a few weeks old. French government officials who had collaborated with the Germans were still being rooted out and shot. Deep layers of corruption had been exposed among those who did business with the Nazis, and rumors were rising of betrayal even within the highest levels of the resistance. France was questioning its own morality and accounts were starting to circulate about the unspeakable atrocities of German death camps. The world had lost its bearings. The auditorium was packed.

At forty, Sartre was already a controversial playwright, essayist, and philosophe-célébrité. He had served two years in the Army right out of university and was drafted again in 1939. After being captured by the Germans in 1940 and spending nine months in a prisoner of war camp, he was released because of poor health, discharged from the service, and allowed to return to teaching. He flirted with joining the resistance but finally devoted his energies to writing and political activism.

His first novel, *Nausea* (1938) was about a dejected academic struggling with the challenges of freedom and responsibility. In 1939 he published a book of short stories including "The Wall," about a prisoner condemned to die who is offered his liberty if he will disclose the hiding place of a friend. He gives his guards a fake address, only to learn later that his friend had moved there. The friend is shot and the prisoner is freed. *The Flies* (1943) was a play about Orestes and his sister Electra who battle against the hypocritical laws of Zeus and kill their mother to avenge their father's murder. Blood everywhere. *No Exit* (1944) was a play about three dead characters locked in a room for all eternity, acknowledging their crimes and debating the meaning of existence. Sartre had captured the mood of post-war Europe in all its absurdity and gloom.

For Sartre, the atrocities of war on both sides, the failure of government, and the discoveries of science (including Darwin and Freud) had shattered the myth of a supernatural being and destroyed the authority of the State. Now, without the traditional moral guidelines, without hope of salvation, he said, we are on our own in the world.

Condemned to be free: Like Nietzsche, he believed if God is not going to work as a source of guidance in life we have to find our own. We are "condemned to be free" (Sartre delighted in oxymorons like this), alone responsible for our actions, our emotions, and the way we live our lives.

Acting without hope: This doesn't mean we shouldn't act; on the contrary, it means we must have the courage to do what we believe is right since there is no authority to guide us. We cannot hope for others to shape our world, nor can we blame anyone else for how our lives turn out.

It is not by turning back upon himself, but always by seeking beyond himself an aim which is one of liberation, or some particular realization [by which] man can realize himself as truly human.[100] — *Existentialism and Humanism (1945)*

The first network law: But then he went further than Nietzsche. In an aspect of his philosophy that is sometimes overlooked, he wrote that since we are each an integral part of the world, we must accept responsibility for the effect our actions have on others, however small and personal those actions may seem at the time.

> Our responsibility is thus much greater than we had supposed, for it concerns mankind as a whole... For example, if I decide to marry and to have children, even though this decision proceeds simply from my situation, from my passion, or my desire, I am thereby committing not only myself but humanity as a whole to the practice of monogamy. I am creating a certain image of man as I would have him to be. In fashioning myself I fashion man.

Those who called themselves existentialists came to be thought of as brooding, unruly, and rude. Sartre was criticized for appearing to say that since there is no God, we can do anything we want. But of course that's the opposite of what he is saying. In an open peer-to-peer network, we are all in this life together. If there is no God, we must each take responsibility for how our actions affect the world, though how one is supposed to decide what is best for the world is never made clear. Sartre could offer no assurance that every man would see things as clearly and philosophically as he did. Hitler and Gandhi, for example, might have different views.

Sartre's philosophy was criticized, too, for ignoring the influence of others in our lives, the love and fellowship they provide, as well as the assistance they might offer as we struggle to choose the right course of action. And this criticism of his philosophy is closer to the mark. It is one thing to live in a world without God, but living in the world alone is hard.

Is this a glimmer of new network awareness? The very opposite of anarchy? If we all exist in a community — he calls it "man" — then each of us has a role in shaping the character of others. And the welfare of the community, in turn, affects us. What seems at first to be a rejection of social obligation may, in fact, be the essential predicate for network man, the first law of living together in the new world. We need not obey the Church or State, but we are inescapably entangled in its network, and whatever we do affects everyone else. The first law of the network, as later amplified by ant expert E. O. Wilson, is live free and thrive together.

Over the course of two hundred years from Kant to Sartre, the idea emerged that man must find a new balance between the freedom of the individual and the organizing power of the State. The old model of strong governments had clearly failed, having cruelly suppressed the talents and imagination of individuals while engaging in ever more careless and self-serving violence. Rousseau's model for individual freedom seemed to be gaining strength, but in another corner of the world, Voltaire's idea of government by an enlightened aristocracy was about to return in force.

Chapter 7
Thinking Together

On December 30, 1945, the official United States delegation to the United Nations traveled north to New York on a special train and rode out to the pier in a convoy of Army limousines with police escorts on motorcycles and red lights flashing all the way. The group, in their top hats and fur-collared coats, included four of the five delegates to the first meeting of the new organization, along with five alternates and dozens of aides and advisors. They were the best American diplomacy had to offer: the Secretary of State, senators, congressmen, and senior politicians, as well as John Foster Dulles, Alger Hiss, Adlai Stevenson, Thomas Dewey, Abe Fortas, Ralph Bunche, General Matthew Ridgeway, and other distinguished men.[101] They were bound on a mission they believed might lead the world into a new and permanent peace after years of war, and they had been told by the State Department they could bring along as much baggage as they wished, but would be limited to one rifle and no more than five hundred rounds of ammunition each.[102]

As they gathered at the rail for a last look at the wintry city skyline, a small car pulled up and out stepped a tall woman dressed all in black. There was a quiet flurry of stevedores and ship's stewards moving luggage, and then up the gangplank, carrying her own briefcase, came Eleanor Roosevelt.

Eleanor Roosevelt [1884-1962]

After decades in the public eye and twelve years as America's First Lady, the facts of her life were known to everyone. Born into the wealthy New York Knickerbocker clan, she had been orphaned at ten, taken in by an abusive grandmother, and then sent off to boarding school in England. There she came under the guidance of Headmistress Marie Souvestre who gave the young girl the skills, courage, and respect for hard work that would mark her long and consequential life. As Souvestre's friend and companion, Roosevelt traveled with her around Europe during the summers, among the poor and underprivileged as well as the wealthy, from the ethnic villages on the Baltic to the Moorish palaces of Spain, absorbing the cultures and opinions of others and developing a deep reservoir of confidence in her own intellectual abilities. For what she was about to do, there could not have been a more perfect preparation.

In 1903, she returned to the United States and joined the College Settlement program in New York City, teaching English and calisthenics to young immigrant women working in the city's garment district.[103] When she was eighteen, she ran into Franklin Roosevelt, her fifth cousin once removed, and after many years of casual acquaintance, they now began writing back and forth to each other. In 1905 they were married, with the headmaster of Groton officiating and former President Theodore Roosevelt on hand to give away the bride. Over the next ten years, the two had six children, of whom four sons and a daughter survived. She wrote later that she disliked sex, calling it "a duty to be borne," and said that "it did not come naturally to me to understand little children or to enjoy them."

In 1918, at the age of thirty-four, Eleanor found a packet of love letters between her husband and another woman, and after that their marriage was irreconcilably changed. Among the people of her class and his, divorce was not an option, but Eleanor found a way to make it work. She moved into her own house on the Roosevelt's Hyde Park estate, took an apartment in New York City, and threw herself into social causes. She continued to be her husband's wise political partner, a loyal helpmate, and an effective speaker on his behalf. Their marital problems were kept quiet and his future never seemed brighter. Tall, patrician, and well-spoken, he rose to become the Democratic Party's nominee for Vice President in 1920.

Then in 1921, FDR fell ill with polio, lost the use of his legs, and spent the next six years recovering both physically and politically. In 1929, with his wife's very considerable help, he was elected Governor of New York on a Progressive Party platform calling for unemployment insurance, aid to farmers, and pensions for seniors. When the stock market crashed, he was a clear and effective voice for relief and recovery while Herbert Hoover floundered, and two years later he was re-elected to a second term as Governor by a 14 point margin. He became President of the United States in 1933 and was re-elected three times.

During those years of depression and war, Eleanor mastered the art of international politics and became a powerful speaker and writer in the campaign for civil rights, the nation's miners, and refugees fleeing the flames of Europe. She made speeches, went to labor union meetings, and stood on line to feed depression workers. When an army of out-of-work World War I veterans gathered for the second time on the Washington Mall to ask for early payment of their bonuses, she walked among them and promised to help. "Hoover sent his army," the men sang. "FDR sent his wife." During the war she toured the UK and the South Pacific, doing everything she could to boost morale. Admiral Halsey later said, "She alone did more good than any other person or group of civilians who had passed through my area."[104]

She fought effectively for the League of Nations and the World Court, and in 1944 led a campaign to accept 100,000 Jews who had escaped the Holocaust, visiting the temporary camps in Europe and the early Jewish settlements in Palestine where she hoped they might find a permanent home.[105] She traveled the world, held regular press conferences, wrote a daily newspaper column, and was a frequent guest on radio programs. Throughout FDR's presidency, she and her husband were allies in the cause, but their marriage was never healed. In his last years of recurring illness and wartime stress, FDR asked her to come back and live with him in the White House, but she refused.[106]

Now, less than a year since her husband's death, named to her new post by his successor, she devoted herself to her new assignment, studying the background files and briefing papers brought to her by Alger Hiss, Ralph Bunche, and others. She paced the decks of the *Queen Elizabeth* — still camouflaged in wartime gray — as she questioned and debated the issues that would come before the new organization the following week. She gave little time to socializing. "I breakfast alone at the captain's table, (Jan 1)."[107]

A Bright Beginning

"I was so frightened getting off that boat," she wrote. "I knew what the British thought of Franklin, and what they expected of me." But she need not have worried. Old friends greeted her with laughter and affection; long-time allies of FDR extended a welcome with tears in their eyes. She had lunch one day with

Winston Churchill, and tea the next with the royal family, including young Princess Elizabeth, then nineteen, though she wrote later that the king and queen were "far removed from life, it seems."[108] American GIs camped out at Claridge's just for a chance to say hello, and native Londoners stopped her in the street to thank her for the aid America had given during the war. The press crowded around her wherever she went.

A week later in Westminster Hall, fifty-one nations convened to establish the rules and procedures of the new organization. Six committees were created through which the UN would do its work, and Trygve Lie, the Norwegian politician and labor leader, was named the first Secretary-General. There were meetings every day, and full-blown debates in every meeting. The outline of a new post-war world was being hammered into shape. Roosevelt wrote:

> They beg me to stand for world government and seem to ignore the stark reality that Russia would be out at once, and our Congress would never have let us go in. We couldn't get any of the Big Three powers to give up their veto. We will have to crawl together... until all of us have gained more confidence in each other than we now have.[109]

But finally, on January 24, five months after two atom bombs had incinerated 200,000 Japanese, the United Nations adopted its first official resolution, establishing a commission to (a) control atomic energy and ensure its use only for peaceful purposes, and (b) ensure the elimination from national armaments of atomic weapons and all other major weapons adaptable to mass destruction.[110]

There were also caucuses and side meetings every day. At one point the eighteen women delegates from eleven countries gathered in Roosevelt's office to promote the role of women in the conference, under her leadership. They wanted a permanent commission on the status of women and a focus on equal rights for women throughout the world. She wrote in her notes that she never had much enthusiasm for the idea, and preferred working together with the men on an equal basis.

Roosevelt was assigned to Committee III, responsible for social, cultural, and humanitarian matters. It may have been thought that there was little to fear from this elderly, congenial widow, but she shortly proved to her colleagues the depth of their misunderstanding. The first issue presented to the committee had to do with 250,000 refugees from the Holocaust and two million refugees from Russia, Poland, Hungary, and the Eastern Bloc who had escaped Stalin's rule. Now they pleaded for help from the new organization, fearing that if they were forced to return they would be imprisoned or killed.

The Soviets wanted the UN to order them back, claiming that every state or community has a right to control the comings and goings of its citizens. Arguing that case before the committee was Andrei Vyshinsky, the chief prosecutor of the Stalin purge trials in the 1930s, notorious for the imprisonment and execution of nearly a million minorities, dissidents, wealthy landlords, and political opponents. "Give me a man," he famously said, "and I will find the crime." Brilliant, soft-spoken, and brutal, he claimed that the refugees were traitors to the State, quislings, troublemakers, and criminals. Whatever other natural rights and freedoms may be claimed for individuals, he said, a government must have the power to maintain an orderly state and to cleanse its society of disruptive elements for the greater safety and happiness of its people. Send them home, he argued. They are our problem and we know how to deal with them.

In a speech given on February 12, Roosevelt argued against the Russian view, saying that people of the world deserved the right to choose their nationality. The refugees were dissidents, not traitors, and they should be free to live as they wished in a land of their choosing. The UN must consider first the rights of man, she said. We must focus on "what makes *man* more free, not government."[111] After twenty hours of heated and closely argued debate, her view prevailed. The UN took the side of the refugees, and when it was over she and Vyshinsky shook hands. She said she admired his determination and hoped that one day they might see things eye to eye.[112] Speaking passionately, specifically, and without notes, Roosevelt had established herself as a smart, politically savvy new voice on the world stage, and she became the talk of the delegation.[113]

Before returning to the US, Roosevelt visited the refugee camps in Germany and saw their plight first hand. In an experience that seared her heart, she witnessed the smoldering remains of a world where individuals had no rights.

Once fertile land had been destroyed. Mass graves now marked where the death camps had been. Towns and cathedrals had been bombed to rubble, and thousands of survivors still wandered among the ruins, more dead than alive.

> There is a feeling of desperation and sorrow in this camp which seems beyond expression. An old woman knelt on the ground, grasping my knees. I lifted her up, but could not speak. What could one say at the end of a life which had brought her such complete despair?... You can write and talk all you like about it. I have done my best. But to people who have never seen or heard anything similar to it, it is practically impossible to get it across.[114]

On the basis of her success at the London meeting, Roosevelt was asked by Secretary-General Lie to develop a plan for a permanent Commission on Human Rights, and she went immediately to work. She organized three weeks of discussions in a room at the Hunter College Library on the Upper East Side of Manhattan. There, and in the sessions that followed that spring, her little committee of world-class jurists, philosophers, politicians, and academics looked deep into the history and philosophy of human rights and charted a course toward a new social contract that balanced the necessary powers of the state against the essential freedoms of the individual. Still doing her daily column, her monthly article, her radio interviews, and handling her now endless requests for dinners and public speaking, she nonetheless drove her small committee hard, seeking clarity and relevance in the sometimes errant debate.

At one point René Cassin, the distinguished French jurist and intellectual leader of the group, went on for twenty minutes without pause and then gestured to the interpreter to translate — s'il vous plaît — at which point the poor young woman turned red, stammered, and ran out of the room. Roosevelt, fluent in French, stepped in and provided her colleagues with a very credible summary of what had been presented.[115]

The Soviets frustrated the process at every turn, watered down the work wherever they could, and in the end abstained from voting. But a plan for a new Commission on Human Rights was produced, and President Truman asked Roosevelt to present it to the UN's first General Assembly when it convened again in October.

That summer, in addition to her regular writing obligations, she now began her autobiography. She was busier than ever. Then in August, she was in a car accident that broke off her two front teeth which were replaced with two slightly smaller porcelain teeth, pleasantly moderating her iconic Roosevelt profile.

Eight weeks later she was up and working again at full steam. In October 1946, the UN General Assembly convened in Flushing Meadows, New York, site of the 1939 World's Fair. She plunged into discussions with her fellow delegates, and on the Humanitarian and Cultural Committee she found herself again at odds with Vyshinsky, the Russian representative. Again the issue was the resettlement of wartime refugees. Again she refuted the Russian argument and beat the Russians down, now with anecdotes and evidence from recent personal experience. And at one point, after she had given a particularly eloquent plea for justice, the whole room broke into a very undiplomatic round of applause. Her plan for a UN Commission on Human Rights was accepted.

When the Commission on Human Rights convened in January 1947, Roosevelt was chosen chairperson by acclamation, and over the course of the meeting she worked the new Commission hard, saying to them if you want to shorten the days, shorten your speeches. It soon became apparent that if the Commission was to do more than merely adjudicate complaints it needed to be proactive, creating a universal declaration of human rights to guide all nations and communities in their struggle for a new balance between the State and the individual. A committee was formed to draft such a declaration, and Roosevelt herself took the reins. As a canny denizen of the political world, she knew her time was limited. Harry Truman might not be re-elected to office, in which case her seat at the UN table would pass to someone else and her opportunity would be gone. She had two years.

Groups Make Better Decisions

Over the last two decades, there has been a growing body of research into what makes groups like Roosevelt's Human Rights Commission successful. What are the essential ingredients of collective intelligence, as this activity is called? The answers all seem to focus on three aspects of the group's work, true for networks as well: (a) the diversity of the group, (b) the process of converging on a consensus, and (c) the work of communicating the result to a larger audience. Eleanor Roosevelt's success brilliantly demonstrates how these elements work together.

Diversity: It is now commonly understood that a more diversified group usually produces a more successful answer. Groups whose members have cognitive diversity — different ways of approaching a problem — outperform groups with stronger adherence to doctrine, higher levels of skill, or more relevant demography. The members bring to the problem different points of view and different areas of expertise. The diversified membership is better able to identify and correct any weaknesses in a possible solution and keep in memory a broader range of relevant knowledge. Thinking different helps.[116]

It is also important that members understand each other well enough to see how the other individuals are thinking and feeling. Called "theory of mind," this is the capacity of each member to hold a working understanding of each of the other members in mind and to keep that as a guide to the effectiveness of their own actions.[117]

Like random mutation for Darwin, diversity in the group leads to new ideas; weaknesses are challenged, strong new views are supported, and a better solution survives. The collegial nature of networks lends itself to a new model for decision-making that might not have been possible a hundred years ago. In fact, one might argue that truly complicated situations cannot be understood by one person, easily overwhelmed by experience, prejudice, or desire. They can only be understood by groups thinking together.

Convergence: The process of moving to a solution requires a leader of uncommon sensitivity to the social needs of the participants, and at this Roosevelt was a master. She knew about men. She was the mother of four ambitious and successful sons, the niece of a president, a governor's wife for four years, a president's wife for twelve, and a lifelong up-close observer of powerful friends and enemies jostling for influence. Now she set a clear and lofty goal before her group, nurtured a common vocabulary, won the trust of each of the participants, and provided in return the unconditional respect and support that encouraged them to consider competing ideas. But Roosevelt's achievement may be explained by a second surprising element identified in recent research by Anita Woolley: those groups with more female members had a higher collective social sensitivity, leading to a higher collective intelligence and a higher rate of success. Convergence is a social exercise, and women seem to be better at that.

> The highest form of knowledge... is empathy, for it requires us to suspend our egos and live in another's world. It requires profound, purpose-larger-than-the-self kind of understanding. — *Bill Bullard, High School commencement speech in 2017. He attributed the thought to Mary Ann Evans, the nineteenth-century novelist who wrote under the name of George Eliot.*

Communications: The third essential element for success is the ability to communicate the group's solution to a larger constituency. Roosevelt was not as naturally eloquent as her husband, and there were no great writers on her team. She insisted that the declaration be presented in simple language, and even at the end she sent it back to the drafting committee to be rewritten in plainer words. But her passion for the idea, her unparalleled knowledge of the lives of the powerless and underprivileged, and her experience with the human rights issue all had an indisputable eloquence of their own.

The key to the success of her project, though, was her insight that the statement had to be aspirational, not legal. In the past, the Peace of Westphalia, the Congress of Vienna, the Treaty of Paris, and others had been concluded under the auspices of the Pope, a separate power, or a convention of emperors. The participants accepted the new rules and went on their way. But Roosevelt knew the time was long past when human rights could be settled by a few and imposed on the many. A very different model was now required.

She knew if the Commission attempted to write a legal document and get it passed by the member states, the lawyers would take over and the whole declaration would wither into semantic debate. Instead, she proposed that the work be communicated as a set of guidelines to be interpreted and implemented by each nation according to its own legal customs and traditions. Let us act as a community, not as a government.

A New Community

"Thinking that our work might be helped by an informal atmosphere," Roosevelt recalled in her autobiography, "I asked a small group to meet in my [Washington Square] apartment for tea." Present were Chinese philosopher P. C. Chang, John Humphrey, a Canadian diplomat, and jurist Charles Malik of Lebanon.[118] The central problem was clear. The Soviets thought the western culture of individualism had allowed capitalists, unconstrained by government, to amass great wealth, while the unprotected masses suffered poverty, class conflict, and abuse of their human rights. Conversely, the US and Europeans felt that excess government control over people suffocated their initiative and blocked the evolution of society as a whole. In Russia under Stalin, millions had died in prisons and penal camps simply because they dissented from the official view.

Finding a common understanding in this conflict was daunting, but Roosevelt's secret weapon was, as always, hard work, patience, and a deep instinct for fairness. She put the task before the group:

Many of us believe that an organized society, in the form of a government, exists for the good of the individual; others believe that an organized society in the form of a government, exists for the benefit of a group. We may not have to decide this particular point, but I think we do have to make sure, in writing a bill of human rights, that we safeguard the fundamental freedoms of the individual. If we do not do that, in the long run, it seems to me, we run the risk of [perpetuating those] conditions which we have just tried to prevent, at great cost to human life.[119]

Perhaps the most startling aspect of the Declaration as it emerged is the number of economic rights it proclaims — in part as a result of Roosevelt's debates with the Russians. The Declaration included a remarkably liberal post-war view of how a future social contract should work. In addition to the traditional rights of liberty, freedom of speech, a fair trial, and an equal voice in government, the drafters called for the controversial right to work as well as a standard of living adequate for health and well-being, including food, clothing, housing, medical care, and necessary social services. Still deeply bruised by the worldwide depression, the drafters claimed that men and women everywhere had a right to community-supported security in the event of unemployment, sickness, disability, widowhood, old age, or other loss of livelihood in circumstances beyond their control. If people could not eat or sleep safely at night, they could not dream. And if they could not dream, then life would have no upward arc.

The declaration also called for free and compulsory education at the elementary and fundamental stages, with technical and professional education equally accessible to all based on ability. In 1947, it was too early for people to see the coming of the "information age," but it was clear to Roosevelt and her committee that we were moving into a world where knowledge would replace labor as the basis for a new economy. And access to knowledge must be available to everyone.

But in addition to those legal and economic rights, the document claimed three freedoms essential to a networked world:

• Freedom of thought, conscience, and religion, in teaching, practice, worship, and observance.

• Freedom to hold and express opinions without interference, as well as the freedom to seek, receive, and impart information and ideas through any media and regardless of national frontiers.

• Right to privacy of person, family, home, and correspondence.

These rights shall be limited solely for the purpose of securing due recognition and respect for the rights and freedoms of others, and of meeting the just requirements of morality, public order and the general welfare in a democratic society.[120] — *Universal Declaration of Human Rights (1946)*

As the drafting process went forward, Roosevelt was negotiating language with the many members of the Commission one on one, finding small accommodations in the spirit of this great endeavor. But when the Human Rights Commission met again in Geneva in November 1947, the Russians again rebelled, charging the US was guilty of hypocrisy, claiming new rights to equal housing, health, and social freedom while violating those rights in its own country. Roosevelt met these concerns with polite resistance, and she worked to keep the discussion at a high, factual level.[121] While disclaiming any professional legal knowledge herself, she persisted in probing the facts beneath the Russian argument, and more than once proposed that the US would willingly submit to an independent investigation of rights violations in its own country if Russia would reciprocate. The Russians always demurred.

In June 1948, the Human Rights Commission met to debate the Declaration for the last time. The Russians had sent in a new representative, Dr. Alexei Pavlov, Soviet spokesman and debonair nephew of the famous behavioral psychologist. No organization committed to drafting a "Universal Declaration of Human Rights" was going to come down in favor of government power and collectivism; Pavlov could not possibly succeed in turning the group in a new direction. But he could confuse, distract, derail and delay the work, and he tried very hard to do that. He challenged the human rights records of all the nations involved and insisted that the committee acknowledge that every citizen has a duty to the State that transcends any personal freedoms. He eloquently attacked his colleagues and then frustrated their efforts to respond, proposing amendments to every article.[122] From Roosevelt's memoirs:

> On one occasion, it seemed to me that the rash accusations he brought up against the United States... were proving a real detriment to our work.... I banged the gavel so hard that the other delegates jumped in surprise and, before he could continue, I got in a few words of my own. "We are here," I said, "to devise ways of safeguarding human rights. We are not here to attack each other's governments, and I hope when we return on Monday the delegate of the Soviet Union will remember that!" I banged the gavel again. "Meeting adjourned!" I can still see Dr. Pavlov staring at me in surprise. But this maneuver may have had some effect because his orations were brief and to the point for about a week after that.[123]

Harry Truman unexpectedly won re-election in November 1948, beating Thomas Dewey who had been FDR's opponent in 1944. Had Dewey won, Eleanor would almost certainly have been removed from the UN delegation.

On the evening of December 10, 1948, at the Palais de Chaillot in Paris, the UN General Assembly met to consider the Declaration. With the President of the UN, the Secretary-General, and the President of the Security Council crouching like gargoyles on a dais above her, Roosevelt came to the speaker's podium to make her final argument:

> We stand today at the threshold of a great event both in the life of the United Nations and in the life of mankind. This Universal Declaration of Human Rights may well become the international Magna Carta of all men everywhere. We hope its proclamation by the General Assembly will be an event comparable to the proclamation of the Declaration of the Rights of Man by the French people in 1789, the adoption of the Bill of Rights by the people of the United States, and the adoption of comparable declarations at different times in other countries.
>
> The central fact is that man is fundamentally a moral being. That the light we have is imperfect does not matter so long as we are always trying to improve it... No man is by nature simply the servant of the state or of another man... the ideal and fact of freedom — and not technology — are the true distinguishing marks of our civilization.[124]

In the next hour, the General Assembly voted to approve the Universal Declaration of Human Rights with forty-eight nations in favor, and eight nations abstaining — including the Soviet Union, Yugoslavia, Poland, Saudi Arabia, and South Africa. No one voted against it. When the tabulation of votes was over, the entire United Nations assembly rose to offer Roosevelt a standing ovation, the only time in its history it has ever done so.[125]

Over the next twenty years, her dream of a Universal Declaration of Human Rights became widely accepted as the new norm for balancing the interests of an orderly state against the freedom of the individual. It has led to more than seventy human rights treaties in governments around the world and serves as a model for national, regional, and world courts everywhere. Though not enforceable as law, it has become the standard for government restraint and justice for people of all nations.

In 1948, Eleanor Roosevelt was named the most admired woman in America and one of the ten most important people in the country, along with her friends Harry Truman, George Marshall, and General Eisenhower.[126] In the years that followed, she continued to be active in international human rights issues. She kept up her schedule of daily columns, monthly articles, radio broadcasts, and books, and was an indefatigable activist in the fields of civil rights, rights for women, and other progressive causes. There was a joke among the men who worked with her during the drafting of the Declaration: "Dear God, make Eleanor tired." But she never slowed down and died in 1962 at the age of seventy-eight. In his eulogy for her, her dear friend Adlai Stevenson said:

> It takes courage to love life. Loving it demands imagination and perception and the kind of patience women are more apt to have than men — the bravest and most understanding women. And loving takes something more besides — it takes a gift for life, a gift for love.

> Eleanor Roosevelt's childhood was unhappy — miserably unhappy, she sometimes said. But it was Eleanor Roosevelt who also said that one must never, for whatever reason, turn his back on life. [Hers was] crowded, restless, fearless... She walked in the slums and the ghettos of the world, not on a tour of inspection, nor as a condescending patron, but as one who could not feel complacent while others were hungry, and who could not find contentment while others were in distress. This was not a sacrifice. This, for Mrs. Roosevelt, was the only meaningful way of life.[127]

It may never be possible to form the kind of world government H.G. Wells and others had envisioned, but in the two years that Roosevelt led the international debate on human rights, she carried forward Rousseau's belief that man is naturally good, she blocked the most recent efforts to re-establish Voltaire's notion of a controlling aristocracy, and she planted the seeds of a new world community. She made a claim for intellectual as well as political and economic freedom. She proved that when people "undertake to reason," as Voltaire put it, they could respectfully argue their deepest beliefs even as technology barreled forward to make such discussions more immediate, more vivid, and more central to our lives.

She contributed a personal morality to the community when competing government ambitions, tangled in red tape, seemed to cancel each other out. She was a leader in a new world, a network man, rising from out of nowhere to teach us how to dream together about important issues. Like Teilhard at the edge of the Gobi Desert writing mystical letters to his friends, like Grace

Hopper who said computers ought to start talking among themselves, or like Rousseau, the crazy French rabble-rouser who said men should be free to follow their hearts, these philosophers, technologists, and internet pioneers show us new ways to think together. Armed with little more than their own moral and intellectual energy, they emerge, inspire, organize, and explain the potential of a new network world in ways that few traditional leaders have ever done before.

Chapter 8
A Flatter World

There will come a time, maybe fifty years from now, when delegates gather from around the world to converge on a standard protocol for all international networks, an agreement that stitches them into the kind of noösphere Teilhard was talking about, transcending the customs and restrictions of thousands of public and private systems and establishing standards for information interchange, privacy, intellectual property protection, truth in messaging, and freedom of political and commercial speech. And when that meeting is called to order it might be instructive to remember the daunting challenge faced by those who struggled to give birth to the United Nations, how they stumbled forward, how they did some things right and many things wrong, and how, perhaps inevitably, they tried to design a governing framework for the new network world with administrative tools and ideas that were decades out of date.

Thirty years earlier on the eve of America's entry into World War I, President Woodrow Wilson had pleaded with the US Senate to think of world peace not as the traditional one-time settlement of great combatants putting down their arms, but as a modern commitment to dialogue, an ongoing, difficult, and respectful give-and-take among equals he called a "community of power."

> If it be only a struggle for a new balance of power, who will guarantee, who can guarantee, the stable equilibrium of the new arrangement? Only a tranquil Europe can be a stable Europe. There must be, not a balance of power, but a community of power; not organized rivalries, but an organized common peace.[128] — *Address to the US Senate, 1917.*

The United Nations was conceived of as just such a forum, but it quickly reverted to a more primitive enforcement tool, intended to reassert the power of the victorious few. The strongest nations of the world would form an alliance to prevent the smaller and presumably less law-abiding nations from encroaching on their neighbor's territories, running sorties against their people, and otherwise engaging in the international economic and military mischief that has so often led to war. In May 1944, inviting the great nations to a conference on world peace, President Roosevelt said if rogue governments "started to run amok... or grab territories from their neighbors," the new organization would "stop them before they got started."

The Fall of the UN

Dressed in the lofty language of peace and human rights, the United Nations was presented as a venue where disagreements could be amicably resolved and nations could achieve what Rousseau called a "civil state" of equality and mutual support, helping each other rise to their highest potential. But old habits die hard. Walter Lippmann, a columnist and prominent spokesman for the liberal establishment, echoed the aristocratic sentiments of Voltaire: "The responsibility for order rests upon the victorious governments. They cannot delegate this responsibility to a world society which does not yet exist, or has just barely been organized."[129] And, as always with aristocracies, some thought they were more equal than others. The problem from the beginning was that five of those victorious governments, the United States, the United Kingdom, France, Russia, and China, had themselves been the most dangerous and destabilizing predators in the past, and they had no intention of surrendering any freedoms of their own.

At the first organizing conference held at Dumbarton Oaks in August 1944, a deep and general distrust of Stalin derailed all but the most routine decisions, and in the end the delegates could not agree on how many nations would have a vote in the new organization, or which, if any, should have a veto. The Russians insisted that any action by the Security Council could be blocked by any of the five founding members; an issue could not even be raised for discussion if one of the Big Five objected. And when the conference ended, that disagreement had still not been resolved. At Yalta, three months later, Roosevelt, Churchill, and Stalin agreed that the fifteen-nation Security Council could discuss any issue raised, that the veto powers of the Big Five would not apply to "procedural" issues, and that if any power was involved in a dispute it would have to recuse itself from the deliberations. The number of countries permitted to vote was juggled around to everyone's satisfaction and the trio agreed that a conference of the fifty allied nations would convene in San Francisco at the end of April to draft and approve the UN charter. The first outline of a world government was born.

But by April, the Allies were sweeping into Germany, the Russians had taken Berlin, and FDR was dead. The war in Europe was over and Japan was girding for a final battle to the death on its own shores. In San Francisco, 1,726 delegates arrived, along with 1,058 clerks and international bureaucrats, 2,636 reporters, 4,500 telephone operators and other support staff, as well as volunteers from the Red Cross and the Boy Scouts.[130] The nations newly joining the discussion resisted the notion of a world alliance dominated by five powerful countries, and Australia led a movement to limit the veto powers being proposed. But when the conference closed two months later, the original Yalta formula was approved, and at the San Francisco Opera House on June 25, Harry S. Truman made his first public appearance as President to sign the agreement and declare that the UN "must keep the world free from the fear of war."

It has not done so. Five years later, in 1950, with the support of China and the Soviet Union, the North Korean army crossed a boundary drawn between the Communist and non-Communist populations, confirming the world's fear that Stalin and Mao Zedong planned to advance their Marxist influence over Asia as well as Eastern Europe, using nuclear weapons if necessary. With China and the USSR boycotting the Security Council, the UN voted to support the South, and the United States sent in its army. But after three years of fighting and 1.2 million soldiers and civilians dead on both sides, a truce was declared and the boundary between North and South Korea remained as before.

Then it happened again. Vietnam, like Korea, was divided into the North, under Communist rule, and the South, a corrupt dependency of the United States. In 1955, when guerillas from the North began crossing into the South, the UN was stymied once more. Russia did not boycott the process this time but along with China, stayed in the room to veto every decision by the Security Council that seemed to favor the South while the US vetoed every decision that favored the North. The UN was powerless; the war escalated; and over the next ten years, about 1.5 million soldiers and civilians died. The North ultimately gained control over the whole country; Communism became the unifying political regime; and now, after all that expenditure of money and lives, a prospering Vietnam is all Communist and the thirteenth largest trading partner of the United States.

In 2003, the United States government alleged that Iraq was harboring weapons of mass destruction and intended to use them against America, but the UN's chief weapons inspector showed that the evidence presented by the US was contrary to his own on-the-ground examination. The debate proceeded, and during the days that followed ultimatums were proposed, additional testimony was heard, and the Iraq government offered to stand for a complete inspection. The US launched a vigorous back-channel effort to influence the position of the other Security Council members.[131] It was later alleged by *The Guardian* that National Security Advisor Condoleezza Rice had directed the National Security Agency to spy on the Council members during the debate, intercepting telephone and email communications in their offices and their homes.[132] In retrospect, it is clear that the United States was using the UN not as a tool to keep the peace or defend against terrorist threats but to sanitize the American effort to gain greater control over the oil fields of the Middle East. And the other European powers were driving toward the same goal. In the end, only four of the fifteen nations supported the US, and the UN withdrew from taking any action. A month later, the United States invaded Iraq, toppled the government, and laid waste to its major cities at a cost of $2.4 trillion[133] and at least 151,000 Iraqi dead.[134] Weapons of mass destruction were never found.

In past worldwide health emergencies, the UN has acted quickly to coordinate and deploy medical assistance, exactly as its founders had hoped. But in recent years, with the United States taking an often-hostile position toward the organization's activities, the group has fallen silent. In the months following the outbreak of COVID-19, the most serious epidemic since the Spanish Flu in 1918, the Security Council declined to hold any meetings on the crisis for fear of embarrassing China, where the outbreak began.

In early 2022, Russia recognized rebel-held regions of eastern Ukraine as independent states and surrounded its neighbor with the largest troop mobilization since WWII. But Russia is one of the five nations that can veto anything the Security Council does, and it did so. Hours later its Army rolled across the border.

It should be acknowledged that in Angola, Somalia, Darfur, Bosnia, and elsewhere, the heroic efforts of the UN's peacekeeping forces have mitigated the effects of local conflicts, so long as the interests of the major powers were not at risk. But the effort by a few responsible governments to prevent war and impose a rational order upon the world has largely failed.

The Rise of NGOs

In one sense, that no longer matters. The days are long gone when three old men could meet for a week at the ancient summer palace of the Tsars and settle the affairs of the world. At the end of World War I, the great empires of the West had fractured into upstart nations all scrambling for their own voice, and by the end of World War II it was clear that the UN, or something like it, was needed as a forum where these voices could be heard. But no sooner did the outline of a world government appear, than those elite nations leading the campaign began to see their political might slipping away. New stateless corporations and non-government entities appeared, including religious movements, political insurgents, and industrial cartels over which traditional governments had little control. Now the very idea of world government seems obsolete.

America, for one, has lost influence over its largest corporations. Among the biggest US companies, 35 percent of the shareholders are not American,[135] and 40 percent of the employees live and work outside the United States. At least sixty of the largest US companies paid no federal taxes in 2018, including Amazon, Delta Airlines, Chevron, General Motors, John Deere, Halliburton, and IBM.[136][137] Budweiser, Burger King, Trader Joe's, General Electric, and 7-Eleven are not even American-owned.[138][139] Geography no longer matters. In a network world, statehood is a charming but apparently irrelevant concept.

At the same time, transnational corporations and international non-government agencies have ballooned across the world, including charitable and non-profit entities as well as stateless terrorist organizations and e-commerce networks. The number of international non-government organizations has risen from 5,000 in 1990 to an estimated 70,000 in 2018,[140] and their impact is more powerful and pervasive than that of any empire in history. The resources of the private Bill and Melinda Gates Foundation, for example, have become more significant in world public health than the UN's World Health Organization.[141] The Contact Group for Piracy off the Coast of Somalia (CGPCS), a private consortium of government and non-government intelligence, legal, and naval resources, has become more effective in fighting piracy than any national military entity.[142] According to a study by the One Earth Future Foundation,[143] groups like these are now working through stable peer-to-peer frameworks and alliances to coordinate and control a vast segment of the international economy. And none of them go to the UN meetings.

> The ever-more-crowded governance stage means that States' ability to control or regulate [global economic growth] has diminished, while non-state actors' efforts to shape or tame it have increased.[144] — *Who Governs the Globe (2010)*

Information networks are flattening the traditional hierarchy of world government. From the beginning of the 21st century, thanks to the explosion of private, worldwide information networks and transportation systems, the affairs of the planet have fallen increasingly into the hands of Al Qaeda, ISIS, the Taliban, Boko Haram, the international oil and pharmaceutical cartels, Apple and Microsoft, Boeing, JP Morgan Chase, Walmart, Amazon, Amnesty International, Greenpeace, and others. Even transnational criminal organizations are employing network technology to advance their activities, recruit new members, and wage war against rivals.[145]

The One Earth Future Foundation concluded: "Data concretely shows that states are no longer the sole — or in some instances, even the most crucial — actors in the existing world order."[146] Networks are.

We have been looking at this problem through the eyes of Voltaire who saw government as a hierarchical, rules-based activity, managed by a fraternity of enlightened leaders. But in fact, a new network of people and organizations has emerged from the ground up. Rousseau's self-organizing "general will" is rising into view, and the question of who will lead such organizations now presses hard upon us.

For all the scale and power these organizations offer, leadership is missing. The new international networks serve themselves. They coordinate their activities for mutual benefit, and no doubt work carefully to avoid arousing a predatory instinct in each other. Some are truly charitable, some are high-minded and altruistic, but they seem to share no central idea of where the world as a whole should be headed.

It is one thing to leave behind the ancient model of social power arranged in a hierarchy of rank and privilege and instead let the world be guided by the "general will." That trend is clear and compelling. But that alone may not address the larger issues of environmental health, climate change, arms proliferation, social and economic inequality, or world hunger that threaten our happiness and wellbeing. Even Rousseau's stag hunt problem omits this larger question. In that model, who was it that sent those men out into the forest in the first place? Who inspired those villagers to make a personal sacrifice in the name of a larger hypothetical good? And what role does village leadership play as the hunt goes forward? Rousseau never tells us. And neither does Voltaire. In a non-hierarchical organization, how will that leadership be expressed? When Voltaire's pampered philosophers disappear from the scene and Rousseau's rambunctious rabble rule the streets, where shall we look for purpose, strategy, correction, and the sense of social fairness necessary for survival?

Chapter 9
Science Dreams

Writers have been writing about the future forever, and on the issue of how new technology will change our lives, their works have been imaginative and even prescient. But ironically, what those writers saw that captured their interest was not scientific, it was social. They realized that a worldwide network meant far more than just a series of connections, more than the hum of messages flashing back and forth at higher and higher speeds. They saw new social rules, new customs, new assumptions about knowledge and values, and new ways to govern how we behave toward each other. Rising networks, they thought, would require a new network society.

Science fiction is how science dreams, and from the earliest days of the computer, the idea of a large mechanical "brain" evoked a nightmare of new and powerful forces taking over the world. Still recovering from the totalitarian horrors of Hitler and Stalin, people heard brainwashing stories coming out of the Korean War and watched newsreels from Mao Zedong's China that showed government-enforced social engineering already operating on a massive scale. Commies were dismantling family life and drowning love, imagination, and initiative in a sea of faceless conformity. The Western world was on edge.

At home, tales of Communist spies were everywhere in the news. Stimulated by reports about the Mark I computer, demonstrations of radar, and rumors coming out of Los Alamos, science fiction writers began to write about a vast network of "electronic brains" controlling the details of our lives in a way that might destroy our most human characteristics.

Theodore Sturgeon [1918-1985]

Theodore Sturgeon's sci-fi novel *More Than Human*, published in 1951, was the earliest and most successful instance of what is now a popular motif — a group of misfits creating a community of the mind more powerful than any political, military, or scientific entity. In the book, he raises two questions: (a) is it possible that a group of people thinking together might be as powerful as any technology? And (b) what would such a network be like if it had no conscience, no basic morality, no compassion?

The story unfolds in three acts. First, we meet the characters: a twenty-five-year-old idiot, an eight-year-old girl who can will things to fly through the air, two black toddlers who teleport themselves at will, and a genius baby who invents an anti-gravity machine that threatens the world economy. In the second act, they band together and learn to function as a single unit called the "gestalt." In a sometimes-confusing psycho slam dance of sharing memories, piercing veils of amnesia, and pushing self-destructive thoughts onto the enemy, the group lurches about, a collaborative of wildly dysfunctional children trying to save the world. But in the final act, the gestalt acquires a last member who provides a conscience. They are organized and led by a reasonable man who gives the group a clearer purpose.

The idea of sharing thoughts in a psychic network was not new to Sturgeon, but his final observation was both novel and important. Networks may connect our thinking, he suggests, but that is not enough. They must have a conscience, a purpose, a set of values, and a standard for truth or they become a formless twitter of anonymous voices, a danger to themselves and others. Sturgeon was trying to show us that to emerge as a useful element in our lives, the network had to function not just as a connection but as a community. The network needed to grow a soul.

Isaac Asimov [1920-1992]

The same year, Isaac Asimov began the science fiction saga *The Foundation*. He expanded it to three volumes, let it go dormant for nearly thirty years, and then further expanded it to include four more books, including *Foundation's Edge*, completing what was called in its 1966 Hugo Award "The Best All-Time [Science Fiction] Series." The books turn on the premise that Hari Seldon, a "psychosocial engineer," having foreseen the pending collapse of the current galactic government, has recruited the brightest minds he can find and set them up at the far end of the star system to collect all the world's knowledge so it can serve as the basis for the next civilization.

One of the ideas offered by Asimov was that a network might be structured as a distributed storage and retrieval device. In "Gaia," a section of the *Foundation's Edge* novel, he describes how the planet Gaia has become a single interconnected network capable of extending its awareness through agents placed secretly across the galaxy, communicating instantly with the central collective and able to alter the minds of others within a limited range. The Gaia mind stores its knowledge in distributed objects — in millions of humans, large-brained animals, and even in water, trees, or geological formations, each remembering and communicating knowledge about itself and the life it leads. And as the series ends, Asimov asks casually whether this network mind might one day gain a will, an independent morality, and an attitude of its own toward the human race.

Gene Roddenberry [1921-1991]

In the stories of Gene Roddenberry, creator of *Star Trek*, we are presented with a darker prospect. Networks are in control, having long since replaced the ancient gods. But scattered across the far reaches of the galaxy, egomaniacal creatures still lord over civilizations, crushing the human spirit and lusting for even greater power. In the typical Star Trek plot, the *Starship Enterprise* encounters a planet in thrall to an old Greek god retired from Earth and now longing to be worshipped as he was in the past ("Who Mourns for Adonais"). In another, God is a crazy old man who kills anyone who doesn't believe in him ("Star Trek: Final Frontier"). Or he is an Oz-like computer with the face of a snake, holding his worshippers in slavery ("The Apple"). In Roddenberry's world, the forces we should fear are errant life forms or malfunctioning machines, ever intent on turning us into mindless zombies. The *Enterprise* destroys them all and goes boldly on its way.

Up from the bones of our most ancient monsters, Roddenberry conjured an alternative force with god-like power, a malevolent unity of souls. In an extraordinary if frightening vision of the future, he described the Borg Collective, a group mind that assimilates individuals, even civilizations, into a common consciousness — not that different from Teilhard's vision — allowing its members to share the same thoughts and be regenerated by the hive in the event of damage or trauma. This collective network can react more quickly and more successfully to threats and opportunities, omniscient, omnipotent, and superior to all others in the galaxy. And against this force stands the hero, Captain Kirk, risking his life every Thursday night to protect our freedom and right to individuality.

George Lucas [1944-]

The *Star Wars* saga, too, is the simple hero story of a young warrior going out into the world, in this case accompanied by the obligatory wisecracking sidekick, the pretty girl, the robot, and the wizard. But George Lucas flips the script, putting a mystical new network at the service of the virtuous and rigorously trained Jedi knight. This time the network is straight out of Teilhard's notebooks. It is a cosmic unity called "The Force."

Obi-Wan Kenobi, the Jedi master, describes it early in the first film:

It's an energy field created by all living things. It surrounds us and penetrates us. It binds the galaxy together. — *Star Wars, A New Hope (1977)*

Individuals are sensitive to the force by nature or can become so through training. They can detect the presence of other sensitized individuals across interstellar distances and feel emotional disruptions as worlds explode. They can call upon the force to guide or augment their actions, use the force to raise a spaceship out of the swamp, choke an impudent admiral, or control the mind of a menacing guard.

"The Force is what gives a Jedi his power."

Parallel to the Force and competing against it for control of the galaxy is the Dark Side. Drawing on the anger, greed, and evil in people, this alternative network overcomes an individual's instincts for good and turns him instead to a life of hatred, pitting him against those, including our hero, who seek truth and justice in the world.

Arthur C. Clarke [1917-2008]

The undisputed heavyweight champion of science fiction writing over the last century is certainly the mild-mannered Arthur Clarke, who for more than sixty years, wrote many of the most scientifically interesting, eloquently imagined books we have about space travel, life on other planets, and future societies here at home. He was interested in the stars from early childhood. When war broke out over Britain, he served as a radar technician, and when it ended, he went up to Kings College and got a double first in mathematics and physics in two years at the age of thirty-one.

Clarke was the first to see that a satellite in geostationary orbit could serve as a communications relay point. A signal beamed to it from earth could be rebroadcast to receivers on the globe below, making a worldwide network practical for the first time. His confident little paper on that subject was published in 1945. By 1946, his passion for space travel had elevated him to chairman of the British Interplanetary Society, a gathering of fledgling space geeks debating the practical aspects of rocketry and the best strategy for landing a man on the moon. All the while he was contributing papers to scientific journals about space flight, computers, and future technology while trying his hand at short stories. By 1951, he had turned to fiction writing full time.

It was 1956. Computer scientist Alan Turing had just famously killed himself rather than continue to live alone in a world that denied him love. Clarke, also gay, decided to leave England and move to the island of Ceylon, now Sri Lanka, a former British colony then of ten million people off the southern coast of India. There for the next fifty years, he turned his thoughts to the future.

He was obsessed with the question of whether there might be some omnipotent entity in the universe. Calling himself a "pantheist" and a "crypto-Buddhist," he was steadfastly opposed to religion, describing it as "the most malevolent and persistent of all mind viruses. We should get rid of it as quick as we can."[147] "The greatest tragedy in mankind's entire history may be the hijacking of morality by religion."[148] The possibility of a sentient network haunted his writing.

Clarke's deep knowledge of space travel and predilection for exotic jackets made him a popular television interview during the first extraordinary years of America's mission to the moon. He was knighted by the Queen in 2000, and other honors descended upon him in his last years. A prescient scientist in his own right, he said he wanted to be remembered for his fiction.

2001 (1968): In his most famous work, he concocts a gauzy techno-mystery in which an astronaut becomes one with some sort of celestial super-mind. In the course of exploring one of the moon's craters, scientists have uncovered a black crystalline monolith, apparently placed there to monitor the evolution of man and guide him along the right path. When the excavation proceeds and the light of the sun falls upon it for the first time in three million years, the monolith begins to emit a piercing radio signal connecting it to something far away on the distant moon of Saturn. The decision is made to trace the path of the signal, and as the main story begins, Dr. David Bowman is piloting the *Discovery One* toward Saturn, along with his co-pilot and three colleagues in hibernation chambers waiting to be awakened when the planet comes into sight.

But HAL, the onboard computer, precipitates a failure in one of the circuit boards, and when Bowman tries to fix it, HAL breaks the atmospheric seal on the spacecraft, killing the co-pilot and three colleagues. Bowman escapes in an emergency pod and continues on the voyage alone, and as he approaches the Saturn moon at last he sees a second monolith, similar to the first. The monolith opens, swallowing Bowman and his space pod, and the last message we hear is "The thing's hollow — it goes on forever — and — oh my God — it's full of stars."

In the final act — more clearly presented in the book (by Clarke) than in the screenplay (by Stanley Kubrick) — Bowman is transformed into a non-corporeal "star child" that can travel space forever. The star child returns to earth where nations are locked in a dangerous military standoff and he destroys a nuclear warhead that has been placed in orbit around our planet. Mankind is saved once again.

Childhood's End (1953): But in his best book, Clarke presents his idea of a future force, and like Lucas, Roddenberry, and Asimov, he sees it as some kind of shared mind. Clarke imagines a fleet of large silver spaceships settling silently over the major cities of the world, slowly quieting international strife and bringing the human race to a new level of peaceful cooperation and productivity.

Thus pacified, the world experiences an explosion of scientific knowledge, but without the stimulus of strife and competition, all forms of creative art cease. No new works of painting, literature, or music are produced for a generation. The human race is too intent upon savoring the pleasures of the present; utopia is here at last. Later, when the creatures from the silver spaceships — the Overlords — provide a magical system for seeing the reality of history, people realize that their religious myths have no basis in fact, and religion completely disappears from the planet. As he tells the story, Clarke cannot disguise his glee:

> Within a few days, all mankind's multitudinous messiahs had lost their divinity. Beneath the fierce and passionless light of truth, faiths that had sustained millions for twice a thousand years vanished like the morning dew. All the good and evil they had wrought were swept suddenly into the past and could touch the minds of men no more.[149] — *Childhood's End (1953)*

After a lifetime of peace and pleasure, a new generation of children appears, equipped with extraordinary mental powers including prescience, telepathy, and the ability to visualize other worlds in deep space. As these children grow, they fall silent. Like today's teenagers texting alone in their rooms, they frequently retreat into trance-like isolation for hours at a time, mystically communicating with each other over an unseen network, contemplating the fathomless complexities of the universe.

> Like an epidemic spreading swiftly from land to land, the metamorphosis infected the entire human race. It touched practically no one above the age of ten, and no one below that age escaped.[150]

The Overlords now confess that they have come to protect and assist the birth of a new race, explaining that their own species, while highly developed, is no longer capable of evolution. "Our potentialities are exhausted, but yours are still untapped. [You] are linked in ways we do not understand, with powers... that are now awakening on your world."

As we are above you, so there is something above us using us for its own purposes. We have never discovered what it is, though we have been its tool for ages and dare not disobey it... You call us the Overlords, not knowing the irony of that title. Let us say that above us is the Overmind, using us as the potter uses the wheel.[151]

"In a few years it will all be over, and the human race will have divided in twain. There is no way back, and no future for the world you know. All the hopes and dreams of your race are ended now. You have given birth to your successors, and it is your tragedy that you will never understand them... Indeed they will not possess minds as you know them. They will be a single entity as you yourselves are the sums of your myriad cells.[152]

William Gibson [1948-]

Born and brought up in the American South, William Gibson was a tall, bookish, lonely child, nursed on the horror fantasies of H.P. Lovecraft, *The Twilight Zone*, and science fiction magazines, which he described as "abundant, perpetually replenished, and a freely available source of oxygen. You saw things differently in extraordinary company."[153] In high school, he became a serious sci-fi fan, went to science fiction conventions, and sank into the worlds of Robert Heinlein, Theodore Sturgeon, the darker mysteries of Philip K. Dick, and the eccentric writing of William Burroughs, Thomas Pynchon, and Terry Southern. He determined to become a writer himself.

In 1967, he announced to his draft board that his "one ambition in life was to take every mind-altering substance,"[154] but the board was uninspired by his enthusiasm and the war went ahead without him. These were the hippie years, years of coffee houses, folk music, dreams of traveling in space, and the emerging mythology of big computers. They were years of race riots and Woodstock, an escape to Canada, kicking around Europe and the Mediterranean and finally settling, married, in Vancouver. By 1977, at the age of thirty, he had a child. He was back in college, majoring in English, and starting to sell science fiction stories to the pulps. Then in 1982, after meeting Terry Carr at a convention, Gibson was invited to contribute a novel if he wished to undertake it. He would have a year to get it done.

Neuromancer (1984): The result was one of the most successful science fiction novels of the twentieth century. In it, Case, a brilliant computer cowboy and ex-drug addict, blacklisted by the hacking fraternity and high on the hit list of an angry drug lord, is hired by the mysterious Armitage to hack a worldwide computer network called the Matrix and retrieve a data file containing the reconstructed consciousness of Neuromancer, a superconsciousness locked away deep in the network, having taken the form of a young boy living with the reconstructed consciousness of Case's long-dead girlfriend, Linda Lee.

Through a series of complex hacking tests and brilliant victories, Case frees Neuromancer and as the story ends, the newly liberated super-entity has found another superconsciousness as powerful as itself, transmitting from across the galaxy. Case is cured of all vestiges of his former addiction, and when he visits Neuromancer one last time he sees that his own consciousness has been cloned, and is now waving to him from the leafy glades of cyberspace where he lives with Linda Lee.

The tale is full of nightmare imagery, drug addiction, psychic and bionic reconstructions, and devious intelligence constructs. It is ironic, intentionally obscure, and deeply reflective of the world at the time. The economy of Japan has risen up out of the gurgling cyber-swamp. Human augmentation has reached its natural and malevolent maturity, and vast databases guarded by complex codes and protocols now shelter avatars and mutants living in rainy slums rank with communicable viruses, spies and counter-spies, and an endless supply of mind-altering substances. Gibson's dark vision, so eloquently evoked in techno-baroque detail, became known in science fiction circles as cyberpunk, the new standard model for depicting the future of our species.

The Matrix itself, as Gibson calls the network, is a lawless domain like Arthur Clarke's Overmind, with no higher authority, no central government like the world of Star Trek, no aristocracy of scientists and Asimov intellectuals. It is every criminal for himself, an intergalactic sprawl of global corporations, violent Yakusa gangs prowling the solar system, and cyber-villains armed with powerful technologies enlisted in the traditional pursuit of wealth, domination, and revenge. And against this evil network struggles a perverse version of the lonesome samurai longing to be whole again.

Given Gibson's background, the technical sophistication of this novel was unexpected. He was computer illiterate and wrote the story on a 1927 portable Hermes typewriter he later described as "the kind of thing Hemingway might have used in the field."[155] He didn't have a personal computer until 1988, or an email address until 1996. But what made this work even more unexpected was Gibson's invention of cyberspace. The future network he dreams of is not just an electronic system for sending messages back and forth, which had been written about for more than a century. Nor is it limited to a community of like-minded participants sharing their thoughts, which Teilhard had dreamed about in 1915. It is a shared consciousness, an entirely fabricated metaverse in which we live and act and change each other's lives. Leaving our physical bodies slumped over a flickering screen, we enter a shared virtual space of real and imagined people with real and invented tools, inflicting on each other the pains and joys of "life."

The French philosopher René Descartes thought the only world we can know for certain is the world of the mind. Our knowledge is limited to what we perceive through our sometimes unreliable senses. But in the seventeenth century, the mind was a solitary place with seating for one. What Gibson saw was that the mind could be opened to others, not only the ones we bring along in our imagination but also real people who have jacked into the system at the same time. In *Neuromancer*, the network became a place, a new agora beyond the limitations of the physical world, beyond its laws and customs, beyond the boundaries of time and space, where participants establish communities, trade resources, form unlikely alliances, and go to war. The network, conceived as a tool for global communications, had become a world in itself.

'The Matrix has its roots in primitive arcade games,' said the voice-over, 'in early graphics programs and military experimentation with cranial jacks.' On the Sony, a two-dimensional space war faded behind a forest of mathematically generated ferns, demonstrating the spatial possibilities of logarithmic spirals; cold blue military footage burned through, lab animals wired into test systems, helmets feeding into fire control circuits of tanks and war planes.[156] — *William Gibson, Neuromancer (1984)*

From a technical standpoint, what Gibson imagined is very likely to come true. In time alternative reality will offer an ever-present overlay to experience, a heads-up display, a signal blinking at the edge of our glasses, supporting our decisions and sometimes clashing with them. Then networks, real and virtual, will co-exist, and occasionally collide.

What William Gibson imagined in *Neuromancer* was a network of false people, false places, and false values, made vivid and intoxicating by computer-generated detail. It was a virtual world where every player was a participant, dealing not only with programmed avatars pretending to be people but with real people pretending to be avatars. Characters in his novel share intimate thoughts and emotions in this digital play space. They fight battles, fall in love, and wound each other in deeply psychological ways.

Cyberspace. A consensual hallucination experienced daily by billions of legitimate operators, in every nation... A graphic representation of data abstracted from the banks of every computer in the human system. Unthinkable complexity. Lines of light ranged in the nonspace of the mind, clusters and constellations of data. Like city lights, receding.[157]

Operating beyond government, beyond geographic boundaries, beyond the pesky laws of physics and biology, beyond the conventions of civilized society, this is a network connecting us in ways we have never imagined, in an infinite community of communities. But for Gibson, the network of the future will be more than that. It is a shared consciousness involving humans and non-humans alike.

A Future World

What are we to make of these visions? Among the best science fiction writers of the last fifty years, there are several points of consensus on how an emerging global network will change the human race.

Geography has disappeared: Throughout this literature, there are new eusocial collectives, hives, swarms, committees, and alliances of deeply communicating creatures whose combined intelligence is greater in scope than that of any individual. And they are indifferent to national boundaries. In nearly every case, the works portray a future interconnected in a high-bandwidth network extending down into all but the lowest classes of society. In the future these writers have imagined, people will share knowledge and guidance beyond the limits of language and geography, in real time, without benefit of a superior controller or intermediary. The fiction of the '50s and '60s did not explain how these collectives would work; it was a vision of social revolution without borders, offered long before the technology appeared that could make it possible.

Humans will reach new powers of cognition: Superior intelligence, analytical ability, and mystical insight are commonly supposed to characterize the members of our future species, particularly with regard to brain/mind processes. Robert Heinlein imagined a "Fair Witness" who could dispassionately record and analyze the facts of any event.[158] Thufir Hawat, in Frank Herbert's *Dune* novels, is a mentat-for-hire with cognitive powers that exceed most computers.[159] Just as Homo sapiens were recognized as different when they first appeared in the forest, these "super" beings of the future will be recognized as different. As children, they will appear with their faculties fully formed, not taught to them by mentors of an older time, and they will remain connected to others of their kind. But as envisioned by science fiction, they invariably lack an important faculty of their predecessors, and it should give us pause. The inhabitants of networks described in this fiction emphasize analysis and reason rather than imagination or enhanced emotional understanding. They do not feel.

Except in a very few cases, the networks fail to facilitate the exchange of attitudes and emotions, and it is a deficit even the greatest writers sense. In a goodbye video made for his friends on the occasion of his ninetieth birthday, Arthur Clarke expressed a longing for this dimension in human communication that even he had failed to incorporate in his vision of the future:

Technology tools help us to gather and disseminate information, but we also need qualities like tolerance and compassion to achieve greater understanding between peoples and nations... I hope we have learned something from the most barbaric century in history, the twentieth. I would like to see us overcome our tribal divisions, and begin to think and act as if

we were one family. That would be real globalization.[160] — *Arthur Clarke,*
The Final Goodbye (2008)

Religion and politics will fade away: In the future as imagined in science
fiction, the ideas of organized religion and nationhood have been transformed
into an instinct for individual spirituality. In an interesting interview with Carl
Sagan, the astronomer, and Dr. Stephen Hawking, the physicist, Clarke quotes
Nehru: "Politics and religion are obsolete; the time has come for science and
spirituality."[161] Our traditional idea of God is now nowhere to be seen except
as a twisted, malevolent, malfunctioning computer. As nations lumber against
each other in the fog and blood of war, weakened from battle and obsessed with
self-aggrandizement, something new will emerge to guide our lives.

A flatter social world: Information is fragile. Every time it is restated,
transferred, or simplified it becomes degraded by misunderstanding and bias.
So decisions in the future should be delegated out to the primary fact space
whenever possible. Fast, wide-band networks allow us to do that, shifting from
traditional top-down "authority" hierarchies to flatter, more collegial structures.
And that often means that organizations of the future will be led from the
middle, not the top. Our greatest hero literature reflects that change.

El Cid, the fictional Spanish nobleman of 1000 AD, was cast out of court
then fought his way back as a warlord, conquered the enemy, and became the
ruler of all Valencia. His story glorified the monarchy and gave every young
man a reason to worship the king. Arthur of Britain gives us a similar tale; a
young boy, wisely mentored, takes up a magical sword and becomes the
virtuous and all-powerful king, the object of our love and loyalty. In 1844, the
most popular novel was *The Count of Monte Cristo* by Alexandre Dumas about
a young naval officer, unfairly accused and imprisoned by his family's enemies.
The hero escapes, exacts revenge, and rises to his new station as a clever,
resourceful, and wealthy aristocrat, replacing the flawed king as the object of
our admiration.

But by the middle of the twentieth century, the heroes of our fiction come
out of the people, do great deeds, and then go back to their village. In *High
Noon*, Gary Cooper faces the outlaws alone, prevails, and then throws his badge
of authority in the dirt. In *Star Wars*, Han Solo, the irascible and antisocial
warrior, leads Luke and his ragtag alliance to defeat the Imperial Empire, then

returns to his samurai life. In *Neuromancer*, Case is the wounded hacker, recruited for his extraordinary technical skills, who defeats the faceless systems of a global media conglomerate, defies the laws of the intergalactic police, and finds resolution, alone again, in the infinite halls of cyberspace.

The transformation to a flatter world has been most vividly demonstrated in the evolution of *Star Trek*, the best-known science fiction story of the last fifty years. In the original series that ran from 1966 to 1969, William Shatner as the iconic Captain Kirk made his decisions alone at the ship's bridge, the ultimate manifestation of the organization's top-down hierarchy. But when the series was revived as *Star Trek: The Next Generation* from 1987 to 1994, Patrick Stewart as Captain Jean-Luc Picard convenes his senior officers around a single table where they share diverse but complementary skills and responsibilities. Except for matters involving the navigation of the ship, the decision structure has changed from a military squad to a team of equals, from Captain Kirk's crisp decide-and-delegate hierarchy to the more collegial model of consensus and cooperation.[162] Picard treats his team as respected experts in their fields; he trusts them. Information is shared; they think together.

What science fiction tells us about the future is that people will reach conclusions based on a sense of what most of the others in their chosen community believe, even when it may be contrary to their own experience and self-interest. Thinking together is what the network technology enables, and where science fiction tells us we are headed. If we are all sharing our lives in an intimate, always-connected community, then, as Teilhard suggested, the moral force that guides us in the future will no longer be the authority of the all-powerful Church or State but something new and humble, rising out of us.

Chapter 10
The Age of Aquarius

Nietzsche and Sartre argued that the great institutions had failed, leaving us stranded and alone in a world where nothing made sense anymore. The Judeo-Christian doctrine of love had been forgotten in the Church's scramble for institutional power, while the empires of Europe, fighting for survival, had become convulsed in pointless and costly wars. The institutional world was in ruins. Individuals were free (Sartre says "condemned") to make it on their own as best they could.

When computer technology began to infiltrate our lives, the hope was it could normalize an historically unruly labor force, get everyone in line, and make life more automated and easier for the aristocracy to control. But ever smaller and more versatile personal computers brought new freedoms to individuals instead, and then connected them in network communities whose reach and power we have scarcely begun to recognize.

Developments in brain/mind science and the counter-culture mindset of the '60s, including the use of mind-altering drugs, encouraged the idea that people could discover new levels of personal awareness and creativity within themselves. Through meditation, exercise, and training they could shake free of old social and intellectual constraints and dance in a new and happier world. The bible of this movement was *The Aquarian Conspiracy*, an exuberant exploration of the idea by Marilyn Ferguson, its high priestess and informal leader of a worldwide network of enthusiasts and practitioners.

Marilyn Ferguson [1938-2008]

Ferguson was far out and in the right place. Sometimes it seems the West is divided into Europe, America, and California, and that was the case in 1980. While America was riding a revival of traditional religious faith and Europe was gnawing on the bones of existentialism, life in California, as Harold Bloom described it, was an "orange grove." Rising out of the ferment of the '60s, the

New Age was a creature of the personal potential movement, a smoky, bare-it-all sing-along celebrating the collapse of a hundred years of American "normalness" and the opening of society's new frontier. Marilyn Ferguson saw how this vision and the enabling technology would change the community and she became an enthusiastic and seductive advocate, leading her flock in new directions. Bloom said she was the movement's high priestess and its most enthusiastic (and uncritical) chronicler. She was an evangelist, and her comprehensive and charismatic catalog of New Age activities struck a responsive chord in America, in Europe, and around the world.

Alvin Toffler had just published *The Third Wave*, arguing that in the coming Information Age there would be less standardization and more individual or artisanal production, as well as a shift away from the nation-state toward tribal and religious loyalties. Marshall McLuhan was advancing the idea that new technology would connect us in a "global village," inherently amoral and free from the constraints of a ruling class. Suddenly you would be able to say anything to anyone anywhere.

At CBS in those years, the news division had a manual that soberly instructed its editors to "tell the audience what they need to know." A department of Standards and Practices at each network enforced a narrow model of morality based on white, suburban, middle-class, Judeo-Christian traditions. Nothing could be broadcast that appealed to prurient interests, referred to homosexuality or women's rights, questioned God or religion, or was deemed contrary to the prevailing political view. In 1969, the folk-singing/comedy duo the Smothers Brothers had their prime-time variety show canceled for allowing Pete Seeger to sing an anti-war song on the air. But now cable offered to free us from all that. Satellite dishes on the roof would soon connect every household to a wide world of education, healthcare, and true democracy.

The personal computer emerged as the engine of this revolution. Steve Jobs, Steve Wozniak, and their friends were stealing components from their Silicon Valley employers, building the computers in a garage, and watching as a new technology whose potential they scarcely understood themselves empowered individuals, even elementary school students, in an astonishing array of unexpected applications. Jobs, co-founder of Apple, declared the potential of home computing "insanely great," and his personal net worth went from $1 million in 1978 to $100 million in 1980. He was then twenty-five.

It was an age of bumper stickers. It was a time of promise.

Ferguson was a young Irish-American woman from Colorado with two ex-husbands and three kids, a struggling freelance writer who found a new home in Los Angeles, a life-changing inspiration in transcendental meditation, and a modest income running a newsletter she had started about discoveries in brain/mind science. In the process, she began to sense a "massive realignment" in society. She called it a paradigm shift, but it was more like a poorly organized prison riot, an overthrow of the established hierarchy she thought had largely failed — in medicine, in politics, and in social organizations. Father did not know best.

The Human Potential Movement. The argument of Ferguson's book — and of New Age writing in general — was that expanded consciousness would bring the individual up to a fresh level of insight and creativity, newly able to exploit the tools Doug Engelbart was imagining. In an age where information was equally available to everyone, the network model of many to many would be a more productive organization scheme than the traditional one-to-many hierarchy.

New Age ideas unblock the mind, clarify our motivations, and create a feeling of new opportunity, even if only for a moment. One correspondent quoted in Ferguson's book wrote:

> Suddenly I was overwhelmed by the beauty of everything I saw. This vivid, transcending experience tore apart my limited outlook. I had never realized the emotional heights possible. In this half-hour solitary experience I felt unity with all, universal love, connectedness. This smashing time destroyed my old reality permanently.[163] — *Marilyn Ferguson, The Aquarian Conspiracy (1980)*

And another:

> "One day in the spring while taking a walk after meditating, I had an electric feeling which lasted about five seconds in which I felt totally integrated with the creative force of the universe. I "saw" what spiritual transformation was

trying to do, what my mission in life was, and several alternative ways I might accomplish it."[164]

At the height of their popularity in the 1980s, New Age ideas were adopted by schools, sports teams, military units, and even prison groups where expanded consciousness training was found to result in a more open and productive environment. Businesses tried "consciousness-raising" techniques among their executives. Stanford University's Graduate School of Business included meditation, "dream work," and a discussion of the "New Age Capitalist" in its curriculum. In 1986, managers from IBM, AT&T, and General Motors held a conference to discuss how metaphysics and mysticism might help them compete in a world market.[165]

In her book, Ferguson goes further to argue that a clearer understanding of one's own mental motivations and obstacles can be the basis for a new personal morality, a guide to successful action in a complicated world. You are free to do your own thing if you dare. She compared the challenge of gaining control over your life to the American Revolution. The founding fathers were committed to getting rid of the king and becoming sovereign. Today, she said, we are doing that again.

> What we didn't realize was that there is political tyranny and there is tyranny of our own minds. How do you become your own king; how do you learn to govern yourself? We are at the brink. We can keep doing these useless reforms that don't get us anywhere, or we can work on the instrument itself [the mind] which is the cause of our wars and our injustices and our violence.[166]

From Rousseau to freedom: It is a straight line from Ferguson back to Sartre's declaration that we must become our true selves, to Nietzsche's "will to power," and to Kant's "moral law within." We no longer need someone else to provide incentives or absolution. She said we are in charge of our own lives.

It follows that there is no "good" or "evil" in the world, no sin or guilt, only fear and negativity that block us from reaching a new spiritual level. New Age believers tended to accept the Eastern idea of Karma, a cosmic balance, and a continuation of our higher self after the death of the body.

Those filling out the Aquarian Conspiracy questionnaire commented that their experiences had forced them to give up their previous assumption that bodily death ends consciousness. Despite their disaffiliation with formal religion, 53 percent expressed strong belief in such survival and another 23 percent said they were "moderately sure," a total of 75 percent. Only 5 percent were skeptical and 3 percent disbelieving.[167]

The benefits of understanding one's fears, conflicts, and motivations had been well documented, and bringing those feelings to a level of conscious consideration, Freud's primary insight, has certainly proved to be important for good mental health. The continued discovery in the 1970s of the mind's extraordinary nature, as well as Ferguson's ongoing survey of all the latest neuroscience, gave this fizzy consciousness-expansion talk a feeling of immediacy. There was the sense that we were on the edge of something magical and transforming, and she was a popular speaker around the world, applying the lessons of her research to everything from education to politics to women's rights. But the moments of enlightenment, peak performance, or profound creative power she spoke of were rare and difficult to sustain, and for most people the benefits, while seductive, were hard to confirm.

Her ideas about networking, on the other hand, were sound and delivered with an infectious wink of anarchy. If you were running an eighteenth-century British Man-of-War it made sense to organize the men along strict lines of class and function, ascending through ranks from the lowest and least worthy tar to the captain who held the power of life and death over everyone in his little wooden world. But in the late twentieth century, when technology had put all the information in the hands of everyone on board, a more horizontal network arrangement offered a way to divide the tasks more logically and get the benefit of everyone's unique talents and opinions.

Networks gave everyone a voice, and sometimes everyone was speaking at once. She writes:

Networking was now a verb, and it was done by conferences, phone calls, air travel, books, phantom organizations, papers, pamphleteering, photocopying, lectures, workshops, parties, grapevines, mutual friends, summit meetings, coalitions, tapes, newsletters... Experiences and insights were shared, argued, tested, adapted, and shaken down into their usable elements very quickly.[168]

Comparing the network to the human brain:

The network is an alert responsive form of social organization. Information moves in a nonlinear fashion, all at once, and in a meaningful way.[169]

Networks are the strategy by which small groups can transform an entire society. Gandhi used coalitions to lead India to independence. He called it "grouping unities" and said it was essential to success. The circle of unities thus grouped in the right fashion will ever grow in circumference until at last, it is coterminous with the whole world.

While most of our institutions are faltering, a twentieth-century version of the ancient tribe or kinship has emerged: the network, a tool for the next step in human evolution.[170]

Holistic: Her favorite word was "holistic." The specific meaning of that term is that the whole is visible in the part. The soul and meaning of the group is visible in each of its members. In a holistic entity, the essence of knowledge, memory, functionality, and even will is distributed throughout, not clustered in the upper regions of some ideological ziggurat, vulnerable to dizziness and decapitation. But Ferguson used it as a dog whistle to crypto-anarchists. Down with the bosses and their corrupt politics, their stupid wars, and their failed economies; down with the powerful and the proud, striding around in their know-it-all hats telling us (young women particularly) what was right and wrong. There was about her writing a deep, "Don't Tread on Me" resistance to authority of any kind, that peculiarly American instinct for individualism that goes back to the beginning.

A network has no leader; leadership passes from one member to another. [Quoting Carl Rogers], 'we've had a few Thoreau's, but never hundreds of thousands of people, young and old alike, willing to obey some laws and disobey others on the basis of their own personal moral judgment.'[171]

She believed the founding fathers had a mystical understanding of individual worth and the power of freedom. They had tried hard to build that into our new form of government, but she thought they might be disappointed to see what we have done with it. Nonetheless, she remained optimistic.

Quoting Theodore Roszak, professor of counter-culture at California State, Ferguson added that while the power of the network makes an organization more functional, it also vastly enriches the lives of its members.

> Whatever their stated purpose, the function of most of these networks is mutual support and enrichment, empowerment of the individual, and cooperation to effect change. Most aim for a more humane and hospitable world.[172]

And then, given a little encouragement, she leans forward in a conspiratorial whisper and suggests that the way to change a system is to cast it into chaos and wait for spontaneous self-organization to re-form the members in a new and more powerful pattern. Her friend Ilya Prigogine had just received the Nobel Prize for his theory of dissipative structures, showing how this works with chemicals. Friedrich Hayek argued that the economy was a continuing spontaneous re-ordering. Michael Polanyi thought science was a process of alternating chaos and renewal. Paul Krugman thought cities were examples of random self-organizing systems. Ferguson saw the pattern in all this:

> As to the nature of the change, we can tell you very little... it spreads explosively, like the formation of crystals around the next nucleus in a saturated solution.[173]

Let the explosions begin.

There are two problems with the way she saw this future. She continually falls under the spell of language, thinking that an argument so beautifully stated must therefore be true. We are dazzled. Our powers of reason are overwhelmed:

> God is experienced as flow, wholeness, the infinite kaleidoscope of life and death, Ultimate Cause, the ground of being that Alan Watts called 'the silence out of which all sound comes.'[174]

Repeated examples of this kind of enigmatic oracularity among New Age poets and songwriters can be an impediment to further serious consideration.

The second is what we might call the "cosmic crystal" maneuver. Drawing on her prodigious command of science and her friendship with geniuses whose knowledge is past all understanding, she often cites an example from the latest research in neuroscience, living systems, or physics and then applies it to human behavior as if what is true in one realm must, therefore, be true in another. Spontaneous self-organization, for example, may work in saturated fluids, but the idea that a city suddenly without government or infrastructure could spontaneously reorganize itself along new and superior lines might be dangerous to take seriously.

In its brief ascendancy in the 1970s and '80s, the New Age movement created fellowship at a new level. Everyone who believed was talking with everyone else. It was an optimistic world, full of new science and neo-pagan mythology, free of doctrine or religious structure of any kind. Full of hope. After the Vietnam War and before the appearance of the internet, it was a time when fellowship was experienced as a network, the intimacy of which had probably not been seen since the Christians held their meetings in the catacombs beneath the streets of ancient Rome.

High Above the Center Ring

Marilyn Ferguson was a good friend of mine for many years, though I confess I didn't always return her calls. A two-hour session with her on the phone — and it was rarely less than that — was the verbal equivalent of a mixed martial arts match; everything was at stake and you had to keep up. She took a wild, antic delight in scampering through ideas lofty, silly, and impossible at the same time, and a bout with her was always a dizzying, intoxicating, sometimes punishing adventure. She had an encyclopedic knowledge of the brain/mind literature and expected you to move fast, punch hard, and show her your best tricks. We interrupted each other all the time, leaping over the obviosities and bringing in or sweeping aside whole swaths of thought, taken as read, so we could get more quickly to the next new idea.

We dragged one realm of knowledge on top of another and turned them both like bits of colored glass in a kaleidoscope, bringing out surprising patterns in each. Like kids trading marbles, we swapped insights or new ideas we had collected since our last meeting. We reveled in the ability of an apt and agile phrase to capture a complicated truth — she was a grandmaster at that: "Nobody knows as much as all of us know."

You didn't get very far into the topic of the day though, before realizing how unorthodox her thinking was. She believed in sensing the current of the world's thoughts and going with it like a kite in the wind. She had a scheme for a three-dimensional holographic sound that was somehow tied in with an old love affair or a former husband. It was never clear which. She wanted to start a publishing cooperative that would treat authors with respect — a charming fantasy but doomed, of course. She told me she communicated with the dead — the gone-yonders, as she called them — and said her secret friend was Thomas Jefferson, who often told her how disappointed he was to see the current state of the nation. She was experimenting with very short bursts of automatic writing — taking dictation from spirits. She felt those sessions liberated her from the constraints of conventional thought, and she sent me what she had done so far. To paraphrase James Russell Lowell writing about another mystic, Edgar Allen Poe, I think Marilyn Ferguson was three-fifths genius and two-fifths sheer fudge.

When we last got together, a year or so before her death, she was living, with a man, I think, in a rusty old Los Angeles factory that had been converted into an artists' commune. We had beers and a microwave supper in a dingy serve-yourself café the residents had put up in one of the empty studios, and we talked. The millions she had made from her best-selling book were all gone. Her publisher had abandoned her and she was estranged from her children. But she was as brilliant as ever, insightful and funny in her impudent, Colorado way, full of beans and pushing the envelope of ideas about human potential and the future of thinking together. She was making notes on a new book she was going to call "Uncommon Sense," and she talked about a new network model that was deeply spiritual (not religious) and maybe closer to what Teilhard had envisioned.

When she called me in the late summer of 2008, she said she had been diagnosed with narcolepsy. She was sleeping sixteen hours a day and having difficulty working for more than thirty minutes at a time. Her doctors were treating her with experimental drugs, which I think she was augmenting with some of her own, and she was trying to get her life organized at last. And in the middle of all that, she died of a heart attack. I wrote to her daughter, offering to return the papers her mother had sent me, but I never heard back.

I tell you this for two reasons. First, when ideas are moved to the abstract layer of philosophy or literature they are often bleached of the ambiguities, the contradictions, and the personal foibles that give them beauty, broader meaning, and a kind of human truth. Reading Marilyn Ferguson's ideas without knowing who she was or understanding the tenor of her times is like judging a circus from a circus poster. You have to smell the sawdust and the elephants. You have to feel your heart leap at the sight of the trapeze artist, swinging by her ankles high above the center ring.

But the second reason is more important. Marilyn Ferguson was the new Homo colloquium, the Network Man. I think she knew she was living an unusual life, but if I told her she had ascended into Teilhard's noösphere sooner than the rest of us, she would have cocked her head and laughed. Now, on the other side of the internet revolution, we can see with astonishment how she was able to conduct her life high at the outer edge of reality.

All of a sudden she was a clearinghouse for research papers, unpublished books, and speculative schemes in pseudo-science and social transformation. She was on the phone with a pantheon of visionaries, Nobel laureates, and swamis like Buckminster Fuller, Werner Erhard, Ilya Prigogine, Fritjof Capra, Al Gore, and Ted Turner. First through her *Brain/Mind* newsletter and then through her book, she was breathlessly keeping up with the leading edge of neuroscience and revolutionary social change, even as she served as hostess of the longest-running permanently floating virtual cocktail party in the Western world. She knew everyone and kept everybody at his best, every thought spinning, and every insight aptly phrased and in circulation until it found a rooting place in this theory or that witty op-ed piece for the *Times*. "It was tremendously helpful because [she] bound people together and informed us of each other's work," physicist Fritjof Capra said later. "Marilyn Ferguson's main achievement — and it was a tremendous achievement — was that she sustained this networking of the alternative culture and New Age movement long before there was an Internet."[175]

She lost herself in it. She had lost a grip on her personal life, her health, and her financial wellbeing, but I don't think that mattered to her at all. She was living life in the matrix with more joy and energy and carelessness than the rest of us would have dared.

Leaving Marilyn, hugging her for the last time in the cold shadows of that café, I was aware of how pale, small, and as it turned out ephemeral our physical lives are. But in another sense I knew that our parting was irrelevant, nothing to be concerned about. I would always have the gift of her luminous intelligence, her vital, almost childlike curiosity, and her sloppy heart, winking like the fiddler's daughter and beckoning us toward a new world.

Chapter 11
Truth is Local

Then, with no help from government, high-technology corporations, or the academy, a dream of the world's knowledge available over a single network suddenly sprang to life, along with a radically new kind of community that could make such a miracle sustainable.

The vision of a world library had been around for a hundred years; nothing new there. Technology was now producing computers fast enough and cheap enough to put that library on every desk, all interconnected as Grace Hopper said they should be. The editing software necessary to build the library had even been written. But now came the dream of a knowledge-sharing network breaking all the rules, a crazy, free-wheeling information world entirely unlike anything that had gone before, and deeply unsettling for those who believe that truth is absolute and must be respected. It was an idea Rousseau himself might have come up with, turning the world's knowledge aristocracies upside down.

Jimmy Wales [1966-]

In January 2001, Jimmy Wales and Larry Sanger, two internet entrepreneurs, were faced with the fact that their new online encyclopedia, Nupedia, was going nowhere. The original plan had been to invite experts in different fields to create items that would then be reviewed by qualified peers and published online — a process sanctified by nearly two thousand years of scholarly publishing. This is how serious truth had always been arrived at.

But this time it wasn't working. At thirty-two, Larry Sanger had a Ph.D. in the theory of knowledge from Ohio State and was a believer in the academic process. He was the editor, trying to pump up the content. His partner, Jimmy Wales, was thirty-five, the money guy and a lover of encyclopedias from his youth in Huntsville, Alabama. A precocious home-schooled student, Wales had entered college at sixteen and completed all but his thesis for a Ph.D. in finance before going to work as an options and foreign currency trader. In six years, he had made enough money to retire and start Boomis, an adult content search site on the wild new worldwide web. But that began to falter as competitors, including *Playboy*, flocked to the opportunity. Nupedia was his second try at a free online service, and now that, too, was stumbling at the starting line.

> The [original] idea was to have thousands of volunteers writing articles for an online encyclopedia in all languages. Initially, we found ourselves organizing the work in a very top-down, structured, academic, old-fashioned way. It was no fun for the volunteer writers because we had a lot of academic peer review committees who would criticize articles and give feedback. It was like handing in an essay at grad school, and basically intimidating to participate in.[176] — *Jimmy Wales (2007)*

Searching for answers, Sanger met for tacos with an old friend, Ben Kovitz, who suggested that the new wiki software might offer a solution to Nupedia's editorial bottleneck. Invented by Ward Cunningham, the open-source system had been designed to let programmers write and edit items while allowing others to freely comment, argue, and correct. It offered none of the academic checks and reviews Sanger was used to, but it might remove the procedural impediments that Nupedia contributors faced. And it could keep track of all changes. If every contributor's history on the site was visible to all, contributors might aspire to a reputation for quality and discipline.[177] And that, in turn, would ensure the editorial quality of the content. It worked for hackers — the new generation of free-wheeling computer anarchists — and it might solve Sanger's problem. With nothing to lose, the two men decided to give it a try. "Humor me," Sanger wrote on the Nupedia discussion forum a few days later. "Go there and add a little article. It will take all of five or ten minutes."

The new system took off. There were 150 articles submitted within weeks, and by the end of the year, there were 20,000 entries in eighteen languages, with 350 regular contributors. Instead of the hallowed tradition of selecting experts, having peer reviews of every item, and judging the accuracy of the information based on the credentials of the contributors (Voltaire would have been pleased), here was an entirely open regime where anyone could write anything, and anyone else could correct it. Something very unusual was happening.

Sanger was unhappy with the constant confusion of disrespectful contributors anonymously challenging long-standing "truths" and nitpicking each other's articles. He saw little legitimate scholarship in the process and feared that this new Wikipedia scheme was turning out ever-increasing volumes of junk. He argued with Wales that Nupedia's more regimented approach was the reliable road to truth and that more experts should be recruited. But Wales saw something different. In college, he had read an article by Friedrich Hayek arguing that truth is local. In "The Use of Knowledge in Society (1945) ,"[178] the Austrian economist wrote that when information is dispersed in a network, the most accurate information comes from those who are closest to the event or issue being described. A network that can harness this decentralized and undiluted knowledge and make it available to others will deliver information more efficiently and more accurately than any traditional "scholarly" system that tries to bring it into conformity with the central library. That radical libertarian sentiment became a fundamental part of his worldview, and when Sanger left the project in 2002, Wales applied it. Nupedia would be shut down and Wikipedia would go forward as an open-source encyclopedia. Anyone could contribute, anyone could edit the content, and the most useful knowledge would emerge from the honest efforts of volunteers, each competing to establish a reputation for research, accuracy, and insight.

Two radical ideas made Wikipedia important: of course, the information would be available to everyone in the world — that was obvious to all who were watching the technology unfold. What was radical was the idea that information would *come* from everyone in the world. Without credentials or institutional adornment, unbeholden to any guild of scholars, the contributors would offer their own work with only their reputation to recommend it. Teenage hackers, retired professors, and people in love with knowledge pitched in, all as anonymous, diverse, and as well-intentioned as the reading world. Wikipedia represented what Michael Foucault called a "radical redistribution of social power."[179]

The second idea was that the quality of the information would be debated and determined by the collective, based on conventionally accepted sources. What Rousseau called "the general will." Wikipedia denies the reliability of ecstatic revelation (faith). It explicitly eschews the authority of insight and imagination and gives no weight to the contributor's experience, academic standing, or eloquence. It is the ultimate flattening of our knowledge aristocracy, contrary to thousands of years of priesthoods, mandarins, scholars, philosophers, and scientists. It is free as Nietzsche said we should be free, and prone to the same dangers.

Today the open-source, online encyclopedia is updated every minute by thousands of contributors working autonomously in a network that stretches around the world. Without the discipline and imprimatur of publishers, this is a system that explicitly avoids art, opinion, and original research. If Gutenberg replaced "truth" with knowledge, Wikipedia is replacing knowledge with information. It will not lead to political or intellectual revolution, but it will arm with information those who have that goal.

Three Big Ideas

Wikipedia is not quite the network envisioned a century ago by Teilhard de Chardin, but it embodies three ideas that may be important as we continue to evolve in that direction.

Truth is local: For the last four thousand years — at least as long as there has been a way to write things down — communities have been largely characterized by a shared body of knowledge. It provides history, drama, and inspiration to their culture, a repository of established science, recipes for living, and moral guidance in their lives. And the mechanism for determining what is or is not included in that knowledge base has nearly always been some kind of central bureaucracy — the Church, the king, the academy, craft collectives, or societies of scholars. So the idea that such knowledge might now be opened to contributions by everyone in the community is truly radical. It is one thing to distribute knowledge equally to the whole world — the internet makes that possible. But Wikipedia allows the whole world to participate in *creating* that knowledge, as well. It gives everyone an equal voice. And like Gutenberg's little press, that changes everything.

With the establishment of Wikipedia, Wales and his colleagues wrote the second law of networks. Truth is local. The most accurate description of any issue usually comes from the person closest to the facts, though the idea that anyone should be allowed to contribute to the community knowledge base may seem as irresponsible as the idea that everyone should be allowed to vote. But Hayek argued that in a world where it is no longer possible for any authority to maintain a central, up-to-date library of global knowledge and experience, there is no practical alternative. The best and most important new ideas always struggle for acceptance at the far perimeter of society; the latest data will always be slow in making its way into the standard model. The fact is that a community that can quickly and wisely incorporate these innovations into its knowledge base will thrive in a changing world, and a community that cannot will, as E. O. Wilson once wrote, live in grass huts and die young of diseases they don't understand.

Most people are basically good: The second idea that makes Wikipedia successful addresses the concerns rising from the first. How do you deal with the chaos of having everyone talking all at once, even those who are malicious or misinformed? How can a world of uncredentialed amateurs compete with a hierarchy of robes? The answer is that contributions by new members are reviewed, and all contributions are subject to changes and additions by others. In practice, this means that nearly all articles on Wikipedia have been written and edited by two or three people and reflect the discussion and debate on the talk pages and editorial forums the system supports.[180]

Contributors may use screen names, but their identity on the network is persistent and the history of their behavior is available to all. So there are no anonymous hits, and malicious or erroneous efforts can be quickly reversed. Those who repeatedly thwart the rules are permanently expelled from the community.

The process of review, comment, and acceptance is rigorous. According to a study by the Wikimedia Community Department, 10 percent of the contributions surveyed were considered "better than average," and 47 percent of the items were deemed acceptable by Wiki standards. Twenty percent fell below the standard for acceptability and 23 percent were rejected as "vandalism," deliberate efforts to compromise the quality of information or the reputation of the person or organization described.[181]

In his testimony before the US Senate Committee on Homeland Security in 2014, Wales said he had watched the emergence of collaborative systems among programmers who write what they need and openly share and correct the contributions of others. He saw that with the lightest of controls, the community of contributors could police itself and produce good quality work in a system that was transparent and equitable. But he acknowledged that finding the right mix of discipline and independence was difficult. "Something [is needed] between a police state and anarchy; people are free, but respectful of the rules. A balance between openness and control [is needed] that puts power in the hands of the community."[182]

Wales is often quick to correct the impression that this is "the wisdom of crowds" or mob rule. Decisions are not made by a majority, or by groupthink which relies on social pressure to drive outliers toward consensus. Instead, he argues, it is a process of reasoned debate, back and forth within a self-selected group of participants, known to each other, with their reputations for intelligence and honest collaboration on the line.

> The truth is that people who are eager to push bizarre theories based on random speculation by lunatics do not generally find a fact-based, open culture of dialogue and debate to be to their liking. I think this is one of the huge benefits of Wikipedia, it allows ordinary people a quick way to rely on a resource where good people have thoughtfully sorted through the noise to arrive at a broad presentation of the truth.

> Basically, what I think works in a wiki is to trust people to do the right thing and trust them as much as you can possibly stand it, until it hurts your head and makes you scared for what they're going to break. Because that is what works.[183] — *Jimmy Wales (2004)*

It ought to be fun: "It should be exciting. It should be creative. For me, that's what makes life worth living, is having creativity and productivity, building things that are useful." Jimmy Wales' idea of fun is to do something constructive and helpful with his time, and he says the contributors feel the same way. He says they, too, are motivated by a desire to be productive, to be of use to others, and be recognized by their peers for having done meaningful work. But some of the fun of Wikipedia is also social. There is in everyone a longing to belong. A sense of fellowship is essential to any successful community, and Wikipedia works hard behind the scenes to reinforce the tradition of fairness and equality among the contributors, removing onerous restrictions and obstacles to productivity.

Even the hunt for accuracy has some of the aspects of a game. When a contributor submits a particularly good item, others with interest in the subject often award a Wikipedian note of praise that becomes a part of the author's public record. And when the item is offensive or wrong they pounce. It is easy to click on the contributor's name and see his or her history of activity on the site, both positive and negative, so every contributor is held to account for items, edits, and comments. The resulting environment of praise and shame creates an incentive for each contributor to aspire through hard work to higher rank and prestige in the volunteer organization.[184]

Rules for a Flatter World

In the long rise of our species from simple hunting groups to a world of people thinking together, Wikipedia is an important waypoint, and the details of its unusual operation deserve our attention. In nearly twenty years of existence, the organization behind the encyclopedia has developed rules that are peculiarly appropriate to the future of a networked world, and very different from traditional models. Sartre gave us the first law: each of us is responsible for the effect of our actions on the other members of the community. Hayek gave us the second law: truth is local. The most accurate account of any situation is likely to come from those closest to the fact space. And now Wales gives us the third law.

You are what you do: In the Wiki organization, there is no rank, only reputation. In the ultimate example of Sartre's existential idea, a Wikipedia contributor is known by contributions made and instances of praise received from other Wikipedians. A personal page may note language and technical skills, subject specialties, history of contributions, and whatever quirky characteristics the contributor chooses to highlight, available to all by clicking on the name wherever it appears on a talk page. Custom favors geeky, self-effacing humor, while mentions of political or ideological views are discouraged. Most contributors use only screen names; real names, titles, degrees, and academic or corporate credentials are very rarely disclosed.

As of 2019, there have been more than thirty-one million contributors registered. Half of them are under twenty-two years of age, 61 percent are college graduates, and about 84 percent are male, typical of the hacker community from which its earliest contributors were drawn.[185] The organization recognizes about 132,000 registered editors active at any time, and 1 percent of these are responsible for creating or shaping about 77 percent of the content.[186] According to one survey, half the active editors spend at least one hour a day editing, and a fifth spend more than three hours a day.[187] So the largest and most active encyclopedia on the internet is mostly the product of several thousand young educated males around the world, together adding an average of six hundred new articles a day.

Tiers of control: Within the ranks of Wikipedia volunteers, there are seven tiers of senior editors with commensurate levels of authority.

Founder: Jimmy Wales compares his authority to that of a British monarch whose "power should fade over time; an advisor helping people think about the bigger picture. I will be replaced by institutions within the community." He says he enjoys the respect of the community "only as long as I act thoughtfully and in fairness and justice to everyone, and consistent with the consensus of the community."[188]

Stewards: Beneath the founder are currently forty Wikipedia Stewards acting across all the languages, each one elected by at least 80 percent of active editors in all of Wikipediom, usually after years of active leadership. A third of these are native English speakers, though the vast majority are also fluent.[189] They have broad rights to block pages, remove contributors, make content changes, resolve disputes, and make administrative decisions consistent with the spirit and purpose of the organization.

Check-users and oversighters: Beneath the stewards are two classes of senior editors who have access to the contributor's real IP address so they can confirm that any individual is represented by only one user identity. They can suppress users' contributions, comments, identities, and other materials when they think suppression would improve the quality of the content or help resolve a conflict, and they can ensure that each contributor is authentic and unique, not a proxy or a fake name. Along with stewards, they are required to disclose their real identities to the Wikipedia Foundation. They are the organization's bulwark against fraud, vandalism, malicious behavior, and the other natural failings of any online community. If in their enthusiasm they make a wrong call, they are expected to acknowledge their error and apologize. They are the membership police.[190]

Below these senior levels are tens of thousands of administrators, bureaucrats, and "rollbackers" who carry the load of content editing. They are often assigned to projects, special subjects, or categories of contributions, and they are the content police. Administrators must be elected by at least 80 percent of members voting. They have usually been active members for several years, have created well-regarded articles, have participated often in editor forums, have a long history of good edits, and have no blocked articles to their name.[191] Senior editors have a private communications network that allows them to discuss content issues in confidence.

Two structural elements are critical in making Wikipedia work: (a) all contributors and editors have one and only one persistent identity, and (b) every action by every contributor is part of the permanent record available to every Wikipedia user. There are no anonymous participants. Well-behaved contributors are publicly praised, and miscreants are expelled from the community. The members police themselves.

This is the Panopticon effect. In the late eighteenth century, economist Jeremy Bentham proposed that prisons be built in a circular fashion with cells arranged symmetrically around a central guard station so all prisoners could be under observation all the time by each other as well as by the guards. Bentham said the condition of being under permanent observation by one's peers would be a powerful force for conformity, as has since been demonstrated by countless societies, corporations (open office designs), cities (surveillance cameras), and even countries (China's emerging facial recognition and Social Credit System). Networks like Wikipedia uniquely allow people to govern each other. In the stag hunt problem posed by Rousseau, for example, it is less likely that anyone would abandon his post to chase the rabbit if he knew that his dereliction would be immediately known to everyone else in the village.

The process is the product: With 18 billion pages viewed a month,[192] Wikipedia is the fifth most popular website in the world.[193] There are nearly five million articles in the English language Wikipedia, and twenty-three million more in the other 286 languages. A 2005 study by *Nature* magazine examined the quality of the site's scientific content and found an average of four errors per entry, only slightly higher than the three errors per entry found in the *Encyclopedia Britannica.*[194] These metrics suggest that this all-volunteer, all-amateur, non-profit, and devoutly egalitarian organization has largely become what Jimmy Wales called "a free encyclopedia of the highest possible quality [available] to every single person on the planet in their own language."[195]

It is popular within the Wikipedia community to say that its success is due to the group's core belief: there is no truth, there are only reliable sources. But behind that commitment lies a process of editorial discourse and debate that may be the organization's real genius. What makes Wikipedia work where many social networks have failed is the scrupulous fairness and civility with which the editorial debate proceeds. On the forums and talk pages rarely viewed by most users, content is argued and refined, following a dozen rules quoted so often they each have their own geeky acronym.

Four rules deal with the nature of the content on the network:

Reliable sources (RS): Wikipedia is not a source, it is a compendium of sources. Unlike Britannica or similar traditional encyclopedias, Wikipedia offers no independent "expert" overview, it summarizes overviews written by others.

No original research (NOR): Nothing is included that has not appeared elsewhere in a legitimate publication. Even when novelist Philip Roth wrote to correct a fact about one of his books, his correction could not be included until it had been published elsewhere.[196]

Write from a neutral point of view (NPOV): Items must be written without bias or advocacy. Even the most controversial topics are dealt with evenhandedly, with both sides then actively editing any aspect of the coverage they feel is unfair. Public relations language is quickly removed, disputants are silenced. Vandals, slanderers, propagandists, trolls, spammers, and hoaxers are identified and often expelled from the community. Even entire organizations are blocked. After six months of persistent revision, reversion, and argument, the Church of Scientology and dozens of individual members were blocked from contributing or commenting further.[197]

No conflict of interest (COI): If the author or editor of the item has a conflict of interest it must be declared and the author must withdraw from further editorial participation.

Three rules address the nature of the editorial debate:

Assume good faith (AGF): Despite occasional evidence to the contrary, editors are required to respond to any criticism as if it had been offered in good faith. According to Wikipedia expert Dariusz Jemielniak, claims of content ownership are discouraged, and an editor should not be upset if someone edits his or her lines. The ethos is to get it started, then make it right.[198]

No gaming (GAME): Editors are expected to advance their views on merit alone, and not "seek gotchas and loopholes," or "reprimand other editors for minor errors instead of simply correcting them."[199]

Etiquette (EQ): Discussion is expected to be polite and respectful, and views should be advanced based on facts and sources, not on rank, experience, or power in the community.[200] Two rules are similar: no personal attacks (NPA) and civility at all times (CIV).

Three rules govern behavior within the community:

Do not bite newcomers (DNB): Within the Wikipedia community there is a strong sense of belonging, and it is against the rules to criticize new editors unduly. Those who seek higher ranks are expected to show a multi-year history of advice and assistance to newcomers.

Forgive and forget (FORG): Editors and contributors are also expected to turn the other cheek. Wars break out on the talk pages with editors advancing competing interpretations, competing sources, and different facts. Conflict is not a bad thing. Changes get unchanged. Edits made are reversed and restored and reversed again until a neutral accommodation is reached or a senior editor calls a halt. Despite the hurt feelings that result, editors are cautioned to put past disagreements behind them in the name of a higher goal.

Consensus (CON): The most difficult, and possibly most important rule is this: Wikipedia is not a democracy (DEM). Resolutions are not achieved by voting or polling the participants, which in Wikipedia thinking only drives participants apart. Reasoned argument and exploration are encouraged, allowing all views to be aired until a fair resolution is arrived at that may satisfy no one, but which represents the most reasonable view.

The opposite of aristocracy: With so many rules, one might expect to see a drift toward bureaucracy, but the Wikipedia ethos also includes a hacker's anti-authority instinct to do what is right, even when it is "wrong." The present is in power over the past, and in a modern non-hierarchical world, editors are expected to make their own decisions.

No one is immune from criticism. In 2010, Jimmy Wales' original editor Larry Sanger sent a letter to the FBI claiming that Wikipedia was hosting pornographic pictures of children, and Wales reacted immediately, deleting seventy-one sexually explicit pictures, including classical art and anatomical drawings. An uproar ensued, his deletions were reversed, and the reversals were reversed. The stewards thought that by acting alone without discussion, Wales had run rough-shod over proper procedure. He had offended the sense of community, and the process they had all agreed to follow. Some said his privileges as founder should be revoked.

"Nobody has such authority," one steward insisted. "You behaved like a vandal... abusing your status in the evilest way anyone could imagine... You have destroyed all confidence people had in you." Petitions were circulated, Wales was accused of behaving like a dictator, and the argument raged on until, in the end, he apologized:

> We were about to be smeared in all media as hosting hardcore pornography and doing nothing about it. Now the correct storyline is that we are cleaning up. I am proud to have made sure that storyline broke the way it did, and I'm sorry I had to step on some toes to make it happen.[201]

Hundreds of editors rallied to remove him as the "founder," while only a few dozen took his side. Wales agreed to relinquish many of his editorial privileges in editing and blocking material, and when the controversy subsided six months later, he was still the "founder," but his position in the organization had been transformed. Dariusz Jemielniak, Polish professor of organizational behavior, trustee of the Wikimedia Foundation, and one of the forty stewards at the time, writes that as Wales was freed from management responsibilities, he evolved from the charismatic head of a movement to an inspiring icon of the Wikipedia world. His vision, self-effacing humor, unswerving devotion to the Wikipedia ideals, and respect for the voices of others had raised him above the fray.

Wales' decision to reduce his powers and apologize to the community ended his role as a day-to-day executive and began a new existence as the spirit of Wikipedia, permanently present in the organization's memory, and more powerful than ever before. He opened the way for the next generation of management.

There are challenges ahead. The number of new editors joining the Wikipedia community has declined steadily since 2007. The software for entering and editing an item is complex and redolent of a programming style popular more than a decade ago when it was written. The topics covered reflect the interests of the young white male editors, and lack the broad balance of a traditional encyclopedia. In the beginning, there were many items about video games and porn actresses, for example, and fewer items about Elizabethan poets, though that has moderated somewhat. The rules have become laws rather than guidelines, and there is a risk that Wikipedia might descend into a brittle bureaucracy.[202]

The Bigger Picture

In a larger sense, Wikipedia has survived while other great encyclopedias including *Britannica* and *Encarta* have failed, but it has not achieved their often-magisterial scope. Some *Britannica* articles were written by world experts — Einstein, Trotsky, Madame Curie — and could run to three hundred pages. Wikipedia today lacks balanced coverage of the arts, literature, science, history, religion, philosophy, and the great ideas. It lacks the range and wisdom of a more disciplined editorial view, a larger intellectual framework within which to locate the information the editors have collected. And in its present form, the online encyclopedia is unlikely ever to match the gravitas of its print predecessors.

The fault, if there is one, may lie in Jimmy Wales' longtime loyalty to the ideas of Friedrich Hayek. According to Francis Fukuyama, Hayek's great insight was that "individual human beings muddle along, making progress by planning, experimenting, trying, failing, and trying again," independently engaging in innovation and discovery. And that is a good description of how Wikipedia operates today. Like Rousseau, Hayek believed that individual freedom, as he called it, was a more promising road to human success than any plan that might be dictated by the kind of elitist central government Voltaire had in mind. In what has become the prevailing conservative philosophy for the last fifty years, Hayek argued that government has no claim to a higher vision or morality, and is often corrupted by the prejudice and perfidy that occur naturally at such altitudes. He said people should, therefore, be free to manage their own affairs.

But critics of Hayek have argued that the individual freedom he advocates cannot be fully enjoyed without the health, education, defense, and monetary infrastructure that only community government can provide.[203] We have seen for fifty thousand years that people hunt more successfully in packs than when they go out alone. And packs require leadership, strategy, and shared resources. A selfless understanding of the community's long-term needs seems somehow essential for real progress.

So it is with Wikipedia. The encyclopedia as it stands is an active worldwide network of information gatherers, laboring alone and in uncoordinated anonymity, each instantly updating his or her corner of the content, and scrupulously linking the material to supporting sources. And as such, it is the largest compendium of information ever assembled.

Wikipedia is a remarkable new invention, entirely the product of the network world. But compared to Teilhard's noösphere of knowledge, alive to the thoughts, opinions, and emotions of mankind, it is still just a rough-hewn model of what is possible, and of communities sure to come.

Chapter 12
Big Brother

In the spring of 1947, Eric Blair headed north again to Jura, a stony little island off the western coast of Scotland. His friend David Astor offered him a four-bedroom cottage there and he had used it several times over the last year, trying to complete a book he planned to call *Last Man in Europe*. Now he was returning for a final push. At six-feet-two, Blair was a gangly, cadaverous looking man with a thin pencil mustache, a heavy smoker of roll-your-own shag tobacco dressed in sometimes shabby bohemian fashion, frugal by nature, soft-spoken, and aloof. And he had recently been diagnosed with tuberculosis, a persistent infection of the lungs that was always fatal in those days. The cottage had no electricity, but included gas to cook and heat the water, storm lanterns to light the night, peat to burn in the evening, and a battery-powered radio connecting him to an England still digging out from under the rubble of World War II.[205] At forty-five, Blair was determined to finish his story about how, by turning a network into a virulent weapon of lies and intimidation, a government might one day control even the way people think.

Thought Control

Whoever controls the network controls the truth. People thinking for themselves can topple an empire, and every government in history has fought to keep that from happening.

Emperor Qin, who ruled China in the second century BC, sought to stamp out any disagreeable ideas, and remove from history the evidence of any notable personage other than himself. Particularly all traces of Confucius.

I request that apart from the annals of Qin all the records kept by scribes be burned... Should any person dare to cite the "Poetry" or "Documents," he should be executed in the marketplace.[206]

When the Spanish conquered the Americas, they collected and destroyed centuries of Mayan literature. In 1562, Bishop Diego de Landa, charged with bringing the Roman Catholic faith to the Yucatan peninsula, ordered that all indigenous works should be burned, along with virtually all records of the ancient Aztecs who had in turn systematically destroyed the literature of all the worlds they had conquered.

We found a large number of books in these characters and, as they contained nothing in them which were not superstition and lies of the devil, we burned them all, which they [the Maya] regretted to an amazing degree, and which caused them much affliction.[207] — *Bishop Diego de Landa*

In the 1930s, the government of Germany collected and burned works by authors they deemed "degenerate," including Thomas Mann, Marcel Proust, Sigmund Freud, Victor Hugo, Ernest Hemingway, James Joyce, H. G. Wells, and Karl Marx. When the Allied armies took over Berlin, they, in turn, drew up a list of thirty thousand titles deemed supportive of German "militarism" and ordered that they should be collected and destroyed.

Modern networks present a more difficult problem, but in China, Russia, Saudi Arabia, and even the United States, efforts by government to control people's thinking persist, often with enthusiastic corporate connivance.

China: Faced with the rapid acceptance of Wikipedia and its independent editorial structure, China first sought to intercept network users trying to reach pages that were inimical to the regime, secretly replacing the original Wikipedia information with look-alike pages that were more friendly. But Wikipedia moved to a secure system that encrypted the information between the user and the database, frustrating the government's ability to see who was looking for what. Since June 2015, the Chinese government has blocked all access to the site. Google, too, has been blocked, replaced by Baidu, a very functional but content-compliant search tool.

And from the earliest days of the COVID-19 pandemic, China has exercised close control over how the media — particularly the internet — treated the subject. The Cyberspace Administration, created in 2014, directed news media to shape public opinion, discount any public health warnings, promote the positive actions of the government, and suppress any negative reports. Private contractors and bots were employed to flood the news and internet channels with false reports favoring the party line and to muzzle any unauthorized voices.

All Cyberspace Administration bureaus must pay heightened attention to online opinion and resolutely control anything that seriously damages party and government credibility, and attacks the political system.

When reporting on limits on travel, controls on movement and other prevention and control measures, do not use formulations like "lockdown," "road closures," "sealed doors" or "paper seals."[208] — *Cyberspace Administration of China (2020)*

In 2010, the government began building Sesame Credit, a wide-ranging database of personal information designed to determine the "trustworthiness" of each of its 1.4 billion citizens. The system now contains individual health records, legal judgments, credit history, financial transactions, traffic violations, personal shopping, internet browsing history, and social media activity for all Chinese citizens. Social standing is based on such elements as job and school performance, financial status, traffic violations and not sorting household trash, as well as other indiscretions. It can also be lowered if the person is known to be associating with others of low social credit standing. Sesame Credit's Technology Director, Li Yingyun, said that in the new social credit system "Someone who plays video games for ten hours a day would be considered an idle person... Someone who frequently buys diapers would be considered probably a parent, who on balance is more likely to have a sense of responsibility."[209]

As of June 2019, twenty-three million airline tickets were denied to individuals deemed untrustworthy by the system. Their children have been turned away from private schools and universities, while those with high scores receive preferential consideration. "Trustworthy" individuals get reduced waiting times in hospitals and government agencies, hotel discounts, low bike rental fees, better rates on bank loans, and favorable consideration on job offers.[210]

But under Xi Jinping, president of China since 2013, the country has moved beyond trust systems. According to a harrowing investigation by Geoffrey Cain, reported in *The Perfect Police State*, surveillance cameras are now in place nationwide, including in the living rooms of those suspected of dissent. Everyone is being watched; children are encouraged to report on their parents, and any unusual behavior is investigated. The apparatus of authority is unpredictable and opaque, and according to Cain, the Chinese people live in a "gray cloud of fear."

Now even Chinese students abroad seem to be in the crosshairs. Social media and websites in the United States, Europe, Australia, and elsewhere are monitored by the Chinese government for any critical references to President Xi or his administration, and with the police standing by, parents in China call the students and tell them their digital communications are now being watched and they must stop their unpatriotic activities.[211]

The arrival of the COVID-19 virus has given the Chinese government an opportunity to dramatically expand surveillance of its citizens. Facial recognition systems built by Western technology companies now feed a massive AI network designed to track the movements of all citizens, while DNA and biometric data is gathered on everyone as part of the government's "anti-virus precautions." Even Chinese-made smartphones, the only kind Chinese citizens can buy, are equipped with apps that report the user's location, activity, and transactions back to the authorities. Video cameras on every street are used to identify people not wearing face masks, and home power consumption data is used to identify anyone who might be leaving the house during a quarantine.[212]

Under the rubric "Safe Cities Initiatives," these surveillance, facial recognition, and AI network technologies are being packaged and sold to other like-minded governments, along with pre-crime strategies for identifying and arresting individuals deemed "likely" to commit a crime.

This exporting of technology is a core part of China's larger "Belt and Road" initiative, intended to boost the country's economic leverage in the region. Over the last twenty years, China used its cheap labor costs to attract hi-tech computer, communications, and biotech companies, then exploited those relationships to gain — some say steal — technology secrets and jump-start hi-tech industries of its own. Now Chinese companies, operating as an arm of the government, sell their competitive products at discount prices or short-term debt to more than fifty countries in South America, Africa, and the Middle East — including Pakistan — displacing Western products and creating a new technological and trade dependency. Embedded in all this technology are the secret processes, protocols, and payoffs of a deep network, invisible to the user and reporting loyally back to China, all with the goal of raising China to a position of trade and technology dominance in the developing world.

In the seventeenth and eighteenth centuries, naval technology and strategies were the weapons with which the great European empires competed for control of the world's resources and markets. Now, through deep network technology, information control, and third-world debt, China is colonizing Asia and Africa. Networks are the high seas on which the boundaries of new empires are busily being drawn, along with the battle lines of the future.

> The vast ocean of data, just like oil resources during industrialization, contains immense productive power and opportunities. Whoever controls big data technologies will control the resources for development and have the upper hand.[213] — *Xi Jinping, on becoming president of China in 2013.*

Russia: Similar efforts to control the thinking of a community have emerged in Russia. In November 2019, Vladimir Putin, president of Russia, told a meeting of linguists that "as for Wikipedia, it [would be] better to replace it with the new Big Russian Encyclopedia in electronic form. At least that will be reliable information, presented in a good, modern way."[214]

Meanwhile, the Kremlin has taken a broader approach to the problem of information disseminated beyond state control. The country's Internet Sovereignty Law, passed in early 2019, requires Russian internet service providers to install software that can "track, filter, and reroute internet traffic," according to Human Rights Watch, allowing the state telecommunications agency to "independently and extra-judicially block access to content that the government deems a threat."[215] Now, according to Rachel Denber, Human Rights Watch's Deputy Europe and Central Asia Director, "The government can directly censor content or even turn Russia's internet into a closed system without telling the public what they are doing or why."[216]

Saudi Arabia: Long one of the most restrictive media regimes in the world, it is accustomed to meting out harsh punishment to individuals and organizations who speak ill of the ruling family. In 2003 the Law of Printing and Publication required all media to be licensed by the government, and specified that nothing should be published that conflicts with Sharia Law, threatens public security, or "stirs up discord among citizens." The law was extended in 2007 to cover the internet and all electronic media. According to the public prosecutor's office, persons found guilty of "producing and distributing content that ridicules, mocks, provokes and disturbs public order, religious values, and public morals, or whose writing may be considered damaging to the reputation, stability, and security of the country may be subject to a fine of three million riyals ($800,000)."[217]

United States: In non-totalitarian countries, private sector trust networks now allow a user to look up the risk of doing business with any given person or company. In the United States, Trooly.com, one of several startups focusing on trust rating, is a search engine that scans three billion pages from about 8,000 sites, including birth and death certificates, money laundering watch lists, and the sex offender registry. It also searches the "dark web" that is not indexed by Google or the other conventional tools. Finally, Trooly searches social media including Facebook and Instagram, mining the information for individual and business behavior that might present an abnormal risk to partners, customers, and clients.

Facebook, the social media giant, has already begun a program designed to predict the trustworthiness of its subscribers, saying it is part of the company's effort to fight disinformation on the network. Users are ranked on a scale based in part on how often the user flags content that is trusted by others. The company does not disclose the full basis for its ranking.[218]

What makes the Facebook initiative stand out is the breadth of the personal information database being compiled. An early 2019 report from the *Wall Street Journal* claimed that of seventy smartphone apps it tested, eleven were sending sensitive information to Facebook without the user's knowledge, even if the user did not have a Facebook account.[219] FloPeriod, for example, was sending information about the ovulation cycle of its users, and whether they said they were trying to get pregnant. Realtor, the real estate app, sent listing information viewed by its users to competing brokers, and multiple health monitoring apps were capturing heart rates and other medical information for sale to others.

In late 2019, *The New York Times* identified five US companies in the business of determining the trustworthiness of individuals, based on a comprehensive analysis of data from emails, e-commerce activity, online reviews, personal pages, and smartphone activity. In one case the reporter got a copy of her file: it was four hundred pages long.[220]

The Brennan Center, a non-profit research organization focused on privacy and social media, recently reported that the Los Angeles Police Department has contracted with several high-tech startups to mine Facebook and other social networks and identify individuals who are likely to commit crimes in the future. This determination is based on demographics, buying habits, messages exchanged on social media, and the messages exchanged by social media friends. The project also includes the creation of fake avatars designed to engage potential criminals in incriminating exchanges.[221]

Eric Blair [1903-1950]

Writing at the end of the Second World War, the premonition that governments might behave like this was the core of Blair's new book idea. By the spring of 1947, he was a well-respected book reviewer in London literary circles, an essayist, and a post-war English socialist who wrote often about the plight of the poor and the dysfunctions of Stalinism. He had grown up among England's middle classes and attended Eton on a scholarship, but was too poor to go on to university. Instead, he went off to Burma and joined the police for five years, then knocked about in Paris and London, taught high school a bit, and tried to write. But his efforts at poetry, social criticism, and literary commentary fell largely on deaf ears, and in 1937, at the age of thirty-three, he went to Spain along with liberal idealists on both sides of the Atlantic to join the Republicans fighting against the fascist government of General Francisco Franco. Here was a real-life reenactment of H.G. Wells' *War of the Worlds*, the power class against the people.

Stephen Spender called it a "poet's war." It was the few against the many, dictators against democracy, militant nationalism against the noble dream of communism — a fight for everything Blair believed in. But it was also a war of lies and misinformation, and it changed his view of where the world was headed. In the next war, he later wrote, truth and reality would be the first casualties.

> For the first time, I saw newspaper reports which did not bear any relation to the facts... history being rewritten not in terms of what happened but of what ought to have happened according to various party lines... This prospect frightens me more than bombs.[222] — *George Orwell, remembering the war.*

At the front, he found a nightmare of military incompetence, an army poorly organized and equipped, marauding gangs of no political allegiance stripping the countryside of firewood and food, and an atmosphere even among his comrades of backstabbing, conspiracy, and paranoia. But he fought for the cause and cheered his fellow soldiers on with dreams of the future until, wounded in battle, his lungs weakened by fever, he was accused of advocating socialism, labeled a "Trotskyite," and forced to escape the country to avoid a Franco prison.

Back in London, in the midst of an economic depression, he saw the people of England struggling for survival, oppressed and deluded by an uncaring and duplicitous aristocracy, then cozying up to Hitler. He thought with his recent military experience and first-hand knowledge of Stalinist complexities there might be a literary future to be forged in such circumstances. He could do essays and maybe a book or two, published under the pen name he had adopted so his socialist writing wouldn't embarrass his parents: George Orwell.

But in September 1939, the Germans invaded Poland and Orwell was swept up in the war effort. Declared physically unfit for military service because of his lungs, he joined the Home Guard, began writing pamphlets, and launched a series of patriotic and anti-Stalinist programs on the BBC, learning the mechanics of censorship, propaganda, and bureaucracy. He was particularly concerned about the rising tide of oppression in the Soviet Union. Show trials in Russia were famously sweeping up dissidents and executing them in secret.

For prosecutors, the intent to commit a crime was the same as committing one, and in a world where the information apparatus was entirely under government control, intent was easy to prove. Stalin's picture hung in every apartment, children were called to testify against their parents, and even an innocent gesture could be officially interpreted as sedition. Science was discredited. Trofim Lysenko, the powerful director of the Soviet Academy of Agricultural Science, disputed the idea of genetics and evolution, and under his regime thousands of scientists who refused to renounce such revolutionary theories were fired from their posts and forced into poverty. Other dissidents were imprisoned or executed as enemies of the state, paralyzing a generation of Soviet biologists.

In 1944, he finished *Animal Farm*, a parody of Soviet-style communism, but had trouble finding a publisher. It was obviously an anti-Stalin satire at a time when Stalin was Britain's necessary ally, keeping Hitler bogged down on Germany's eastern flank. A dozen publishers rejected the manuscript, including one who said there was no market for "animal stories." Another publisher accepted the book and then turned it down on the recommendation of a man in the Ministry of Information who was later unmasked as a Soviet spy. On the verge of publishing it himself as a two-shilling pamphlet, Orwell finally got an advance of £100 from Secker & Warburg, who agreed to do the book if they could find enough paper to print it on.[223]

The book came out, the reviews were favorable, and Orwell's friends were sending him encouraging notes. He was seeing real writing income for the first time in his life. But he thought his next book would be even bigger. The idea was to project the current crimes of Stalinism into the future and portray a society ruled by manipulating the information available to its citizens. History, culture, and the media would be swept aside. "Whoever controls the present controls the past."[224] This time the government would not merely destroy the record of past civilizations. It would create an alternative history in its place.

The protagonist of the new novel is Winston Smith, a mid-level bureaucrat in a world ravaged by war. Smith works in London for the Ministry of Truth, rewriting history to support the government's ubiquitous propaganda. He has become secretly disaffected by the dishonesty and manipulation of it all, and is exploring the shadows of resistance when he meets Julia, who also works for the government writing simple saccharine novels and pornography for popular consumption. Smith wants to debate the merits of life under Big Brother, but Julia says, who cares. "It's always one bloody war after another, and the news is all lies anyway."

Winston and Julia begin an affair, sharing their doubts and dreams as well as a cheap room among the proles, the lowest caste in society. But like everyone, they are watched by their neighbors, spied on by devices in their own world, and finally arrested by the thought police. Sent to a re-education camp, they are tortured and brainwashed. Each betrays the other, and as the book ends, Winston is sitting in a café, cheering news of the government's latest victory over what he knows is an entirely fictional enemy. He realizes that he has come to love Big Brother.

To some extent, Orwell was following in the footsteps of Aldous Huxley who had taught him French at Eton. Huxley had published *Brave New World* fifteen years earlier, a similarly dystopian portrait of the future where people are genetically bred, trained, and drugged to serve the purposes of an all-powerful government. And Huxley, in turn, was following in the footsteps of H. G. Wells. Huxley was a public advocate for mind-altering drugs who moved to California in 1937 and became a prophet of the human potential movement that would later so charm Marilyn Ferguson and Doug Engelbart.

Like Wells, Huxley, and others before them, Orwell imagined a new information network that would enable and enforce an oppressive, all-powerful regime. In particular, he described the Telescreen, a common household display that brought into every room the news as the government wished it to be known, including programmed propaganda, entertainment, and crowd-pleasing minutes of hate, love, and patriotic fervor. But the Telescreen could also capture every whisper and every sigh, zoom in on facial expressions, and see into the most private corners of every citizen's life.[225] O'Brien, Smith's inquisitor in the book, tells him that thought control is all that matters: "We control the truth because we control the mind."

What makes this book so interesting today is not the prescience of Orwell's technical invention or even the details of how a totalitarian government would come to dominate all aspects of life, but the idea that all this could be achieved by controlling the network. A few anonymous bureaucrats, acting behind the scenes, could determine what information was and was not available to the people. By creating phony wars and crises, with blow-by-blow accounts in the media, government could promote patriotism and enlist the uninformed masses in support of whatever campaign was expedient at the time. By launching widespread surveillance, the government could track and eradicate dissent, suppress free speech, destroy the notion of privacy, and accustom the population to the idea that history, like truth, was best left to the powerful few.

Big Brother Lies

The tactics of Big Brother reflect those Orwell had observed in the rising Stalinist regime, and they fall largely into three categories that we see being employed today: (a) government falsely frames its activities to make them appear benign, (b) it prevents the publication of all dissenting views, and (c) it promulgates a wave of misinformation designed to confuse the facts and shape public opinion in its favor.

False names: In Orwell's novel, the program of government lies is run by the Ministry of Truth, silencing dissident voices and actively spreading propaganda across the landscape. The Ministry of Love is in charge of brainwashing, the Ministry of Plenty deals with rationing, and the Ministry of Peace runs a phony war, designed to promote patriotic fervor and political support. Orwell even invents "doublespeak," a language for the purpose: "War is peace," "Freedom is slavery," and "Ignorance is strength."

Censorship: The second and most visible strategy of the government is to silence any public or private disagreement, punish all who question the rules, launch constant byzantine investigations of those who seem to be straying from the party line, and promote a feeling of fear and paranoia among the people. Media that question the prevailing view are impugned or shut down. Fake news. Voting and other forms of democratic participation are gerrymandered, suppressed, and challenged in court. Neighbors are encouraged to spy on neighbors. Dissenters are "re-educated" and in some cases become in Orwell's quirky language "unpersons," all traces of their existence lost down the "memory hole." In this dystopian world, thinking together means thinking alike.

Disinformation: But the most powerful weapon in Big Brother's arsenal is a strategy developed by Stalin. Dezinformatsiya is the trick of using trusted public networks to spread lies to deceive the people. The effort includes creating information that is false but credible and disseminating it over the media, supported by phony documents, expert testimony, and other traditional indicators of truth. A steady stream of conflicting information creates confusion and fatigue to the point where people give up on finding the truth. And even if the effort fails to persuade, the reliability of the media itself is thus permanently impugned.

In the run-up to the invasion of Iraq in 2008, the American government flooded the news media in the US, UK, and Europe with fake information, phony documents, and unsubstantiated "intelligence" to prove that Iraq was harboring weapons of mass destruction.[226]

By November 1948, after a year and a half of writing and re-writing, Orwell had a final manuscript of the book but, unable to find a typist who would move up to Scotland for the duration, he set about retyping it himself in his sickbed at the rate of several thousand words a day. But Orwell was in and out of the hospital by then, and suffering pains in his chest. In December he sent the manuscript to his publisher, who called it "amongst the most terrifying books I have ever read." The book was published in June 1949, under the revised title, "*1984*," and it was recognized almost immediately as a masterpiece, even by Winston Churchill, who told his doctor he had read it twice.

But his own time had run out. In January 1950, in his room at University College Hospital, he suffered a massive hemorrhage and died alone.

The Spectacle

Orwell saw clearly how government could manipulate the networks to create an entirely new level of thought control. But he could not have anticipated a newer force in the Western world, managing the information by which the masses of people live their lives.

In most authoritarian countries the networks are controlled and manipulated by the government to stay in power. But in the United States and the Western world, social media and news networks manipulate their content to gather a crowd and promote advertising revenue. Traditional newspapers, magazines, and radio which once dominated the advertising business, now get a little more than 8 percent of the revenue in the United States. TV and radio get about 27 percent, and online networks — mainly Google, Facebook, and Amazon, got about 64 percent of the total $242 billion advertising budget in 2020.[227]

Teilhard knew nothing about the media in 1915 and could scarcely have imagined how today's networks could become so separated from reality. But as early as 1967, philosopher Guy DeBord predicted a grim future when authentic social life would be replaced with a simulation he called the "spectacle," by which he meant the media. "All that once what was directly lived has become mere representation."[228]

Jean Baudrillard, whose work is often cited as the basis for the movie *The Matrix*,[229] expanded on DeBord in 1981, in an analysis that is as useful today as it was then. He identified four stages of simulation in which the ideas and images offered in the media move from being a fair representation of reality to a cynical self-serving substitute:

• The first stage is a faithful report. The media recognizes reality and tries to present an accurate account. This, they report, is a picture we took of a man walking a dog in the neighborhood yesterday.

• In the second stage, the media acknowledges the original reality but declares all reports other than their own to be fake. We took this picture of the man and his harmless little dog ourselves. Trust us. Those other pictures you see were taken with a digital camera that enlarges, pans, and otherwise distorts the image. They are obviously fake news.

• The third stage obscures reality, sowing doubt on whether we can ever be certain of what happened. Experts are confused. Maybe the dog thing happened, maybe it didn't. We're looking into it for you.

• The fourth stage denies the provability or relevance of any original reality that may be contrary to their view. Facts don't matter. Those rumors you heard about men and dogs running through the neighborhood are unimportant in our fast-paced post-factual world. Old news. Stay tuned for a panel of experts on the reality of modern life in suburban paradise.[230]

For DeBord, the world presented by the media is a timeless simulacrum, perpetually current and correct. It is easy to update the story with a click, erasing any history to the contrary. In the new world, reality is whatever the media says it is.

2084

If Orwell wrote the book today he would have to devote a major section to the rise of social technology, including billions of tiny communicating processors that shape our days, nudging us toward choices that benefit the infomediaries who stand behind the curtain, writing the algorithms and running the deep network.

Alex Pentland, Director of the Human Dynamics Lab at MIT's Media Lab, is an explorer in this new world. In the technotopia he envisions, sensors worn by workers will monitor their social behavior, nudge them in the direction of social efficiency, and initiate corrective actions where necessary. He says these devices will "automatically measure... and predict human behavior from unconscious social signals, identify social affinity among individuals working on the same team, and enhance social interactions by providing feedback to the users of our system." He calls this the "instrumented society."[231] All we need to do now is work out a new set of laws to handle those legacy concerns for privacy, rights in data, and the inconvenient disruption caused by dissent.

Will people accept and abide by this new arrangement? Pentland says yes. In a process he calls "social influence," each of us will adapt to the condition of surveillance because we will recognize that a more informed society will mean a more efficient government, more productive industry, and richer individual lives:

> For the first time, we can precisely map the behavior of large numbers of people as they go about their daily lives. For individuals, the attraction is the possibility of a world where everything is arranged for your convenience — your health checkup is magically scheduled just as you begin to get sick, the bus comes just as you get to the bus stop, and there is never a line of waiting people at city hall.[232] — *Alex Pentland, 2021*

His research program at MIT is an enthusiastic proponent of such "instrumentation," and it is largely funded by the technology and social media companies who would benefit most in this scenario. Pentland, though, admits that such a society might be vulnerable to the kind of totalitarian manipulation Orwell feared:

> We need to think carefully about the growth and increasingly broad usage of personal data to drive society's systems, and particularly about the safety, stability, and fairness of their design.[233]

But he presses bravely on, asserting that these dehumanizing risks can be averted. As a society, we will constantly encourage the birth of new ideas, he says, and rally around those that work. As members of a conscious collective, to use Durkheim's phrase, each of us will see our role in the group, and now, through the miracle of the network, be aware of each other. We will modify our personal behavior to conform to the group's goals and values, and arrange our lives for the benefit of the system as a whole.

Shimmering there on the horizon, Pentland says, is a vision of an instrumented network operating with a minimum of government. We will be out from under the influence of a ruling class (except the computer scientists and corporations who run the network, of course), the tedious chores of daily maintenance and coordination having been assumed by a world of benign little processors so small they will be "outside the boundaries of human awareness."

Chapter 13
Smoke and Mirrors

Networks can be used by government, the media, and the rising system of processors embedded in our lives to spread false information and manipulate the thoughts and behavior of the people. But even as we struggle to keep the conversation free and open, anonymous participants now regularly appear in the community, practicing widespread fraud and manipulation while social media companies deny responsibility, claim freedom of speech, and quietly profit from the outrage they provoke. At risk is the future of democracy.

Fake Friends

Astroturf and bots: In November 2019, Facebook acknowledged that it knowingly enabled as many as sixty million anonymous accounts called "bots" to post news on the social media platform appearing to support advertisers, political campaigns, and media personalities.[234]

• In the worldwide debate over climate change, a recent study showed that 25 percent of the messages posted on the network were paid for by corporations, political movements, and other climate change deniers all pretending to be concerned citizens.[235]

• In the early months of the 2020 COVID-19 health scare, when stay at home was a controversial containment strategy, researchers at Carnegie Mellon University determined that nearly half of the Twitter messages on the topic were secretly generated by software programs as part of a massive disinformation campaign intended to re-open the economy, pump up the Dow, and support the re-election of the current administration. Of the two hundred million active accounts they examined, 62 percent of the top thousand were bots whose true identity could not be determined.[236]

• A recent analysis by the US/UK Center for Countering Digital Hate found that of the 812,000 anti-vaccine messages they examined on Facebook, 73 percent came from twelve online accounts, posting under various fake names.

Of those that were reported as misinformation, Facebook left 95 percent in place, arguing that the network must honor "free speech."[237]

• In April 2017, when the FCC asked for comment on their plan to roll back network neutrality rules, 80 percent of the comments they received were fake, generated by a consortium of the country's largest broadband service providers, including AT&T, Comcast, and Charter Communications. The FCC then used that response to justify its decision to continue blocking internet content, slowing service, and making people pay more for higher data speeds.[238]

Avatars and illusions: When fake comments and social media messages are inadequate, witnesses are now making "personal" appearances on the network. Holography and other 3D projection technologies show colleagues sitting across the table, not across the world.[239] And the people they portray can be fake.

In 2014, Narendra Modi, then running for Prime Minister of India, created a 3D hologram of himself giving his stump speech and showed it in more than eight hundred locations throughout the country, though in some of the more rural venues where illiteracy is high, the audience believed that the candidate was actually there, and they were confused and mystified when he seemed to dissolve into thin air at the end of the speech.[240] Modi won the election.

The same year, at the annual Billboard Music Awards, Michael Jackson appeared as a hologram five years after his death to perform "Slave to the Rhythm" with a live five-piece band and sixteen real dancers. In a gold jacket, white T-shirt, and brick-red trousers, he rose as if from a throne and walked down several steps before breaking into his trademark song and dance, including a moonwalk.[241]

In April 2021, a watch company executive stepped into a glass-fronted booth in Schaffhausen, Switzerland and appeared almost immediately as a full-sized three-dimensional hologram in a similar booth in Shanghai where he talked with fellow executives at an industry conference and even unveiled a new watch.[242] Holograms are coming into practical use. Other companies are experimenting with Microsoft's Hololense2 headset to "transport" repair technicians to the scene of the problem, or train Japanese Airlines workers to maintain the latest engines. And now Ikin's RWZ smartphone attachment will project a holographic image of the person on the other end of a Facetime call.

But more important than the re-animation of dead rock stars or the transportation of busy executives is the emerging ability to create a believable avatar from nothing, simulating facial expressions, body language, and tone of voice with such fidelity that when people thirteen to thirty-five were recently surveyed on the topic, 42 percent said they didn't realize their favorite brand spokesperson was computer generated. And half of them bought the recommended product anyway.

Real-life simulation: Now we are on the verge of moving from the easily faked world of Facebook, Instagram, and YouTube videos to a network simulation of real life, and the challenge is more complicated. Soul Machines in New Zealand have developed autonomous artificial humans that can appear on the network looking and sounding like real people. Building on a virtual central nervous system called the Human Computing Engine, powered by IBM's Watson Assistant, these avatars can interpret the speech of others and respond with appropriate facial expressions and empathy.

Greg Cross, Chief Business Officer of Soul Machines, says:

> The question we wanted to explore was: What happens when you create a digital face? Will people engage with it? Will they find that digital face more engaging than a chatbot or a voice assistant? Our view is that, yes, of course they will. That's ultimately the market and business development we've been going on."[243] We're heading into a world where we're going to spend a lot more of our time interacting with machines. We have a fundamental belief that these machines can be more helpful to us if they're more like us.[244]

Miquela, the digital influencer brainchild of Los Angeles-based startup Brud, is a carefully designed artificial teenager on Instagram. Though she admits to being a robot, in between her sponsored posts for Calvin Klein, Prada, and other luxury brands, she regularly confides to her 1.9 million followers about very human experiences like her dating life, quarreling with her BFFs, being bullied, and even being sexually assaulted during a Lyft ride. *Time* magazine named her one of the most influential people on the internet in 2018, but she is not human. A new class of beings is emerging on the network, immune to praise or shaming, beyond the reach of the law, and knowing more about us than our best friends.

Even real people can now be faked. The ability to entirely synthesize videos of well-known personalities and have them appear on the network saying whatever the synthesizer wishes them to say has now reached the point where these "deep fakes," as they are known, look like the real thing. According to a recent study published in the *Proceedings of the National Academy of Sciences*, synthesized audio and video images are now so realistic that they are "indistinguishable — and more trustworthy — than real faces."[245] The problem is not only that fake messages can be made to look realistic, but that real video evidence can now be plausibly claimed to be fake.

Forecasters point to future networks that will include artificial personalities capable of meaningful, emotional, and responsive speech. But we should be concerned that these newly emotional avatars are not members of any human collective. They are motivated not by Kant's inner sense of right and wrong, not by Durkheim's loyalty to a community or a nation, not by altruism toward kin, or by obedience to any body of local or religious laws — can you indict a robot? — but by an undeviating adherence to the instructions of their anonymous programmers.

But a deeper problem is emerging. All these messages — even the best of these messages among real people — lack an emotional dimension that is essential to human discourse, and without that enriching layer of meaning, the network can be a lonely and dangerous place.

Communications of the First and Second Kind

Machines can't wink. The systems we use today and are likely to use for the next decade or so lack the body language, vocal intonations, and facial expressions that allow us to really say what we would say face to face. As a result, the network that is growing to connect us so intimately often ends up concealing a vital aspect of the truth. For example:

As the Iraq War got underway in 2003, the American government claimed that Saddam had nuclear and biological weapons of mass destruction, and based on that claim, the US had invaded the country, toppled the government, and launched a deeply destructive campaign to gain control of the region's oil. But hard evidence was missing, the claim was being questioned, and other governments were withholding their support. Then an old man was captured carrying stolen nuclear material. Messages rocketed up the chain of command to Washington and back: here was the smoking gun. A convoy raced west out of Baghdad, taking J.D. Maddox, an intelligence officer for the US Department of Energy, out to Abu Ghraib to interrogate the prisoner.

> I offered him a cold bottle of water. He cried. My line of questioning was simple: Tell me about the nuclear material you were transporting. His answers also were simple: I wasn't transporting nuclear material; I didn't do it. For a while, I assumed his tears were a ploy. I applied greater pressure: Stop lying to me; tell me where you got it; we know everything. His crying intensified. The truth was that he had been caught with car parts patched together to look like a small radioactive-material container. He was trying to make some money selling the fake bomb to a sucker in a war zone.
>
> My subject protested his innocence and even tried to take my hands in his, pleading for his family's security... I had risked the lives of a dozen soldiers to be there — only to find a small-scale confirmation of the ludicrous false premises under which we had invaded and occupied Iraq. The Iraqi weapons of mass destruction were no more than a bit of improvised sham, a con man's counterfeit goods. In the process, I had stumbled into one of the darkest places in wartime Iraq and into the most revealing truth of the conflict.[246] — *J.D. Maddox, remembering the event in 2020*

On one hand, Maddox knew the official argument for invasion, presented by the US government, embellished by the UK at every step, and transmitted around the world by the media.[247] On the other hand, Maddox had the simple, human, face-to-face plea of a desperate old man whose expressions, tears, body language, and tone of voice could not be faked. He was clearly innocent. The WMD story was false, the invasion of Iraq was not warranted, and the loss of lives and fortune that followed was a colossal fraud. Maddox, now a security consultant and adjunct professor at George Mason University, says he reported his conclusion to the interpreter who promised to pass it up the network to the commanding officer. This old man doesn't belong here, Maddox said. None of us do.

The networks we use today and the ones emerging over the next decade are very good at conveying data but no good at all at conveying the emotional dimension of that data. And as Maddox discovered, facial expressions, body language, and intonation add layers of meaning to the text. This is the music behind the words, and over the last several decades, researchers have argued that communication of this second kind is crucial to human understanding.[248] Vanessa K. Bohns and her colleagues have suggested that face-to-face communication is thirty-four times more persuasive than the same message conveyed by email.[249] Emotional communications capture meaning in ways that text alone cannot.

Zoom isn't much better. According to Madeleine Albright, who served as secretary of state under President Bill Clinton:

I don't think it's possible to overstate the importance of face-to-face diplomacy.

On Zoom, you have no kind of sense of their movements and how they sit and various things that show what kind of person you are dealing with. You can't judge what's going through their minds.[250] — *Madeleine Albright, 2021*

As businesses move from in-office collaboration to remote communication over video links, they may be losing a deeper level of interaction among the members of their staff. Harrison Street, a Chicago-based private investment firm, let its people work from home during the early phases of the COVID-19 pandemic, but after several months of operating in remote mode, called them all back into the office, five days a week.

Personal interactions are what this is all about. Being empathetic, being able to look someone in the eye and shake someone's hand, just listening and sitting in people's offices and bumping into somebody in the lunchroom and sharing an idea — that just doesn't happen over Zoom.[251] — *Chris Merrill, CEO, 2021*

Emotional communication is interactive, suboptimal, speculative, and quarrelsome. It is partial, provocative, half-question-half-answer, born out of disconnected bits without a theme, and growing in a medium beyond the written word. It thrives in a community that tolerates diversity, experimentation, and challenge, coming to fullness in a group where the members know and trust each other. That rarely happens on the network we have today.

Prosody: The human brain has separate systems for handling the two kinds of information. On the left or dominant lobe, behind the ear, is Wernicke's area which plays a major role in interpreting and expressing speech, retrieving words, and presenting them in a meaningful syntax. A related region called Broca's area on the temple of the same side is the portion of the brain mainly responsible for handling speech.[252]

But there is a second area on the opposite side of the brain behind the right ear and at the right temple that is associated with the emotional music of communications. Rhyme, alliteration, or a sing-song cadence are all constructed and decoded here. A shout or a whisper, a rhythmic monotone or a dramatic arm-waving crescendo help convey sarcasm, aggression, skepticism, anger, humor, and love. Great actors plumb the verbal complexities of Shakespeare and through prosody bring those words to life. Criminal trials often turn not on the words of a witness but on how those words are spoken. A sigh, a shrug, or a nervous glance can flip the jury. An accent or intonation often tells us whether the speaker is or is not one of us. But so far we have not found a way to capture this second language on the network, and until we do, we are unable to communicate emotionally because the networks that carry our ideas back and forth have a limited vocabulary for such nuance.

Communications of the first and second kind occur together as the brain mixes left and right, putting the words to music. But more than that, recent research suggests that when the speaker and the listener are fully engaged face to face in this kind of emotional exchange, the corresponding areas of both brains are involved. Italian neuroscientist Giacomo Rizzolatti has suggested that through specialized "mirror neurons," humans have the capacity for shared experiences. In face-to-face communications, individuals mimic the emotions and actions of each other through the direct stimulation of feeling, not thinking. There is something deeper going on here. Rizzolatti says we can think in sync.

Limbic resonance: Down beneath the two halves of the cortex lies curled the most primitive part of our brain, responsible for emotional communication and response. A squirmy clutch of separate hormone-secreting glands control the autonomic and emotional functions of the brain, and through their direct connections with the sensory, olfactory, and visual receptors, they constantly assess the emotional situation and determine the appropriate behavior: fight or flight, desire or disgust, happiness or fear, reward or punishment. Understanding and responding to the emotional signals of others is the oldest and most fundamental task of the brain, and it is crucial to keeping us alive.

In their book, *A General Theory of Love,* Thomas Lewis and his colleagues suggest that the limbic system is the engine of empathy. It operates beyond language, age, and cognitive impairment to evaluate the nature of another's intention — careless, aggressive, friendly, sexual. It communicates with the cortex to color the processes of the conscious mind, and it provides the context and vocabulary for communications of the second kind, enriching the information exchange between the speaker and the listener.[253] When we talk about feelings, we are talking about the limbic system.

Lewis suggests that the actions of one person's limbic system are recognized and reciprocated by the limbic system of another. So in a way that transcends language, memory, and social conventions, we know how the other person feels and we adjust our mood to fit. Aggression triggers aggression. Kindness begets kindness. A trembling touch, a tender smile, a catch in the voice, a slight glistening of the eye — the little signals fly back and forth. One limbic system senses an emotional condition and responds; the other system interprets that response and raises the stakes. Lewis calls this "limbic resonance," the mutual understanding and expression of feelings that complement the words.

This can also happen in groups, as one person's pattern of emotional speech and expression gets mimicked by others. Enthusiasm spreads, a spirit of invention and cooperation infects everyone in what researchers call "emotional contagion."[254] In his provocative explorations into the nature and rhythms of emotion, musician Manfred Clynes suggested that group emotions not only encourage like emotions in others, they discourage opposing emotions. It is harder to express anger when the rest of the group is expressing hope.[255] Harder to be hopeful when everyone else is downcast and discouraged.

Through non-verbal signals that are older than speech, humans share a cooperative, inspirational fellowship. But today's networks fall short of enabling that exchange, and as we move more deeply into network communities, we may be better informed, but we miss the body language, intonations, and smiles that make us feel part of others beyond ourselves.

The Loneliness Machine

The path to alienation: Childwise, a British market research firm that tracks the use of electronic media by British children three to sixteen years of age reports that 93 percent now own smartphones,[256] but those children are paradoxically more likely to feel alone. In her review of this report, Sonia Livingstone, Professor of Social Psychology at the London School of Economics, observes that children spend more than three hours a day on their mobile devices, chatting with friends, watching YouTube, listening to music, and surfing the web.[257] More than half of these children insist on keeping the phone beside their bed at night and say they feel "uncomfortable" if they are ever without a signal.[258]

It has been argued that young people who watch too much television suffer from language development delays, attention deficits, and impaired educational attainment.[259] But recent research has suggested that the use of social media by children might be even more dangerous than TV. In its latest annual Community of Life Survey, the UK Department of Digital, Culture, Media and Sport found that young people aged sixteen to twenty-four who have made the internet a more integral part of their lives are even more likely to feel lonely than those thirty-five and over.[260]

A study by Brian A. Primack and his colleagues found that young adults who spent two hours or more a day on social networks are twice as likely to experience social anxiety and loneliness. Those who visit social media sites more than fifty times a week are three times as likely to feel isolated as those who visit fewer than nine times a week, [261] though correlation doesn't mean cause and effect. As we become more dependent on digital networks for everyday communication, we seem to be losing not only a degree of personal privacy but also the feeling of fellowship with others of our kin. And all this loneliness has a price.

A rising danger: Émile Durkheim was concerned by the surging rate of suicide among those who had been displaced by the industrial revolution. He attributed it to a loss of fellowship among individuals who had come in from the villages to work in the new world of rumbling, nameless mills. And now suicides in the US have reached the highest level in thirty years. While much of this has been attributed to a rise in social and economic alienation among the middle class, researchers have also identified the use of social media as a factor.

Other studies have confirmed and broadened these findings. Using data from the World Health Organization, Ajit Shah at the University of Central Lancashire concludes that "the prevalence of internet usage was significantly and positively correlated with general population suicide rates in both sexes."[262] The new networks fail to connect us emotionally with each other, and the youngest and most ardent users feel that failure most keenly. We are social animals with an instinct for chatter, and if we are to avoid the dystopian vision of a lonely network winding around the world, experts tell us we will need a network that is much better at communicating emotions.

Faking It

Is such a network possible? The best guess of technologists at this point is yes. Over the next few years, the network will not only speed up, become more accessible, and be populated by a new world of tiny processors connecting our lives together without our knowledge, but it will also deepen the level of personal communications in two ways. Through sentiment analysis, we will better understand how our correspondents feel at the moment. And with improvements in augmented reality and holographic projection, we will be able to better present our feelings.

Sensing prosody: For more than a decade now, businesses have used software to scan comments about their products on web pages, forums, and social media, looking for significant mentions, abnormal praise, or criticism. Artificial intelligence tools measure whether the mention is positive or negative, they count comparable mentions, and they place the sentiment in a geographic, demographic, or cultural context. These tools, usually offered by market research or public relations companies, scan the web and help spot a crisis in the making, a shift in opinion, or a problem with service, quality, or price. But as we look forward from this technology we can see it as a precursor to a more commercial manipulation of emotions.

In 2016, Microsoft received a patent for a system that would use mobile software and wearable devices to monitor the behavior of an individual and alert designated authorities or safety personnel whenever there were signs of mood shifts, depression, shouting, use of threatening words, or other expressions beyond what the system defined as "normal."[263]

Affectiva, a Massachusetts startup company, has received funding to build a facial recognition system that can assess the emotional response of users playing video games, engaging in video conversations, or viewing advertising. Early clients of the system include Unilever, Kellogg cereals, Mars candy, and CBS.[264]

According to *The Australian Business Review*, Facebook had been monitoring images, interactions, and network activity on its site to determine moments when younger users were most emotionally receptive to advertising or persuasion.[265] The company responded to this report by explaining that tracking the emotional state of minors was "never used to target people based on their emotional state." They did acknowledge that the research was underway and that they have applied to patent a system that would capture young people's emotions, facial expressions, and moods.[266]

In May 2019, Bloomberg reported that Amazon is building a smartwatch app that can sense the emotions of the wearer based on the sound of the user's voice, and said the company has discussed publicly its desire to build a more lifelike and emotional voice assistant.[267] Microsoft, Google, and IBM, among a host of other firms, are developing similar technologies designed to infer emotional states from images, audio data, and other inputs.

Tone, pitch, accent, inflection, and speed of speech are considered the most important aspects of prosody, and efforts are widely underway to simulate these variables. The confession of an old man in an Iraqi prison was convincing because he was being truthful and sincere. The risk is that in the future, others on the internet will learn to fake that sincerity. On the networks now rising, machines will joke and whisper with you like an old friend.

Chapter 14
The Three Stooges Model

When I started out as an information technology consultant in the late seventies, I heard a story in the company cafeteria about a big piece of research the firm had done for the Department of Defense several years earlier. It was a large project, famous in company lore because the problem was so interesting, the conclusion was so surprising, and the client was so unhappy. The report was buried, but the findings were still being talked about years later.

The research task the client presented was simple: the team would be given access to the records of a hundred US Department of Defense research and development projects and asked to determine what characteristics the most successful of those had in common. Was success due to the budget, the clarity of the mission, the skills and experience of the team, the readiness of the technology, the management methods, or something else? The client thought the critical factor might be the way the team was organized, and the case team's initial review supported that idea.

Three organizational models were identified for closer research. Some of the projects had been organized around the "genius-in-the-middle" model with a very bright leader who imagined the outcome and made most of the decisions. Think Thomas Edison and Steve Jobs. Others followed the "by-the-book" model. Those teams had a clear and careful development program and a strong hierarchical culture, with decisions based on whether the action would bring the desired result within the time and budget allotted. And the third group had followed the "Three Stooges" model, as the team came to call it. Everyone on the project contributed and decisions were based on the debate and convergence of the group. The scope of the work often changed, the budget was overrun, rules were bent, and leadership was challenged, but everyone involved came to work early, stayed late, and had a lot of fun.

The smart money was always on the by-the-book model; NASA and IBM shone in the distance as examples of how thousands of very smart people could work on a complicated task and be dramatically successful. Organization was everything. But the case team's analysis showed that the Three Stooges model was clearly the organization model most consistently correlated with successful innovation. Given a less hierarchical structure, team members were able to speak freely and directly to each other. They felt empowered to challenge old assumptions, try new designs, and correct the course of the project when it seemed to be going astray. Very successful decisions were made by those closest to the problem, supported by groups of people, diverse in their thinking styles, broad in their cognizance of the world, and a little hard to manage.

This was not a model the Department of Defense could incorporate into its culture. The report was shelved and further team presentations were abruptly canceled, but the puzzling results continued to be discussed.

Thinking Together

Since then, other investigations have reached remarkably similar conclusions. A recent study of group dynamics by Google found that the most important element in the success of a group seems to be that the members can participate equally, be equally respected, and be allowed to express their ideas and opinions in a common framework of knowledge and trust.[268] In another piece of seminal research, Anita Woolley and her colleagues at Carnegie Mellon showed the same thing: the most "intelligent" groups in their study were those that gave each participant an equal voice and resisted the tendency to let two or three strong members dominate the process.[269] Groups thinking together seem to make better decisions than individuals, and flatter, more diverse organizations are more innovative and more rewarding for the participants.

Moving from the traditional hierarchical structure to a flatter information team — from Captain Kirk's bridge to Jean Luc Picard's round table — has produced other benefits as well. After the crash of a United Airlines plane in 1977, the National Transportation Safety Board began to focus on pilot/crew communications as a potential source of error — particularly the often observed problem that members of the crew knew something was wrong but were afraid to challenge the chain of command.[270] Over the next few years United Airlines trained their crews to be more frank and assertive toward the pilot, and pilots to be more considerate of other opinions. Crew Resource Management (CRM) training has since become standard for major airlines around the world, teaching teams how divergent opinions should be voiced.

Dr. Gerald B. Healy, president of the American College of Surgeons, has been a longtime advocate of bringing this new organizational flatness into the hospital:

> Operating rooms suffer from the same flaw that once plagued cockpits: Just as crew members had feared questioning their captains, many surgical team members still fear questioning surgeons. Many medical errors could have been avoided if a nurse, resident, or anesthesiologist had felt free to speak up.

> At my department at Children's Hospital of Boston, our medical error rates have dropped to zero after airline pilots taught us team training, and team training resulted in lower death rates, and more satisfied patients in the cardiac surgery program at another New England hospital.[271] — *Gerald Healy, 2008*

In a flatter world, decision-making is a noisy and contentious process involving everyone on the team. And that will take some getting used to. But it promises a way to analyze and decide that is far better than anything hierarchical groups and corporations have ever had before.

The Public Sphere

At about the time the DoD study was taking place, a thirty-three-year-old post-doctoral student at Goethe University in Frankfurt submitted the thesis required of any academic who seeks a full professorship, and in it he traced the emergence of the "public sphere" in eighteenth-century France and the role it played in the overthrow of Louis XVI. He said the revolution was evidence of how government by the few had shifted to a flatter, noisier government by the many. Here was a serious consideration of the Three Stooges principal, the first of its kind.

Jürgen Habermas [1929-] suggested that social and political powers in the past had tried to overwhelm the judgment of their people with "representational" displays of power: the Roman Coliseum was an awesome symbol of the State's might; don't even dream of dissent. Cathedrals were glorious testimony to the eternal power and wisdom of the church; Versailles was a monument to the superior wealth and taste of the king, never to be challenged. But as the printing press and burgeoning international trade made new ideas available to the people, the people started to gather and speak their minds.

The French Revolution signaled a shift from making decisions at the top of a social hierarchy to making decisions at the bottom. In 1789, seven thousand housewives of Paris, waking up to another steep increase in the price of bread, went home for their kitchen knives and then marched for six hours through the pouring rain to Versailles. Coordinating their campaign through the hot new "network" of newspapers, pamphlets, and coffee houses, they captured Louis XVI, dragged him back to face the people, and set an example for revolutions that have rolled on for two centuries around the world.

As Habermas described it, individuals in the late eighteenth century felt newly free to assemble on their own and debate matters of government and religion, unconstrained by their position in society or by the strictures of Church and State. In his words: "Opinion became emancipated from the bonds of economic dependence."[272] Men were not only able to think for themselves, as Kant had suggested, they were now able to debate those thoughts in public. Any idea, work of art, or political opinion could now win legitimacy in the coffee houses and pamphlets of the common people.

But the idea of the "public sphere" as Habermas described it is inadequate in two important ways. First, the public sphere is not an amorphous, transparent world of individuals interacting freely with each other. It is an information community, a network of people, subject to all the strengths and weaknesses Durkheim identified. Networks each have their own standard for determining what is true — ecstatic revelation, the community's body of printed texts, the discipline of science, a tradition of wise men, the eloquence of politicians. And there are multiple communities, spheres within spheres, competing against each other to survive in the outer world. So what is true in one "public sphere" is not necessarily true in another. Some networks with healthy truth systems succeed, and others fail.

And second, that "public sphere" can become corrupted, either by outside forces manipulating the process, or by the members of the community themselves who come to believe in a virtual truth that is internally consistent, supportive of their larger political and religious beliefs, but entirely false.

Network Truth

When the Black Death swept across medieval Europe killing half the population, the teachings of the Church were the standard by which the truth of any situation was measured. In 1348, Pope Clement VI allowed that the plague must be a "mysterious judgment of God," perhaps a misalignment of Mars, Jupiter, and Saturn. He said the forces of evil were loose upon the land, and his response was to blame witches and Jews who were then rounded up and burned. Some of the people formed the Brotherhood of the Flagellants and marched barefoot through the streets, lashing themselves with whips and sticks while crowds gathered to sing hymns. Ecstatic vision was the prevailing standard for truth.[273]

Gutenberg's press changed that, giving birth to an orderly bureaucracy, to laws that could be uniformly followed, and to a more general and systematic understanding of agriculture and the seasons. If it was printed it must be true. And the more people who read these writings, the truer the writings were thought to be.

When the Bubonic Plague struck London in 1665, the city streets were suddenly awash with hastily printed broadsides, sermons, and calls to prayer. A pamphlet by John Graunt tabulated the death count by age, sex, and neighborhood, and the city came to see the affliction as a natural disease it might be able to control. Broadsides counseled people to seek a good diet, fresh air, moderate living habits, and the therapeutic efficacy of London treacle mixed with vinegar and orange juice. Other fad diets and recommendations, hot off the press, suggested perfuming cloths, burning brimstone, boiling vinegar, and avoiding beggars.[274] Publishers, awake to the opportunity, helped fit new ideas to the current paradigms of their community, for better or worse. If there was evil abroad in the world, it took the form of unsold books.

Then slowly the limitations of spirituality and the printed word were recognized, and people began to place their trust in the evidence before them, incomplete, sometimes confusing, but harder to refute. When the Spanish flu broke out in 1918, Colonel William Gorgas had just used science to solve the puzzle of yellow fever and clear the swamps of Panama to make way for the new canal. Madame Curie had received the Nobel Prize for the invention of x-rays that could see the mysteries of the body as it moved and breathed. Science was the new God.

Doctors told the people the flu was caused by bacteria and said they should avoid crowds, wear masks over their mouths and noses in public, stop shaking hands, respect quarantines, and avoid aspirin. But not everyone followed this advice. For the less educated, the idea of bacteria remained a difficult abstraction. Fifty million people died around the world, bodies were piled up against the buildings waiting to be collected, and with mortuaries overwhelmed, families had to dig graves for their relatives.[275] Science, the new truth system, required a new kind of thinking, and not everyone was up to it.

And that is still a problem today. So much of modern science is about things we cannot see or feel. We live in a world of markets we cannot visit, medicine we cannot see, computer tools and software we can only imagine, and reports of sentiment among neighbors we never meet. Science asks us to travel at high speed in a realm we cannot confirm by direct observation. Science, too, is now suspect.

The new basis for determining truth in a network world seems to be the opinion of our friends in the community. American philosopher William James argued that truth is whatever system others will accept as a basis for successful action, including absolute religious, political, or scientific truth if that is what the community has chosen. His point is that no matter what your truth system is — spiritual, legal, scientific, ecstatic — it rarely gets you a result if everyone you deal with rejects that system. Communities then compete with each other to see whose truth system carries them to the greatest success.

At the height of the COVID-19 emergency, when public health experts were offering science as a reason people should wear masks, the president of the United States turned primarily to Twitter and other network media for communication with the nation, regularly repeating false and misleading rumors, and sometimes advocating remedies that "a lot of people are saying."

> "So, supposing we hit the body with a tremendous - whether it's ultraviolet or just very powerful light," the president said, turning to Dr. Deborah Birx, the White House coronavirus response coordinator, "and I think you said that hasn't been checked but you're going to test it.

> "And then I said, supposing you brought the light inside of the body, which you can do either through the skin or in some other way. And I think you said you're going to test that too. Sounds interesting.

> "And then I see the disinfectant where it knocks it out in a minute. One minute. And is there a way we can do something like that, by injection inside or almost a cleaning?

> "So it'd be interesting to check that." Pointing to his head, President Trump went on: "I'm not a doctor. But I'm, like, a person that has a good you-know-what."[276] — *White House briefing, April 24, 2020.*

While print and broadcast media rushed to explain that people should not actually drink bleach or attempt to shine ultraviolet light on their internal organs, social media widely repeated the suggestions, with both positive and negative comments.

According to Pew Research, 62 percent of Americans now get their news from friends on Facebook,[277] which declines responsibility for whether any of their content is true. Within the Fox network community, the opinions of the news department, the on-air hosts, and the president of the United States were echoed, supported, and taken more seriously than science. A study by the National Bureau of Economic Research found that viewers of Fox News, the most-watched news channel in America, were 30 to 50 percent more likely to ignore the recommendations of scientists for staying home, wearing masks, and keeping social distances.[278]

When COVID-19 first appeared in China in 2020, authorities there took a fast and firm grip on testing, contact tracing, and quarantines. The government established an unwavering "truth" about the virus, broadcasting this view not as "science" but as the decision of the people in power. (Habermas would call that "representational.") And the people of China accepted that discipline. Infections dropped quickly, and from January through May, China reported about five thousand deaths, although public health reports from China have been historically dubious.

The US government, on the other hand, ignored the warnings of the Center for Disease Control and Prevention, declined to acknowledge the facts of the virus, and let the narrative be controlled by social media, itself controlled by anonymous bots and special interests. Infections spread, and deaths began to mount. With only a quarter of China's population, America reported twenty times the number of deaths in the same five-month period. Cable news channels took their accustomed positions along the political spectrum and talked mainly about government personalities. Newspapers reported the spread of the COVID-19 virus in a deeper and more quantitative way, but they, too, turned most of their attention to a dispute over what government was and was not doing. Meanwhile, for most people in the country, the truth about the virus came from the network — online news, special websites, and social media.

Virtual Truth

They were not well served. While some special-interest news sites are earnest and comprehensive in their coverage, social media including Facebook, Instagram, Twitter, Snapchat, YouTube, and Vimeo have made little effort to ensure the truth of the content they offer or to confirm the identity of the contributors, the two disciplines that made Wikipedia successful. Even though hundreds of thousands of lives were hanging in the balance. They published what would attract the largest audience. Researchers at Carnegie Mellon University and elsewhere report that half of the COVID-19 content on social media is misinformation or fake news, often posted by bots under the control of self-serving conspiracies. In many cases, the purpose of this deception was to encourage people to gather without masks or protection, shop, dine, travel, return to work as soon as possible, and disregard the recommendations of the US Center for Communicative Diseases.

Under Section 230 of the US Communications Decency Act, updated in 1996, private companies who operate Twitter, Facebook, YouTube, and other social media services in the United States are allowed to edit, block, or remove messages that promote violence or indecency or otherwise violate their terms of service. They may deny access to persistent violators, if necessary. They are also enabled by technology and empowered by law to identify bots and deny them access. But the companies rarely do any of that because it would lower their profits.[279]

Brazil presents an example of how this laissez-faire approach can lead to an information disaster. At the onset of the COVID-19 health emergency in 2020, President Bolsonaro declined to recognize the threat of the virus and said there was no need for a public health campaign. People could get all the information they needed from the news media and social networks. Public discourse was quickly overwhelmed by conspiracy theories, often advanced by special interests and Bolsonaro's own political allies. Hydroxychloroquine, recommended for malaria and lupus, was said to be effective against the virus. (It is not.) Invermectin, widely prescribed in Brazil, blocks COVID infections. (It does not.)[280] Face masks impede the flow of oxygen and cause cancer. (They do not.) COVID-19 is a biological weapon released into the world from secret labs in China. (Probably not.) Vinegar is better than sanitizer for killing the virus on hands and hard surfaces. Vaccines cause cancer, blindness, and homosexuality. They also make you magnetic. Injections are a ruse sponsored by Bill Gates and George Soros to implant microchips in everyone as a way to track their movements and collect personal data, though what Gates and Soros plan to do with all that information is left to your imagination.[281]

By mid-2021, despite vaccines and assistance offered by several other countries, only 13 percent of Brazilians had been vaccinated and the country's death rate had become one of the highest in the world.[282] People wouldn't get vaccinated because their friends wouldn't get vaccinated. The science argument was not persuasive, the media was obviously full of misinformation, and nobody trusted the government. Why should they? Now businesses in Brazil are against the wall; tourism, once a major part of the country's economy, has collapsed. Half the schools are closed and the country's rudimentary internet coverage cannot offer an alternative. By the end of the year the public health department, independent of Bolsonaro, had begun to distribute vaccines, but by any standard, Brazil as a community has failed. Hundreds of thousands of people have died, and the country will not be a competitive business environment again for another decade.

Social media — particularly Facebook — are having an even more corrosive effect in less developed, more turbulent countries where the management has few moderators who can understand the language and innuendo of the hate speech being posted. When whistleblower Frances Haugen disclosed the inner reasoning of the company in a collection of emails, project memos, and management strategy, the full danger of its hands-off attitude toward truth was revealed.

> In Iraq, where violent clashes between Sunni and Shia militias were quickly worsening an already politically fragile country, so-called "cyber armies" battled it out by posting profane and outlawed material, including child nudity, on each other's Facebook pages in efforts to remove rivals from the global platform.[283] — *Frances Haugen, 2021*

In 2020 and 2021, the government of Ethiopia greatly accelerated its war against the rebel Tigray Liberation Front, using hate speech, faked messages, and videos, posted on Facebook, resulting in massacres, gang rapes, and ethnic cleansing throughout the northern region of the country. The United Nations aid chief warned in October that hundreds of thousands in Tigray face famine,[284] and at least 1.7 million people have been displaced, even as the false messages continue. But according to Vice News, a controversial new online news organization, Facebook has done little to block those messages or censor the local government.[285] In Myanmar and other deeply troubled regions, Facebook is being widely used to encourage violence and hate speech in local language and slang that only a native would understand.[286]

It may well be beyond the ability of any company of Facebook's size and diversity of languages to monitor the way dissident forces use its pages around the world. But a new kind of war is breaking out on the internet and, wittingly or otherwise, Facebook and other social media are the arms merchants. After a while, people subjected to such a volume of misinformation redefine their community to block out disturbing voices. Several studies have recently reported that in a world of false and confusing information, people turn for strength to their identity in the group, choosing to blame outsiders for their problems. You lie. We won't listen to you because you are not one of us. Leaders rise among them to affirm this new identity and demonize the outsiders, making things worse by emphasizing the fiction of a people besieged.[287] Belonging is more important than truth.

> The problem is that when we encounter opposing views in the age and context of social media, it's not like reading them in a newspaper while sitting alone. It's like hearing them from the opposing team while sitting with our fellow fans in a football stadium. Online, we're connected with our communities, and we seek approval from our like-minded peers. We bond with our team by yelling at the fans of the other one. [288] — *Zeynep Tufekci, MIT Technology Review, 2018.*

Before the time of writing, what we knew was determined by what we and our friends could remember. That was later expanded to include what we could read. Some who could afford it went to school, bought books, subscribed to newspapers, and were better informed than others. This reinforced a social hierarchy, and for the last several thousand years what most people know about the world and each other has been largely shaped by Voltaire's aristocracy. Now we have a world of colleagues communicating directly with each other. Social rank and credentials matter less, and network truth, buffeted by the winds of hate and greed, is whatever most of the people in our community believe at the moment.

In the networks now rising, education, social status, and subscriptions are less relevant than curiosity, imagination, persistence, and the need to belong. Anyone who asks can know. But with fewer moderators, impartial editors, or fact-checkers of any kind, the public sphere is at risk of becoming a wild, amoral cacophony of con men and crackpots.

Chapter 15

Insurrection

The details are not pretty. We've come a long way from the housewives of Paris wielding their kitchen knives, but anger, violence, mob rule, and big money still play essential roles in today's drama. Children use social media to create national campaigns. Angry self-styled militia, happy to be outdoors with their guns, seize any opportunity to confront anyone who tries to tell them what to do. Billionaires quietly pay to house, feed, and bus supporters to the site of the riot, while politicians use the tumult to raise millions for their re-election. Popular uprisings have become a big and profitable business, and those in power are not going to give it up without a fight.

On January 6, 2021, hundreds of American citizens, angered by the 2020 election outcome, used the power of social networks to coordinate their assault on the United States Capitol, where they planned to overturn the election certification and murder the opposing politicians. Neither goal was reached, but in the process, they attacked the seat of democracy and left a mark on the public mind that will never go away. The "public sphere" in this case remains an angry and fiercely connected community, and as long as the underlying anger is there, the insurrections will continue.

The Social Contract Has Expired

The theory of hierarchical organization as we know it has its modern roots in the eighteenth-century Prussian army, when Frederick the Great turned a horde of mercenaries into tiered battle and support units, establishing discipline, mobility, and a system of layered accountability. As war became more complicated, he saw that even with couriers running back and forth through the cannon fire, the general staff could not keep up with the action at the front. He decided they should focus on the larger strategy, delegate the operational details to the field commanders, and promote or punish those commanders based on the results. Max Weber [1864-1920], himself a Prussian, turned that model into the theory of bureaucracy.

Weber wrote that in business and society, as well as in the army, communities were more effective if they adopted a hierarchical structure with executives arranged in tiers of power and accountability: the leader of each unit would be responsible for the performance of the units beneath him, and share in the profits of those units. The essence of the organization's success, he said, was a system by which the leaders up and down the chain of command could receive timely and actionable information from the next lower ranks and respond with operational objectives, allocation of resources, and oversight of key personnel. Like Durkheim, Weber believed the leader, by virtue of his superior education, skill, and experience, should personify and enforce the values of the group. This was the Prussian Army plus Plato's "souls of gold."

> The fully developed bureaucratic apparatus compares with other organizations exactly as does the machine with the non-mechanical modes of production. Precision, speed, unambiguity, knowledge of files, continuity, discretion, unity, strict subordination, reduction of friction and of material, and personal costs – these are raised to the optimum purging point in the strictly bureaucratic administration.[289] — *Max Weber, Essays in Sociology (1905), English translation published in 1948.*

Alfred P. Sloan broadened this idea, distributing more day-to-day operational control to the lower layers and building the giant General Motors conglomerate on those principles. Chester Barnard, the mid-century management guru, further celebrated the role of the business leader as an impartial decider, a highly skilled communicator, and conductor of the community's information world. Peter Drucker, the management theorist, gave us the modern model of business as a multi-layered knowledge organization designed to bring the facts to the desk of those executives selected for their skills and their dispassionate view of the company's objectives. Later enshrined as the science of "management," strong top-down organizations, not skilled labor, came to be seen as the key to productivity, profit, and even happiness.

With their remarkable post-war success, business leaders became America's new social and economic nobility, and they began using their political powers to reshape the laws for their own benefit. From the 1990s on, workers at the lower levels of the organization were increasingly viewed as nameless and interchangeable. Their rights were weakened, wages were frozen, and campaign finance laws were changed to give greater voice to corporations and special interests. Banks began acting primarily to grow their own portfolios instead of protecting the savings of their customers, and they became the essential middlemen in the rapidly growing digital economy.[290]

From 1978 to 2017, wages of the typical American worker inched up about 12 percent, adjusted for inflation, while executive compensation rose 940 percent.[291] At the end of 2020, as the Dow Jones Industrial Average reached the highest point in history, the richest 1 percent of Americans controlled half the country's money[292] while 50 million Americans, including 17 million children, were unsure of their next meal.[293] In America and around the world, the wealth of hard-working people has shifted into the hands of a new class of gold-plated bureaucrats. Meanwhile, even the costs of education, healthcare, the national highway system, scientific research, and national defense have been moved almost entirely onto the shoulders of the workers. ProPublica recently showed that those at the top of the wealth hierarchy — Jeff Bezos, Elon Musk, Michael Bloomberg, Warren Buffet, and George Soros — pay little or no federal taxes most years.[294]

A post-war generation raised on the soaring cadences of Roosevelt and Kennedy can no longer afford to send their kids to college, buy a second car, or see their children settle comfortably into homes of their own. American corporations in search of greater profits have outsourced semi-skilled production to other countries, and the low-skilled jobs that remain have gone to immigrants who will work for peanuts. Even the necessities like healthcare and education have been taken over by for-profit corporations, drifting beyond reach except through life-long debt. And we have been at war in Korea, Vietnam, Iraq, and Afghanistan for seventy years with little to show for it.

Trust in government has understandably fallen. According to Pew Research, Americans who believed the government was "doing what is right most of the time" plunged from 77 percent in 1964, through the Vietnam war and Watergate, to 27 percent in 1980. It rose again from 1993 to a peak of 54 percent in 2000 and fell through 9/11 and the Iraq War to an all-time low of 15 percent in 2010. In the last ten years trust rose slightly to 20 percent just before the

COVID-19 virus broke out.[295] A CNN poll in late 2021 showed that Americans have lost confidence in the whole democratic process. A survey of 1,378 registered voters on the eve of the 2021 elections showed that 88 percent of Americans are dissatisfied with the state of democracy in their country.[296] 52 percent of Americans (60 percent of Democrats and 24 percent of Republicans) now say politicians have jiggered the voting rules to help themselves, and the results no longer reflect the true will of the people.[297]

At the height of the COVID-19 emergency, 27 percent of Americans refused to take the vaccine because, they said, they don't trust the government to even help them with free medicine.[298]

And this is true around the world. In 2019, the annual Edelman Trust Barometer, a survey of 33,000 online respondents in 28 countries, found that peoples' trust in their government, business leaders, and the media had eroded in spite of a booming world economy. People were afraid that more jobs were being lost to automation, the quality of life was declining for all but the very rich, and everyone in government was on the take. In 2020, in the midst of a pandemic, the survey showed that people everywhere had grown even more angry about ethnic abuse and political corruption. The Edelman report called this a potent "epidemic of misinformation and a loss of belief that what our leaders tell us bears any resemblance to the truth."[299]

Perhaps, as a result, there has been an odd inversion of our traditional standard for choosing leaders: in America, the UK, Russia, Brazil, and other countries around the world, a rough-around-the-edges politician who speaks bluntly is now presumed to be telling the truth. A man who has made billions is thought to be smart, regardless of how that wealth was won, and if it was by cheating the system, so much the better. A man who goes bare-chested among the people and speaks grandly about being "strong," "taking charge," and "fighting back" is thought to be a leader who is upright and honorable himself. And if he speaks frequently about loving the common folk and throwing immigrants and "others" out of the country, then he is a man to be adored by the downtrodden who are searching for a leader, anyone, who seems to be on their side.

In the struggle between aristocracy and the people, two traditional American goals have always been meritocracy and fairness. Anyone should be able to rise through his or her own efforts, regardless of heredity or class. And the distribution of wealth should be fair, even if it is uneven. Riches should flow to those who work hard or have talent and imagination, while everyone pulls together to compete in the larger world. Those ideas now seem to be endangered.

The promise of Voltaire's intelligent and public-spirited aristocrats managing the people's business has faded as well. Our centuries-long agreement that citizens should surrender certain freedoms in return for peace, safety, and equal opportunity has become deeply distorted as the upper layers of government and business throughout the world seem to be extracting an ever-increasing price for their management services.

Implicit in all this from the very beginning has been the assumption that information is scarce; organizing and moving it from place to place is expensive; and therefore decisions need to be made by a few deciders, concentrated in the upper ranks. But in a network world, these assumptions are no longer true. (a) Most of the relevant information is now available to everyone, fast and cheap. The closer the source is to the fact space, the more likely it is to be accurate and timely. (b) Cognitive skills, perspective, and a diversity of experience are alive at all levels of an organization or community, often bringing valuable new insights to existing problems. Why deny access to that resource? (c) Freedom of thought and participation encourages creative insight, gives added meaning to the work, and engenders loyalty toward the community. Now everyone is a decider.

Wael Ghonim [1980-]

And those traditionally excluded from decision-making are getting restless. The networks now rising perfectly fit the needs of a political revolution. In 2011, a wave of protests known as "Arab Spring" swept across North Africa and the Arabian Peninsula, crucially enabled by social media. Protesters were able to coordinate their activities and respond to shifting opportunities faster than authorities could keep up.

Five years later, Wael Ghonim, leader of the movement, spoke about its origins, recalling how, as a young marketing executive for Google in June 2010, he was browsing Facebook pages when he came across a photo:

> ...of a tortured, dead body of a young Egyptian guy. His name was Khaled Said. Khaled was a 29-year-old Alexandrian who was killed by police. I saw myself in his picture... I anonymously created a Facebook page and called it 'We Are All Khaled Said.' In just three days, the page had over 100,000 people, fellow Egyptians who shared the same concern. We worked together for hours and hours. We were crowdsourcing ideas from people, we were engaging them, we were polling collectively for action and sharing news that the regime did not want Egyptians to know. The page became the most followed page in the Arab world.[300] — *Wael Ghonim, 2016*

The rising: Over the next few months, interest in the movement expanded beyond Egypt. The number of visitors to his page swelled to more than three million, and a new knowledge structure emerged spontaneously. The group used multiple languages to reach different audiences and debate different aspects of the revolution: facts and data were discussed in English, France's involvement was debated in French, Arabic was used to reach new members, and the Tunisian dialect was used for local issues and humor.

> I posted an event on Facebook and called it a revolution against corruption, injustice, and dictatorship. I posed a question to the 300,000 users of the page at the time. Today is the 14th of January; the 25th of January is Police Day. It's a national holiday. If 100,000 of us take to the streets of Cairo, no one is going to stop us. In just a few days, the page reached over a million people. Social media was crucial for this campaign. It helped a decentralized movement arise. It made people realize that they were not alone. And it made it impossible for the regime to stop it.

The protest broke out into the streets. The government tried to head off the uprising by blocking access to the internet, and Ghonim was arrested and beaten. Amnesty International filed a protest, and after eleven days he was released to his cheering supporters. "We will not abandon our demand," he shouted. "And that is the departure of the regime." Three days later President Mubarak dismissed the government, delegated power to his vice president, and finally resigned. But in the long run, Ghonim said, the uprising failed and social media became itself a melee of competing opinions and insults:

> We failed to build consensus, and the political struggle led to intense polarization. Social media only amplified the polarization by facilitating the spread of misinformation, rumors, echo chambers, and hate speech. The environment was purely toxic. My online world became a battleground filled with trolls, lies, hate speech.

The uprising lacked the discipline and leadership necessary to turn a mob into a political force. And the government was able to adapt and respond. The Muslim Brotherhood — a fundamentalist movement viewed as a terrorist organization by most world nations — tried to take over the revolution and failed, and then the Army moved in with conventional force. Ghonim and his fellow protesters were rounded up and jailed while the Army established its own social media page to present a false and more favorable version of the events.

Lessons learned: Two years later, Ghonim reflected on the experience:

> First, we don't know how to deal with rumors. Rumors that confirm people's biases are now believed and spread among millions of people.

> Second, we tend to only communicate with people that we agree with, and thanks to social media, we can mute, un-follow, and block everybody else.

> Third, online discussions quickly descend into angry mobs. It's as if we forget that the people behind the screens are actually real people and not just avatars.

> Fourth, it became really hard to change our opinions. Because of the speed and brevity of social media, we are forced to jump to conclusions and write sharp opinions in 140 characters about complex world affairs. And once we do that, it lives forever on the Internet.

> Fifth, today, our social media experiences are designed in a way that favors broadcasting over engagements, posts over discussions, shallow comments

over deep conversations... It's as if we agreed that we are here to talk at each other instead of talking with each other.[301]

Ghonim was later interviewed on *60 Minutes:*

Our revolution is like Wikipedia, okay? Everyone is contributing content, [but] you don't know the names of the people contributing the content. This is exactly what happened. Revolution 2.0 in Egypt was exactly the same. Everyone contributing small pieces, bits and pieces. We drew this whole picture of a revolution. And no one is the hero in that picture.[302]

Nonetheless, the movement toppled four governments and led to the removal of senior ministers in six others. Syria was plunged into civil war, and although the revolt was put down quickly, the long-term effects are still being felt. The power of the Arab League has declined, religious wars have erupted between the Shi'a and the Sunni, a quarter-million people have died at the hands of their governments, and millions of refugees have sought a new life in Europe. Some social media networks have been outlawed, but participation in the remaining networks has doubled. Individuals were empowered by the network to move quickly, spontaneously, and with a single purpose: defeat top-down governments that had been stoutly in place for centuries.

What made Arab Spring fail:

The very thing that made the Arab Spring a shocking historical force–that it was an organic, people-powered movement that had no leader or ideology– eventually cannibalized it. The vacuum swallowed the revolution. In that faltering, there are echoes, and lessons, in the resistance faced by anti-establishment movements in the west, from Black Lives Matter to the challenges to the center ground from the left. What the Arab Spring came up against was a universal conundrum – how to convert the forces that demand equality into those that deliver it.[303] — *Nesrine Malik, 2020*

Swarms: Teilhard saw that the emergence of a worldwide network would trigger a great shift from an orderly world run by a top-down aristocracy of the few to a freer society run by the many. All in each, each in all. And now the revolution he imagined has begun. Like-minded individuals, joined by a common interest and connected in anonymous self-organizing groups have already started to make decisions together through what are being called "social swarms." Often unknown to each other, without any intermediate agency or specified moderator, the members spontaneously communicate online to arrive at a decision: Let's meet at the site of the accident. Let's move to the steps of city hall. Start sending messages to your councilman. Everybody lie down in the street. Now.

Swarms have no leadership and little organization. They expand, contract, and survive the defeat of separate nodes as members act alone in response to the behavior of others in the group. Feedback from the community, often on social media, allows each user to see how his or her position helps move everyone toward compromise and convergence. And they are often motivated to make altruistic gestures even at risk to themselves.

> Ants use chemical traces. Fish detect vibrations in the water around them. Bees use high-speed gestures. Birds detect motions propagating through the flock. Whatever method is used for establishing the interstitial connectivity, the resulting swarms possess capabilities as a group that the individuals alone can't match. For example, high-speed feedback-control among flapping birds enables thousands of starlings to make precision hairpin turns in winds gusting to 40 miles per hour.[304] — *Louis Rosenberg, Human Swarming and the Future of Collective Intelligence (2015)*

But swarms can be raucous and destructive as well, and as we move from the old model to the new one, the media we count on to reflect our behavior is under fundamental stress.

Broadcast television news is the last stronghold of the aristocracy, the only news medium that still takes government seriously. Big Television requires audio and video, and that in turn requires cameras, microphones, lighting, and a live link back to the studio. In order to make the system work, these resources are often positioned in or near the press rooms of the world where the organizations being covered often control the schedule and get preferential access. It's just easier that way. So the news is bent at the source, even before pundits and commentators fluff their hair, straighten their ties, and tell you how it really is.

Cable has further weakened the hegemony of the major networks, and the new trend toward running a TV show from the host's living room may signal the beginning of a final decline. Now everyone is a broadcaster, everyone is streaming live — even the criminals during the crime. Every public person has a studio in the basement, and the capital-intensive apparatus for recording, editing, and broadcasting a television signal is no longer necessary. The news shows even cut away from government press conferences on a regular basis, favoring commercials, sports news, or their own opinions.

Newspapers, once respectful and authoritative, are shifting to the new network model as they must. For many years they tried hard to be fair and sympathetic to as many subscribers as possible, and like the great broadcast networks, they shared a commitment to offering politically balanced coverage. They will be missed. Now the cost of printing and distributing a pound of converted paper to every subscriber every morning has long since exceeded what advertisers are willing to pay for that audience, and as publishers struggle to incorporate graphics, reader forums, and local coverage into their report, a final financial reckoning lies ahead.

Thousands of online news sources, forums, and social media have become the people's publishers, undisciplined, richly opinionated, and often wildly and intentionally inaccurate. The trend is toward media that are open to all, inventive and irresponsible, a rabble with no visible concern for truth.

People are taking the matter into their own hands.

The Children's Crusade

Malala Yousafzai: On October 9, 2012, this fifteen-year-old Pakistani girl, a popular blogger known all over the region for her energetic defense of women's rights to education, was riding home from school when a young man boarded the bus and called out: "Which one of you is Malala?" She raised her hand, and he shot her in the head.

In 2009, at the age of twelve, she had been invited by the BBC to write a blog about life under the rule of the Taliban, and she chose to focus on the fact that women were being denied access to education. Writing as "Cornflower" to hide her identity, the candor and clarity of her posts attracted immediate network attention and support. Her blog became a rallying place for women's rights, and soon she was giving interviews in print and on television. Taliban rebels responded by shutting down all schools in the area, and that provoked an even greater rebellion among the Pashtun people. But Malala was a popular speaker: "How dare the Taliban take away my basic right to education?" As the violence rose, her tribal valley descended into war, the blog stopped, and her father sent her into the countryside for her safety.[305]

Over the next two years, she continued to blog and speak as a prominent rights activist, and at the age of fifteen she was nominated by Bishop Desmond Tutu for the International Children's Peace Prize. Other prizes and international recognition quickly followed.

That got her shot.

But after a year of reconstructive surgery in England, she returned more famous than ever before. She had become a spokesperson for popular education, a worldwide presence on social media, and a living witness to the violence of the Taliban and the resilience of uppity young women. She changed the way women are treated in Pakistan and in 2014, at the age of seventeen, Malala Yousafzai shared the Nobel Peace Prize with Kailash Satyarthi, a children's rights advocate from India. In 2020, she graduated from Oxford, saying: "I don't know what's ahead. For now, it will be Netflix, reading, and sleep."

Greta Thunberg: Inspired by American students striking for gun control after several school shootings in 2018, Thunberg, fifteen, went on strike herself in August 2018, skipping school to stand in front of the Swedish parliament with a sign, and posting her concerns on Instagram and Twitter. Other students joined her within days, settling into a national program of nationwide strikes every Friday.

> You don't have to school strike, it's your own choice. But why should we be studying for a future that soon may be no more? This is more important than school, I think.[306] — *Greta Thunberg, 2018*

By December she had 20,000 students actively striking in 270 cities around the world, including in Australia, the United Kingdom, Belgium, the US, and Japan.

Throughout the spring she spoke to the British, European, and French parliaments, joined in strikes, and wrote eloquently about the failure of government to deal with the climate crisis, traveling everywhere by train to demonstrate carbon-neutral living. When she was invited to address the UN Climate Action Summit in 2019, she sailed across the Atlantic rather than fly, and at the UN she scolded the world's leaders for their inaction.

> This is all wrong. I shouldn't be up here. I should be back in school on the other side of the ocean. Yet you all come to us young people for hope? How dare you! You have stolen my dreams and my childhood with your empty words. And yet I'm one of the lucky ones. People are suffering. People are dying. Entire ecosystems are collapsing. We are at the beginning of a mass extinction. And all you can talk about is money and fairy tales of eternal economic growth. How dare you![307] — *Greta Thunberg, 2019*

After that, there were student strikes throughout the world and coordinated international protests with more than four million students. *Time* magazine named her person of the year in 2019 for her contribution to international awareness of the climate crisis, and she was nominated for the Nobel Peace Prize. In November 2019, when *Glamour* magazine voted her Woman of the Year, she sent them a message of acceptance:

> If a Swedish, teenage science nerd who has shopstop, refuses to fly, and has never worn makeup or been to a hairdresser can be chosen a Woman of the Year by one of the biggest fashion magazines in the world then I think almost nothing is impossible.[308] — *Greta Thunberg, 2019*

"Just say we won"

On his first day as President of the United States, Abraham Lincoln said:

> This country, with its institutions, belongs to the people who inhabit it. Whenever they shall grow weary of the existing government, they can

exercise their constitutional right of amending it, or their revolutionary right to dismember or overthrow it.[309] — *First Inaugural Address (1861)*

In the first week of January 2021, thousands of people in constant network communication with each other rose up. And as between the two rights noted by Lincoln, they chose the second.

At 2:10 a.m., November 4, 2020, the morning after the American presidential election, the votes coming in started to turn. Having established an early lead, President Donald Trump was now beginning to lose in the big blue states, and ABC was even calling Arizona for Joe Biden. He was distraught. "What do we do? What's happening in Michigan?" Rudy Giuliani, Trump's personal lawyer, said "Just say we won."

"What about Pennsylvania?"

"Just say we won."[310]

Instead of respectfully conceding, as has been the tradition in America for more than two hundred years, President Trump's team immediately launched a campaign to halt the election process, sue the states and counties, spread allegations and misinformation on the social networks, fire up his followers, and ultimately direct the Proud Boys and other ultra-right militia groups to march on the United States Capitol. And through it all he led a campaign to de-legitimize the courts, impugn the media, and weaken the process of democracy while raising millions in so-called "overturn the election" money.

This [election] is a fraud on the American public. This is an embarrassment to our country. We were getting ready to win this election. Frankly, we did win this election. We did win this election. — *President Donald Trump, 2:30 a.m. November 4, 2020.*

Stop the count: Within hours, the Trump campaign launched an offensive to block the last stages of the voting process. In Detroit, Philadelphia, Las Vegas, and Phoenix, campaign staffers showed up at the local counting boards, shouldering their way in and shouting that the election officials were scheming to steal the election for Joe Biden. Over the next few days, in all the swing states, the campaign staff made every possible effort to block the counting process, while asserting without evidence that the voting machines had been hacked and the election system itself was a fraud.[311]

• In the following weeks, Giuliani filed suits in more than sixty state and county jurisdictions, seeking to nullify the results of the election based on "fraud." No supporting evidence was presented, and all the suits were dismissed, including two that went to the Supreme Court. Giuliani's license to practice law was subsequently suspended in New York and Washington, D.C.

• In Michigan, Georgia, Arizona, and elsewhere, the campaign launched a new legal offensive seeking to have the state governments nullify the results and replace the official electors with others committed to Trump. Even after the election, the results in Arizona were audited by a state legislature sympathetic to Trump in the hope that the results could be reversed. The audit confirmed Biden's victory.

• At the same time, President Trump pressured the Attorney General and others in the Department of Justice to overturn the results.[312] "People are angry," the President said. "You guys may not be following the internet the way I do." Acting Deputy Attorney General Richard Donoghue pushed back, according to his notes: "Much of the info you're getting is false."

"Just say that the election was corrupt," replied the President. "And leave the rest to me and the Republican congressmen."[313]

• On December 14, 2021, seven states sent false electoral certificates on to the National Archives, naming Trump supporters as the electors instead of those who had been chosen by the voters.[314] The following week, similar efforts were made by the Department of Justice to raise doubts about the outcome in those crucial states, recommending that the states immediately convene a special panel to examine these irregularities.[315] The purpose was to cast enough public doubt on the election that Vice President Pence would have reason to delay certification, and thereby refer it to the House.

• In January, President Trump called the Georgia Secretary of State and in a taped conversation begged him to change the votes in his favor. Similar calls were made to officials in Michigan, Pennsylvania, and Arizona.[316] Trump began to explore with Mike Pence the possibility that the Vice President could stop the certification until all the claimed irregularities could be investigated.

• In the White House on January 4, a highly placed Republican lawyer delivered to President Trump a two-page memo explaining that if sufficient doubts were raised about the election, Vice President Pence could challenge the slate of electors from seven states and set their votes aside. That would send the election to the House of Representatives where Republican states outnumbered Democratic states and each state had one vote. Trump would be declared the victor. According to *Peril*, a book by Bob Woodward and Robert Costa about the last months of the Trump presidency, President Trump endorsed the strategy and urged Pence to go along.[317]

Then the rallies started: On December 12, 2020, the first post-election pro-Trump rally was held in Washington. The Proud Boys, a self-appointed right-wing "militia," led thousands of attendees in chants and gestures of violence. Speakers included the key members of Trump's campaign staff, predicting that he would be returned to office, that he might invoke the Insurrection Act, and that America was otherwise headed for a "bloody war." Trump flew back and forth over the rally in his presidential helicopter and tweeted his approval.[318]

• But with certification of the election scheduled for January 6, just three weeks away, the campaign team needed to crank things up. On dozens of social media platforms, they now started to stir support for a march on the Capitol. Tactical issues were openly discussed on social networks, including which tools might be needed to pry open doors, how to avoid the police, how to smuggle weapons into the city, and how to kill the politicians they might capture.[319] Floorplans of the building were circulated. One message said "Go there, ready for war. We get our President or we die... It is our duty as Americans to fight, kill and die for our rights."[320] Officials at the city and federal level who were monitoring all this decided that the messages did not represent a serious threat.[321]

• On December 14, 2020, the official electors met separately in each state and confirmed the results of the election. Joe Biden had won the presidency by a seven million vote margin, gaining 306 electoral votes to Trump's 232. Those results were then forwarded to Washington where Vice President Pence was scheduled to lead Congress in the final certification.[322]

• Four days later Trump called for a march on Washington. "Big protest in D.C. on January 6th. Be there, will be wild!"[323] The Women for America First, an offshoot of Women for Trump, filed with the District for permission to hold a March to Save America on that date, saying that five thousand people might attend.

• Social media networks were boiling over with messages about the march, many of which were posted under fake names by the Trump campaign and its allies. Trump's fund-raising efforts had gathered nearly $250 million by then to "overturn the election," little or none of which was actually spent to overturn the election.[324]

• In the last days before the rally, Republican Congressmen were seen giving private tours of the Capitol to groups who were later identified as insurgents.[325]

• The day before the riot, Capitol police, the Department of Homeland Security, and the FBI all received warnings that busses of people were coming to the city armed with the intent to overthrow the government. "We can't trust the police, the laws, or the politicians," said one message forwarded by the Secret Service. "It's time to take out all of them and remain a free country on the 6th. We are the law now. It is US that decides our fate."[326]

• The night before the march, the key principals of the campaign including Steve Bannon, Roger Stone, Rudy Giuliani, John Eastman, Jason Miller, Bernard Kerik, Michael T. Flynn, and others of Trump's innermost circle, all met in a war room set up at the Willard Hotel. Trump apparently phoned in to review the last details for the next day's attack and to urge them on in their effort to block certification and overthrow the election.[327]

The big rally: At 9 a.m. the morning of January 6, Trump supporters began massing on the Ellipse, an oval park behind the White House. Bikers, nuns, people wearing versions of the American flag, and others waved banners that read "Save America."

Congressmen Madison Cawthorn of North Carolina and Mo Brooks of Alabama (wearing body armor) told the crowd that it was time to "start taking down names and kicking ass." Eric and Donald Trump Jr. said "We need to march on the Capitol today." Organizers, friends, and hangers-on claimed that violent insurrection was the last chance to save their country, telling them to "fight like hell." And at 11:57, right on schedule, President Trump took the stage. After having pushed stronger, more incendiary speakers off the schedule and onto the rally the previous night, he now had the audience and the media to himself, and he went way beyond what his aides thought he would say.

After reciting a long litany of grievances, he launched into the well-worn claims that the election had been stolen.

In the state of Arizona, over 36,000 ballots were illegally cast by non-citizens. One hundred and fifty thousand people registered in Maricopa County after the registration deadline. More than 22,000 ballots were returned before they were ever supposedly mailed out. Eleven thousand six hundred more ballots and votes were counted, more than there were actual voters. All these claims had been thoroughly investigated and disproven by election officials, local media, and fact-checkers.[328] — *President Donald J. Trump, 2021*

In Michigan, he said, seventeen thousand ballots were cast by people who were deceased. 174,000 ballots could not be tied to registered voters. In Wayne County, poll watchers saw canvassers scanning ballots over and over again. In Detroit, the turnout was 139 percent of registered voters. The morning after the election, after all the voting had ended, 147,000 votes suddenly appeared, 94 percent for Biden. Despite their apparent specificity, these claims had also been found to be based on fraudulent reports and a poor understanding of how the election process worked.[329] But that didn't matter. Even before his speech was over, people in the audience were shouting to each other. "We're going to the Capitol, pass it on."

This was not a speech intended to inform or persuade. Nothing President Trump said was new, and everyone in the crowd had long since accepted the urgency of the cause. It was a speech intended to entertain. It was a costume drama in which the audience dressed up in the stories they loved and acted out their dream of taking over the government. What Trump did in that speech was to focus the people's fear and frustration on democracy itself, and give his followers permission to use violence.

"You'll never take back our country with weakness. You have to show strength and you have to be strong," Trump said. "I know that everyone here will soon be marching over to the Capitol building to peacefully and patriotically make your voices heard."[330]

Some in the crowd had already started out. At 10:58 a.m., before Trump began speaking, a Proud Boys contingent left the rally wearing body armor and carrying radios, smartphones, and baseball bats, marching toward the Capitol building, 1.7 miles up Constitution Avenue.

The attack: At 12:43 p.m., the Proud Boys and several hundred of their followers pushed the police barriers aside and broke into the Capitol building. They may or may not have had President Trump's approval to attack, at this point the evidence is unclear. By the time the insurrectionists had reached the Capitol, they were no longer strategic, they were emotional, united in contagious rebellion, high on rage and urging each other on. Swinging lead pipes and spraying the defending police with chemicals, they broke windows, scrambled up stairways, and streamed into the National Statuary Hall. With one thousand rioters already surrounding the building, and hundreds inside running through the corridors, the Capitol police declared it a riot and requested backup from the District Police.

Within twenty minutes, the rioters had breached both the House and Senate chambers. Pence and other officials were quickly ushered out as the Parliamentarian secured the boxes of electoral ballots and carried them to safety elsewhere in the building. Rioters began to break into the offices of House Speaker Nancy Pelosi and other senior officials, pawing through files, ransacking the rooms, streaming live footage onto the social networks, and posing for selfies. Meanwhile, messages on Facebook and other social media advised and directed the rioters in real time, even reporting where the congressmen and senators were hiding: "All members are in the tunnels under the capital," said one message. "Seal them in turn on the gas."[331]

According to CNN, President Trump, watching the riot on television from the White House, called Congressman Jim Jordan, Senator Tommy Tuberville of Alabama, and possibly others in the chamber urging them to do everything they could to disrupt and defeat the certification process.[332] Recent reports allege that several of those congressmen, news anchors and commentators from Fox News,[333] and even the President's daughter Ivanka[334] pleaded with him to call off the attackers. But when requests began coming in to mobilize the

National Guard, Trump declined to take any action. At the same time, he tweeted: "Please support our Capitol Police. They are truly on the side of our Country." Staff later said he seemed delighted with how the two sides were visibly battling it out.

For the next hour and a half, with staff barricading themselves in their offices and tear gas blowing through the corridors, the United States Capitol was a free-fire zone.

Ashli Babbitt, a Trump supporter, was shot by police as she tried to climb in through a broken window. Two other Trump supporters died of heart attacks, and one died of an amphetamine overdose. One Capitol police officer died of a stroke, and four others died in the following days. A hundred forty police officers were injured. When National Guardsmen finally arrived at 5:40 p.m., authorized in the end by Vice President Pence,[335] the fight was mostly over, and the rioters were trickling out of the building. Only a handful of them were even arrested.[336]

Behind the scenes: Four levels of participants planned and carried out the effort to overturn the 2020 election. President Trump, his lawyer Rudy Giuliani, and a dozen members of his long-time inner circle planned the campaign, fired up the social media, led the legal challenges through the courts, and organized the march on the Capitol. A second layer of several hundred self-styled militia brought muscle to the task. They were the Proud Boys, the Oath Keepers, the Three Percenters, and other militant gangs not affiliated with any political party who seemed driven by the opportunity to tear down the authority they hated, and bully any liberal protesters who might show up.

The third level, called the "normies," is the interesting one. The usual elements were there: Republican Party officials, political donors, white supremacists, and evangelical Christians, as well as ex-military and serving police officers out of uniform. But an analysis of the first 193 people to be arrested, as of the end of January, revealed what the authors of the study called "a far more dangerous problem":

[This was} a new kind of violent mass movement in which more "normal" Trump supporters — middle-class and, in many cases, middle-aged people without obvious ties to the far right — joined with extremists in an attempt to overturn a presidential election.[337] — *The Atlantic*

The normies included business owners and white-collar workers, CEOs, doctors, lawyers, computer specialists, and accountants, drawn there by Fox News, Facebook, Twitter, and the other networks they followed, who sincerely believed that they had been called to action by their President to rescue the country from a stolen election. Only 26 percent had connections to right-wing political action groups. The analysis also showed that the insurrectionists mirrored the American population as a whole, urban and rural, bi-coastal and Midwestern. They were not disproportionately from red states.

> What's clear is that the Capitol riot revealed a new force in American politics — not merely a mix of right-wing organizations, but a broader mass political movement that has violence at its core and draws strength even from places where Trump supporters are in the minority.[338]

The "Insurrection Index," a public database compiled by Public Wise and several voting rights advocacies, lists 1011 individuals, 213 government officials, and 393 organizations who assisted in the campaign to overturn the election,[339] and as the trials go forward in the next few years, we will get a clearer picture of this new force. But it seems now that the network is rising.

Fundraising: There is a fourth layer to the network that attacked the government on January 6, and its members are unlikely ever to be arrested or even identified. A rational person might view the Trump campaign's efforts to sue the states and challenge the legislatures as futile and unproductive, but for the Trump campaign those efforts were a media and fundraising windfall. In the age of social media and crowdfunding platforms, political outrage is big business, and over the course of just a few months, more than a dozen actors attracted hundreds of millions of dollars to "save America." Most of that money went directly into Trump's personal PAC, empowered by law to pay campaign expenses, legal and consulting fees, Trump's properties, and Trump himself. He even sued the Republican Party to keep them from using his name in competing fundraising campaigns. In the end, little or nothing was paid out for campaign expenses or legal fees, and even Rudy Giuliani, who billed Trump millions for his services, got stiffed. Trump continues to flood the networks with disinformation and money-raising schemes.

Although the campaign to overturn the election may appear to be the product of extremists, it has been fed by sophisticated, well-funded national organizations whose boards of directors include some of the country's wealthiest conservatives. Dark-money organizations, sustained by undisclosed donors, have relentlessly promoted the theory that American elections are rife with fraud, and, according to leaked records of their internal deliberations, they have used that as the reason to draft and support state laws that make it harder for non-white and immigrant residents to vote.

Jane Mayer of *The New Yorker* looked more closely at the dark money funding Trump's Save America and found that several foundations and conservative millionaires had been funding attacks on democracy in states across the country for years. In Trump's Save America campaign they saw an opportunity, she writes, to further damage popular support for the election process, setting the stage for a revision of the laws in order to restrict the voting opportunities of working people.[340]

The goal seems to be to permanently alter the structure of American government in favor of a conservative aristocracy.

Chapter 16
Networks Rising

Standing here a hundred years after Teilhard was writing in his battlefield notebooks, we can see three aspects of today's rising networks that were entirely beyond his vision, and a fourth aspect that goes straight to the heart of our wired world, as timely as this morning's headlines.

Deep network: Over the next decade, the network we are familiar with will pale in importance compared to the rise of a much deeper network, connecting us all in a web of unseen sensors, processors, and algorithms. That will streamline industry supply chains and accelerate productivity as the machines and appliances of the world begin talking directly among themselves. In ten years, more than 125 billion separate and addressable processors will shape our daily lives, negotiating on our behalf with no loyalty except to the interest of their handlers. For all the efficiency this may bring, there is a risk that it will also reduce individual freedoms and expand control over our lives, nudging our behavior to serve the interests of a new technocracy whose goals are not our own.

Fake worlds: What Teilhard called the "lustrous surface of our star" has become a world where nothing is true and nobody cares. We are being drawn into a free-wheeling, un-moderated space where many of the people and places we meet are intentionally false. Artificial entities, avatars, and bots distort the information we rely on, pretending to be human but lacking the essential values of any human community. How will we tell true from false? How do we benefit from the great strengths of a new network technology without succumbing to the dangers of *1984*-style propaganda and deception?

A flatter community: The universal availability of information on the network has ignited a political revolution, shifting our social structure from the hierarchies that have ruled the world since ancient times to much more noisy, disorganized, and collegial models. The boundaries of geography and statehood have lost much of their relevance in the modern world. Political power is being taken from the few and distributed among the many, and the social contract has expired. Now everyone has a voice and everyone is talking at once. Teilhard saw none of that.

The rise of a community consciousness: But in one respect Teilhard was profoundly ahead of his time. He saw that the emergence of a worldwide network would trigger a great transformation from an orderly world run by a top-down aristocracy of the few to a freer society where people cared for each other. All in each, each in all.

Set aside the religious aspects of his dream. Strip back the ecstatic language of his notebooks and listen to him for a moment not as a priest but as a scientist. Was he serious? We may dream about a divine peace one day settling over all, gathering us up into a single community of souls and guiding us toward the next stage in our evolution as a species. But how is that supposed to actually work?

Every science fiction writer for fifty years has seen it otherwise, expecting technology to connect us in a world dominated by totalitarian power structures. What makes Teilhard so interesting is how unusual his vision was in this respect. He thought that a network would draw us into an understanding of each other beyond the boundaries of kin and community, with people engaging in a new wave of care, cooperation, and collective intelligence. We might think together, dream together, and together change the trajectory of our species. No one had ever said that before.

For good reason. The forces opposed to such a community are powerful and long-standing:

(a) Arthur Clarke feared that the network will tend to depersonalize our communications and lend power to a hierarchy of media moguls and special interests. The technology could not convey the emotional communications necessary for care, and whatever leadership emerged would be in service to itself. He thought the network world of the future would lack a soul. And he might be right.

(b) Man's institutional selfishness would also seem to make any kind of caring community difficult. Milton Friedman, who won the 1976 Nobel Prize in Economics, wrote in 1962 that in business, at least, the idea of caring for others was wasteful and unnatural.

Few trends could so thoroughly undermine the very foundations of our free society, as the acceptance by corporate officials of a social responsibility other than to make as much money for their stockholders as possible.[341] — *Milton Friedman, Capitalism and Freedom (1962)*

Friedman acknowledges that there may be "social responsibilities" associated with such issues as equal opportunity employment, minimum wage standards, or operating the business in an eco-friendly way, but he asserts that these do not directly benefit the corporation or its shareholders, and therefore should not be supported by its agents.

And there is a lifestyle component to this resistance as well. Any trend toward collaborative, resource-sharing communities is viewed by many in the Western world as a sign of weakness. It runs counter to the concepts of private property, individual freedom, and the legitimacy of power, celebrated as national ideals but long known to serve the interests primarily of the aristocracy. For the eighty million low-income Americans just making it from month to month, for disenfranchised segments of the country, and for undeveloped nations around the world, there is no private property. Individual freedoms are meaningless. And power is strictly a one-way street.

And yet these same collaborative, resource-sharing communities create healthier, better educated, and more economically secure workers for the corporations to hire, and those workers, in turn, are better able to buy the corporation's products. From Rousseau to Darwin to Durkheim, those who have thought most deeply about the survival and wellbeing of the species have concluded that our long-term self-interest demands that we care for each other beyond individual welfare and tribal altruism. But this is a lesson hard to learn, made harder because it is a pay-now, profit-later deal.

(c) George Steiner wrote in *After Babel*, his 1998 study of the world's languages,[342] that there are natural limits to how big a community could grow before rivalries and discord break it into warring factions. When the number of people speaking the same language grows beyond a certain point, he wrote, individuals lose the sense that they have a meaningful role in the community. They have become too-small fish in a too-large pond. And when that happens, members break away to re-establish smaller groups where their lives have more meaning, and they mark the new boundaries with dialect, slang, gang signs, fashions, tattoos, uniforms, buttons, bumper stickers, and even hats.

Thus, Steiner says, contrary to our hopes and the obvious efficiency that would result, there will never be a world language, and by extension, we will never accept the idea that we are all citizens alike in one world.[343]

(d) Local and regional governments will resist the erosion of power that would be inevitable in any political consolidation. Russia, China, North Korea, Saudi Arabia, and other totalitarian regimes seek to assure the wellbeing of their subject populations by controlling information access. And that is likely to continue. Even in the United States, Europe, and other countries where access is more open, private networks like Facebook, Twitter, talk radio, and cable news channels have served to strengthen the barriers dividing today's political and ideological tribes against each other. Conflict is emotionally stimulating and often results in highly profitable audience interest.

It now seems unlikely that the internet will evolve into the single worldwide noösphere of minds that Teilhard envisioned. More likely to emerge will be a system of thinly connected regional networks, defined by language, politics, and cultural characteristics, struggling for sovereignty, competing against each other to see who will thrive and who will fail. The most we can hope for is to become what Eleanor Roosevelt called a "community of nations," sharing certain legal, economic, and humanitarian principles but retaining our many independent national and regional sovereignties and styles.

It is possible that a future flatter world will be a more passive realm of couch potatoes, responding uncritically to lies and disinformation washing over them on social media. George Orwell seemed to think so. On the other hand, it may turn into a noisy, contentious, unregulated world of competition, ad-hoc leadership, and innovation. In all likelihood, we will go in both directions. Totalitarian governments will certainly continue on their present path of treating their citizens as a collective to be managed, while the Western world, including the US and Europe, will continue on its trajectory of greater individual freedom, more open markets, and competing ideas.

We Are Connected

There is still reason to be hopeful. Through private networks and social media, we are already swapping stories, pictures, and videos, joining forums, and debating together all the issues of daily life. People are connected more than ever before, moving from top-down to bottom-up models, spontaneously challenging governments, and even overthrowing them as they did during the Arab Spring revolutions of 2010. We are becoming better informed about each other, and gaining a vision of ourselves in a larger community.

We are a network species, and looking out for others in our community is an instinct. Charles Darwin is remembered as the man who proclaimed that class violence was natural. In 1859, in *The Origin of Species*, he said that bloody conflict among animals of the same species was the process by which the fittest were selected to survive and the weak were winnowed out. But then in 1871, a few years before his death, he published a second book that is less well known, and it seemed to contradict his earlier view. In *The Descent of Man*, he said that even in the midst of this bloody struggle, animals gravitate naturally to social collectives bound together by what he called "sympathy." He had been puzzled by the fact that chimpanzees share food and adopt orphan children, favoring those of their nearest kin. Some successful species included in their hives members who were infertile, functioning as slaves. In other species, members seemed to throw themselves into the path of death when necessary to save the hive. How could this pattern of charity and sacrifice be consistent with survival of the fittest?

Darwin suggested that groups develop what he called "social instinct," what the founding fathers called "virtue," what Rousseau called the "general will," and what Durkheim would later call "conduct," a set of unwritten rules specific to that community, adopted for survival. Members develop a mental model of their group's history and values, and this guides their actions even when they are alone and under stress.

> The social instincts lead an animal to take pleasure in the society of its fellows, to feel a certain amount of sympathy with them, and to perform various services for them, aiding their fellows in certain general ways.

As man advances in civilization, and small tribes are united into larger communities, the simplest reason would tell each individual that he ought to extend his social instincts and sympathies to all members of the same nation, though personally unknown to him. This point being once reached, there is only an artificial barrier to prevent his sympathies extending to the men of all nations and races.[344] — *Charles Darwin, The Descent of Man (1878)*

In time he generalized his theory of evolution to include kin selection, as he called it. Through sympathy and social instinct, members of a group share resources and protect each other. They bring to adulthood a greater number of offspring, passing on these instincts to succeeding generations. Thus, he said, animals act with consideration and kindness toward each other not because of some innate sense of good or evil but from a simple hard-wired calculation: I help you, you help my children. But the old naturalist's late-life idea of man as a kinder and more cooperative species has been largely ignored.

Live Free and Prosper

A hundred years later, Edward O. Wilson, the Harvard expert on ants, gave the ideas of sympathy and social instinct a new and clearer definition. Wilson said that within any group, the competitive individual is the one most likely to survive. But in the larger world of groups competing against groups, the advantage goes to the group that tamps down internal competition and inspires its members to work selflessly together. The key to the success of a community, he said, is altruism, the instinct in individuals to form mutually supportive social networks, often giving up some of their personal ambitions in favor of those of the group. And like Darwin, Wilson argued that groups with a strong sense of kinship and collaboration succeed where others fail.

The self-sacrificing termite-soldier protects the rest of his colony, including the king and queen, its parents. As a result, the soldier's more fertile brothers and sisters flourish, and through them, the altruistic genes are multiplied by a greater production of nephews and nieces.[345] — *Edward O. Wilson, On Human Nature (1979)*

Moreover, he argued, the way modern communities help each other — and thus compete successfully — is through a generous sharing of knowledge:

> Man's destiny is to know, if only because societies with knowledge culturally dominate societies that lack it. Luddites and anti-intellectuals do not master the differential equations of thermodynamics or the biochemical cures of illness. They stay in thatched huts and die young. Cultures with unifying goals will learn more rapidly than those that lack them, and... [further learning] will follow.[346]

The importance of supporting each other in the community was on display in the COVID-19 crisis of 2021. Public health advocates all cited the potential of the new vaccine to protect the person being vaccinated, but people around the world, particularly in the United States, have historically resisted having the government tell them how to live their lives. The fraction of people who trust the government is at an all-time low — 20 percent today compared to 66 percent in the early 1960s.

At the height of the worldwide COVID-19 emergency, a survey of five million US adults conducted by researchers at Carnegie Mellon University, found that 35 percent of Americans would probably or definitely choose not to be vaccinated, significantly higher among Republicans, less educated, and lower-income segments of the population. A third of the country would rather risk agonizing death than submit to the dictates of a bunch of politicians they believe are crooked, self-serving, and entrained to private interests.[347]

In urging people to protect themselves, proponents of the vaccine might be focusing on the wrong benefit. The vaccine also helps prevent individuals from infecting their own families, neighbors, and fellow workers. Even among those who show no symptoms, vaccination reduces the possibility of infecting others by 72 percent.[348] It is understandable that people would distrust the government, doubt the advice of scientists and politicians, and choose to live free of mandates from an aristocracy they don't know and don't like. Sartre, Nietzsche, and Rousseau certainly raised that idea of individual freedom to the level of respected philosophy. But Rousseau and Sartre also said that with networks now connecting us in an intimate new world, our ability to thrive will require us to take greater responsibility for each other.

The point made by Wilson is that in the networks rising today we are all entangled, and to rise together in a complicated and competitive world we must balance individual freedom against the obligations of community membership — get vaccinated against smallpox, stop at red lights, and even mow the front lawn. Live free and thrive together.

We are actually built to care for each other. We humans mate for life and care for our children. Our survival requires that. But Wilson and Darwin before him tell us it is also an instinct among humans to share resources with kin and clan, even to the point of personal sacrifice. Within our community, we share our food and our knowledge. We join with neighbors we don't know to keep the park clean, and we risk our lives in battle out of duty to our tribe. But whether we can learn to see the larger world as a community sharing the climate and the seas is still an open question.

The Social brain: We are a network species not only by instinct but also by anatomy. In 2010, Oxford anthropologist Robin Dunbar suggested that there is a relationship between the size of the human brain and the number of others with whom we can form a trusting and reciprocal relationship.[349] Comparing social behavior and brain size across multiple species over thousands of years, Dunbar suggested that a human's ability to maintain a circle of close friends depends on keeping a model of each friend in the mind — he called it the "social brain" — and this capacity for caring, like the size of the human brain, was evolving very slowly.

About two million years ago, a spurt in brain size included an expansion of the language-connected part of the forebrain.[350] People began to talk to each other. Then the brain doubled in size again about three hundred thousand years ago, enabling our species to plan, socialize, and solve problems. With a thinner skull wall, a higher, almost vertical forehead, and a prominent brow, Homo sapiens began to hunt in packs, breed animals, practice agriculture, work with tools, create family networks, and include art, rituals, and symbols in their daily life. And this is the key: Dunbar wrote that in order to function in a caring group, each man learned to maintain a model in his own mind of his group-mates' behaviors sufficient to see the world as they might see it, to feel the others' fears and motivations as well as his own, and, like great basketball teams or Dixieland bands, guess what his fellow members would do next. It is also true that our own actions are guided by how we might be viewed by the others in the group. We try to be who the network thinks we are. Over time, as the members of small communities gained an understanding of each other, they began to think as one.

This coordination of the group's activities without formal communication was a force multiplier in hunting a woolly mammoth or battling club to club against an attacking tribe. It took training, time, and trust, but the capacity for such relationships within a group turned out to be the characteristic that distinguished Homo sapiens not only from all other creatures in the forest but also from all its predecessors going back to the beginning of time. Those with larger brains were better able to care for each other and work together as a team. The new groups were more productive, more resilient, and had more surviving offspring. And following Darwin's thesis, the caring, better-informed network species thrived.

There are two ways to think about this. As a species, we seem wired to succeed most often when we care about each other. But there may also be an anatomical limit on how many others we can care about. Can intimate non-brain networks, free of deceit and capable of emotional communication, begin to lift this limitation?

Ubuntu

Among the Bantu people in Southern Africa, there is an ethical tradition called "ubuntu" saying essentially that we are each each other. Among the Shona people of Zimbabwe, they say that a "person is a person through other persons."[351] In contrast to Plato's idea that morality and justice should be defined by the better educated few, or Aristotle's idea that we should guide our behavior according to whatever leads us to individual happiness and well-being, the idea of ubuntu is that the best source of moral guidance is the community. Our values, our dreams, and our identities are formed in the context of each other. Echoing the ideas of Durkheim, the members of a community guide us, teaching us to respect the wisdom of elders as the custodians of morality even when their instruction conflicts with our own interests.[352] African humanism, as it is sometimes called, values co-existence and cooperation within the community over the Western tradition of individual freedom.[353]

Eric Yamamoto, professor of law and racial justice, said Ubuntu is the idea that no one can be healthy when the community is sick. "Ubuntu says I am human only because you are human. If I undermine your humanity, I dehumanize myself."[354]

Writing about his work to heal the ravages of African apartheid, Desmond Tutu said "the single main ingredient that made the achievements of [reconciliation] possible was uniquely African — Ubuntu — constraining the members to forgive rather than to demand retribution.[355] Barack Obama, in his eulogy for Tutu in 2013, made the critical point. Ubuntu goes beyond being nice, beyond kindness and generosity. It is a pragmatic way to tap into the resources of others, available when we embrace our common and diverse humanity:

> We achieve ourselves by sharing ourselves with others, and caring for those around us... It took a man like Madiba [Tutu] to free not just the prisoner, but the jailor as well; to show that you must trust others so that they may trust you; to teach that reconciliation is not a matter of ignoring a cruel past, but a means of confronting it with inclusion, generosity, and truth.[356] — *Barack Obama, 2013*

In the history of our species, every great catastrophe has been met by a spontaneous and equally great outpouring of assistance and compassion, beyond the boundaries of clan and tribe, beyond politics, race, religion, and even geography. The catalog of examples is long, but a small illustration will serve. When Oonagh O'Hagan, professor of fashion and textiles at Central St. Martins college in London heard about the shortage of hospital scrubs caused by COVID-19, she got the patterns from a friend and enlisted her students in sewing up replacements. They started a website to coordinate their work, and as more people learned about the project, more people wanted to help. The network quickly expanded to include volunteers outside of the class, then outside the university, and then outside the country as new scrubs flowed in made of colorful fabrics from many cultures and decorated with impromptu and anonymous messages of hope and love.[357] None of these people knew each other at the time, and they never will. But they came to care, and everyone benefitted.

Here's another example. We don't have enough models of everyday caring in our literature, so indulge me:

A Florida woman, herself of very modest means, saw a homeless person on the steps of a convenience store and worried that he might suffer dehydration, she went in, grabbed two bottles of water, and brought them out to the man. She tells what happened next:

> When I came back in, the lady in front of me turned around, hands on hips, and told me that I was just enabling that 'homeless person' (said with a sneer) and that I shouldn't be wasting my money on him.

> It's hot as hell in Florida right now. Mid-nineties with humidity around 80%. It's a good day for heat stroke, and I told her so. I said I'd rather give him a water than call an ambulance.

> I was gonna shrug it off. Let it go. Chalk it up to ignorance and the heat making everybody cranky.

> And then she told me I should be ashamed of myself. That someone should call the police on him, and that it should be illegal to beg for money. That people who give the homeless money just encourage them to stay homeless and that should be illegal, too.

> Ashamed. I should be ashamed for giving some poor old guy a water — it cost a whole dollar, BTW — and I should get in trouble for making sure he didn't stroke out in this heat.

> I guess I look nice. Approachable. Like I wouldn't rip your head off. I am nice, most of the time.

> But not always.

> And I lost my temper.

> I told her to call a cop and report me for buying sh*t at a convenience store.

I told her that I wasn't in the damn mood for crazy right now. That it's a hundred f***ing degrees outside, and I'm hot and tired and sick to death of stupid people. That if she had an ounce of compassion in her whole body, she'd buy him a cold drink, too. That maybe she should figure out why she needs to accost complete strangers. And how's about after that, she back the f**k up outta my face and outta my business and turn back around and not say one more damn word to me.

I'm just about deaf in one ear. I try to modulate my voice. Unless I get angry.

It got pretty loud there at the end. There was dead silence in the store and then someone said loudly "For real!"

And the guy at the front of the line told the cashier to add a sandwich to his purchases for the guy outside.

The guy behind him bought an extra ice cream. The girl behind HIM got change for a twenty 'cause that guy could probably use some cash.'

Every single person in line got him something. Every one, except the now very embarrassed lady in front of me, who slunk out without saying another word.

When I got to the cashier, she didn't charge me for either of the waters, because she was going to take him one anyway. And mine was free because of the entertainment.

When I went outside, he was eating his ice cream and drinking his water with a pile of stuff all around him, a big old grin on his face. He didn't look shaky anymore.

And there, people, is the story of why I hate people. And why I love people. All in the same damned minute.

I sat in the car and drank my water and laughed with tears in my eyes, same as I'm doing now.[358] — *Barbara Mack, 2021*

For all his pessimism, even George Orwell understood the potential of a community caring for its members, and at the end of *1984*, in a short passage we tend to forget, he gave us a glimpse of the proles, 85 percent of the population living in slavery but intimately connected to each other.

> What mattered [to the Proles] were individual relationships, and a completely helpless gesture, an embrace, a tear, a word spoken to a dying man, could have value in itself... They were not loyal to a party or a country or an idea, they were loyal to one another.

> "If there is hope," wrote Winston, "it lies in the proles.[359] — *George Orwell, 1984 (1949)*

Totalitarian and top-heavy systems demand loyalty up and down the chain of command. For all their efficiency, they distract us from each other, discourage conversation, and reinforce the sterile behavior Arthur Clarke feared. We keep quiet and do as we're told. But the open, deeply connected networks now rising invite us to share our lives with others beyond kin and clan. As the old systems give way to more open, unrestricted social networks, a new kind of social cooperation is emerging, beyond altruism. Maybe the ability to connect, care, and collaborate with a much larger number of people is going to be, as Teilhard suggested, the hallmark of a new species.

This shift has been a long time coming, and it is a colorful human story of technology wizards beckoning us into a new world, of eccentric philosophers struggling for centuries to free us from the rule of older religious and imperial aristocracies, and of science fiction writers, futurists, and sociologists imagining dozens of new models for living more freely together. All leading us up to the next extraordinary chapter in human history. Today we are on the verge of a great leap forward in productivity, community care, and collective intelligence. We know this because we've seen it happen once before.

Come back with me across a span of twenty-five thousand years, down over southeastern Europe to the dense forests along the border between Serbia and Bulgaria, to what is now the village of Rabia in the foothills of the Balkan mountains, and to the old Magura caves.

The World's First Selfie

There, if you walk half a mile down into the cool darkness, you will see one of the great paintings of the Stone Age. It was done by primitive man on his long migration from Africa north into Europe, and it shows Homo sapiens — Thinking Man — at the moment of his social awakening. It is the world's first selfie.

The painting appears to depict a harvest dance, a celebration of summer's end when the tribe enjoys one last feast, after which the women and children are sent away to spend the winter months deeper in the cave while the men go out on the long hunt.At the time it was painted, Homo sapiens had been around for about one hundred thousand years and their anatomical advantages over the Neanderthals were fully apparent. They were tall and slight of build compared to their stocky predecessors, relying more on their stone tools than on their muscles. Their enlarged frontal brain had given them the capacity for living in a complex clan-based society, hunting strategically as a group, and expressing themselves in spoken and symbolic language.

They were successful at breeding animals and growing some of the food they needed, and with the last glaciers receding slowly from the slopes of the Pirin Mountains, the skills that had enabled them to survive while other hominids died out could now be applied to hunting the new forests and fishing the rushing rivers for miles around. The time the painting was made would have been a happy one, with even happier times ahead.

The painting seems to move in the flickering torchlight: women are dancing with their arms raised gracefully over their heads while men with erections hover nearby. Dogs and domesticated geese bark and honk around them on the ground. A man with a bow and arrow shows off his skill. Smaller figures — probably children — are playing underfoot while others in the family dance and re-enact the hunt. Geometric figures here and there may count the summer kills or mark significant events of the tribal year. The background is dotted with plants that experts suggest may be mushrooms. But there are no images of gods demanding to be obeyed, no written words to remind the people of their purpose or their past. They are living in the moment, before spirituality. Before writing of any kind. Before science. If there was ever a real Garden of Eden, it might have looked a lot like this.

It is a portrait of our species about to be transformed.

At the time this painting was done, Homo sapiens had grown more skilled at hunting and agriculture and begun living longer, healthier lives. Instead of dying in their mid-thirties, a new generation of elders emerged with a longer experience of hunting tactics, family care, and the seasonal rhythms of the field. As the size of the family grew, these elders with useful knowledge were recognized as contributors, even if their age made them less helpful in the hunt. They knew about healing, about crops, about the weather and the seasons. They remembered old water holes and the habits of herds, and they helped the family make better decisions every day.

With the added life skills and knowledge of these tribal elders, Homo sapiens began to live much more fruitful lives. They were smarter in battle, they had more surviving children, and they could bring down the great beasts in the forest and share the protein with others in their family. According to anthropologist Rachel Caspari, the knowledge available from these elders resulted in an economic and demographic explosion. She writes that the information the elders could offer had "profound effects on the population sizes, social interactions, and genetics of early modern human groups, and may explain why [the new species] was more successful than other archaic humans, such as the Neanderthals."[361]

But the elders sitting around the fire brought another lesson well, and this lesson must have been difficult at first, maybe the most difficult lesson in the history of man: your health and safety depend on others in your community, and their health and safety depend on you. The elders remembered who had married whom. They knew who was and was not a cousin, what favors had been done by neighbors in the past, and how to judge the identity and intention of strangers. For the first time, people began to recognize and enforce kinship with others they had never met. The idea of a "clan" was born, a conscious collective joined by knowledge and beyond the limits of the family.

This, in turn, brought many more people into the covenant of cooperation and mutual support.[362] Larger coordinated hunts were possible. Food and shelter were shared more broadly in times of trouble, and mutual defense pacts were formed to protect new settlements against marauding gangs.

According to Chris Stringer of the Natural History Museum in London, many reasons have been offered for the rise of Homo sapiens: the capacity to produce art, language, and possibly a better brain. But Stringer says that the latest research suggests an even more powerful advantage: "We were networking better, our social groups were larger, we were storing knowledge better and we built on that knowledge."[363]

The rise of this new network connected the family to a larger cooperating community and led to the greatest one-time leap of human productivity in the history of the race.[364] That experience suggests a way of thinking about the impact of networks emerging today.

A Second Transformation

Talking back and forth with others often enough to trace the bumps and pleasures of their days may help us develop a mental model of them, not permanently stored in our memories as Dunbar suggested — his theories pre-date the internet — but available off-brain on the network whenever we want; a kind of on-demand multimedia memory of the world beyond kin and kind that brings us not just the contact information but a more intimate, emotional record of our relationships. We are being drawn by Facebook, Instagram, Twitter, Skype, Zoom, web pages, email, text messaging, and future metaworlds into greater awareness and compassion toward people in a world beyond ourselves, tuning in on each other's lives, forming alliances beyond local boundaries, and sharing beyond the limits of Church, State, and the social aristocracy. We are learning to know together. But more than that, we are learning to care.

Our history suggests that we might think together, dream together, cooperate more fully, and experience a transformation of our species. This is not mysticism. Thomas Hobbes [1588-1679] thought men needed to be ruled. Their lives were violent and contentious, "poor, nasty, brutish, and short," and only a rightful king like Charles II, Hobbes' great friend and former pupil, could bring order and discipline to their world. Centuries of slavery, human rights atrocities, and war have seemed to support his view. But new research suggests that man's first instinct, even from childhood, is to cooperate, choosing actions that will help his friends as well as those actions that will help himself.[365]

Even the 1954 novel, *Lord of the Flies*, which famously portrayed innocent boys reverting to Hobbesian violence after being stranded on an island, is contradicted by the real-life experience of a comparable group of schoolboys, marooned in 1965 on one of the Fiji islands, two thousand miles east of Australia. The boys, aged thirteen to sixteen, organized themselves, planted a garden, captured and raised wild chickens, drank blood, ate fish, sucked on the eggs of seabirds, and managed to light a signal fire. They began and ended each day with a song and a prayer, accompanied by a guitar made from a coconut shell and some wires salvaged from their boat. They tried to build a raft, but it was destroyed in the surf on their first outing. And when one boy fell from a cliff and broke his leg, the others improvised a splint, dragged him back up to their base camp, and cared for him until he healed. They organized themselves into shifts to keep the signal fire burning on the hillside and were finally rescued fifteen months later by a passing fishing boat. They never let the fire go out.[366]

In June 2020, in the wake of the death of George Floyd, a Black man murdered by Minneapolis police, six Nashville teenagers organized a protest rally that grew to include more than ten thousand people. "We all met on Twitter," one of them explained, "And that's how easy it is to do something like this." Jade Fuller, Nya Collins, Zee Thomas, Kennedy Green, Emma Rose Smith, and Mikayla Smith, ages fourteen to sixteen, Black and White, began FaceTiming each other. They formed a coalition called Girls 4 Change and started to promote a city-wide demonstration against police brutality and racism. Nashville police tried to head off the rally by falsely reporting that a tornado was due, but as the crowds began to gather, the girls led the rally to the center of the city and offered water, snacks, and first aid supplies in case they might be needed. They gave instructions to the crowd on how to respond nonviolently to police intervention, they made speeches, read poetry, and lay down in the street in an entirely peaceful, five-hour demonstration:

> "It's your brothers and sisters. It's people in your community, people you know who are feeling oppressed. Their moms and dads are getting killed because of their skin color, because people are afraid of them," Smith told a reporter from the local TV station. "We can all come together as a community to stop what's happening and see that the racism ends in our country."[367]

Former President Barack Obama, commenting on the rising concern about racial justice in the United States, suggested that protestors now come from a broader cross-section of the country than was the case during the race riots of his youth. "That didn't exist back in the 1960s, that kind of broad coalition," he said.

> There is a change in mindset that's taking place — a greater recognition that we can do better. And that is not as a consequence of speeches by politicians. That's not the result of spotlights in news articles. That's a direct result of the activities and organizing and mobilization and engagement of so many young people across the country.[368] — *Barack Obama, June 2020.*

Out of Teilhard's writings and the writings of those dreamers who followed come two big ideas for the future of our species:

Crowdsource government and justice: Freedom and opportunity are gifts we give each other, and the emerging network promises to let members of a community live more openly and peacefully without paying high maintenance fees to bureaucrats. At the same time, the rise of a worldwide network has given people the chance to help themselves. Through direct action such as Tiananmen Square, Arab Spring, and human rights protests rolling across the world, teenagers with network access have changed governments. Imagine what experienced grown-ups could do. The tools of peaceful change are time-tested and reliable, and Teilhard imagined a worldwide network that would connect us all together in such efforts.

There are challenges. Like the highways of old, networks give harbor to some who lurk among us, ready to jump out of the shadows and grab a poorly guarded purse. Many-to-many communication systems are noisy, disputatious, and vulnerable to those who bloviate and deceive. And new technology will make it harder to tell what is real and what is not. We don't know yet how to achieve both individual privacy and public accountability. Everyone who has thought about this flatter world has worried about how leadership will emerge and be sustained.

But through a higher diversity of views that Eleanor Roosevelt taught us to embrace, through the augmentation of cognitive processes Doug Engelbart envisioned, through a deeper sense of responsibility for each other encouraged by Durkheim, Sartre, and H. G. Wells, and through a greater respect for truth and comity, as demonstrated by Jimmy Wales, we are more likely than ever to join in caring communities, competing peacefully and productively as a species.

Seek the Divine in each other: For centuries the Church has stood astride the business of helping each other, but Teilhard's dream offered an alternative. As a priest, he was uttering a profound and unimagined heresy, and the Church was wise to shut him up as quickly as it could. He was suggesting that we might find inspiration and guidance not in the Church but in each other.

> Is the world not in the process of becoming vaster, closer, and more dazzling than Jehovah? Will it not burst our religion asunder, and eclipse our God?[369]

Instead of loving the ecclesiastical apparatus, expecting that our love will be repaid in the next life, we might love each other directly, now, and without distraction. We might care for each other today, not tomorrow, rather than offer our charity to an institution in the hope that it will someday spread the gift around. Living directly is harder to do. Knowing and caring for each other beyond kin and clan is emotionally and cognitively more difficult. But Teilhard dreamed that this new awareness of each other would lead to a great leap in wellness, innovation, and productivity, just as it did long ago in the caves of Magura.

It isn't so much that we can suddenly dream, but that we can dream together. Together we see from different angles a future that trusting communities can build. And if we can create new communities of care, beyond altruism, then the networks now rising around us may be instrumental in one of the great social transformations in human history.

We can do this. In his speech accepting the Nobel Prize for Literature in 1950, American novelist William Faulkner praised the indomitable spirit of humans: "When the last dingdong of doom has clanged and faded from the last worthless rock hanging tideless in the last red and dying evening, even then there will still be one more sound: that of his puny inexhaustible voice, still talking." But Faulkner was wrong in one detail. It will not be one voice talking, it will be more than one. Voices plural, all talking at the same time, gossiping about each other, quarreling over little things, reciting love poems, swapping ideas, singing songs, and laughing. We are a very social, caring, and evolving species, and the future that now lies before us is brighter than ever.

The day will come when, after harnessing space, the winds, the tides, and gravitation, we shall harness... the energies of love. And on that day, for the second time in the history of the world, human beings will have discovered fire. — *from the wartime notebooks of Teilhard de Chardin, 1915.*

Index

Notes

[1] Pierre Teilhard de Chardin, "Phenomenon," in Ursula King, *Pierre Teilhard de Chardin* (Maryknoll, NY: Orbis Books, 2011), 66.

[2] Pierre Teilhard de Chardin, "Heart," in King, 60.

[4] Georges Ifrah, *The Universal History of Computing: From the Abacus to the Quantum Computer* (New York: John Wiley and Sons, Inc., 2001), 121-133.

[5] Kathleen Broome Williams, *Grace Hopper, Admiral of the Cyber Sea* (Annapolis, MD: Naval Institute Press, 2004), 12.

[6] Kurt Beyer, *Grace Hopper and the Invention of the Information Age* (Cambridge, MA: The MIT Press, 2009), 59.

[7] Russell McGee, "My Adventures with Dwarfs: a Personal History in Mainframe Computers," an unpublished manuscript in the archive of the University of Minnesota Charles Babbage Institute (2003) 119.

[8] Williams, 177.

[9] Douglas Engelbart, "The Mother of All Demos, presented by Douglas Engelbart (1968)," *Youtube.com.*

[10] Bush, Vannevar. *"As We May Think,"* *Atlantic Monthly* (July, 1945).

[11] Valerie Landau and Eileen Clegg, *The Engelbart Hypothesis: Dialogs with Douglas Engelbart* (Berkeley, CA Next Press, 2009).

[12] John Markoff, *What the Dormouse Said: How the Sixties Counterculture Shaped the Personal Computer Industry* (New York: Penguin Books, 2006).

[13] Jacques Vallée, *The Heart of the Internet: An Insider's View of the Origin and Promise of the On-Line Revolution* (Newburyport, MA: Hampton Roads, 2002).

[14] Tim Berners-Lee, James Hendler and Ora Lassila, "The Semantic Web," *Scientific American* (May, 2001). At least someone was thinking along the same lines. In 2001, Tim Berners-Lee and his colleagues proposed to expand the searchable web metadata attributes of each page to handle structured information that could be inferred by AI engines. There has since been no significant progress toward this goal, and active research on the so-called "semantic web" seems to have been halted.

[15] Valerie Landau et al.

[16] Romain Dillet, "The Raspberry Pi Foundation unveils the Raspberry Pi 4," *Techcrunch.com* (June 24, 2019).

[17] Julian Chokkattu, "The Display of the Future Might Be in Your Contact Lens," *Wired Magazine* (January 26, 2020).

[18] Mike Elgan, "Why a smart contact lens is the ultimate wearable," *Computerworld* (May 9, 2016).

[19] "The 10 countries with the world's fastest internet speeds," *Business Insider* (May 2015).

[20] Rachel Metz, "Meta is building an AI supercomputer," *CNN Business* (January 24, 2022).

[21] Steve Dent, "Smartwatches may detect the signs of COVID-19 before you know you're sick," *Endgadget.com* (January 18th, 2021).

[22] Shoshana Zuboff, *The Age of Surveillance Capitalism: The Fight for a Human Future at the New Frontier of Power* (New York: Public Affairs, 2019), 236.

[23] Dan Howarth, "Google teams up with Levi's to create interactive denim jacket," *De Zeen.com* (May 26, 2016).

[24] Paul Ziobro and Joann S. Lublin, "Mattel Finds Its New CEO at Google," *The Wall Street Journal* (January 18, 2017).

[25] "The high-tech farming revolution," *BBC* (June 20, 2019).

[26] Daniel Oberhaus, "This New Atomic Clock Is So Precise Our Ability to Measure Gravity Constrains Its Accuracy," *Motherboard.com* (November 30, 2018).

[27] Len Calderone, "Is That a Bug or a Robotic Spy?" *Robotics Tomorrow* (December 5, 2017).

[28] Starre Vartan, "Insect-inspired robots that can jump, fly and climb are almost here," *CNN* (September 26, 2020).

[29] According to several recent studies, these data centers may consume as much as 20% of the world's power in 2025. See Joao Marques Lima, "Data centers of the world will consume 1/5 of Earth's power by 2025," *Data-Economy.com* (December 12, 2017).

[30] Brent Heslop, "By 2030, Each Person Will Own 15 Connected Devices — Here's What That Means for Your Business and Content," *MartechAdvisor* (March, 2019).

[31] Irene Klotz, "Burgeoning Satellite Industry Paving Way To $1 Trillion Space Economy," *Aviation Week* (August 24, 2021).

[32] Mark Harris, "Pentagon testing mass surveillance balloons across the US," *The Guardian* (August 2, 2019).

[33] Lauren Bridges, "Amazon's Ring is the largest civilian surveillance network the US has ever seen," *The Guardian* (May 18, 2021).

[34] Michael Kwet, "In Stores, Secret Surveillance Tracks Your Every Move," *The New York Times* (June 15, 2019).

[35] Stephanie Kirchgaessner and Michael Safi, "Palestinian activists' mobile phones hacked using NSO spyware, says report," *The Guardian* (November 8, 2021).

[36] Stephanie Kirchgaessner, Paul Lewis, David Pegg, Sam Cutler, Nina Lakhani and Michael Safi, "Revealed: leak uncovers global abuse of cyber-surveillance weapon," *The Guardian* (July 18, 2021).

[37] David E. Sanger, Nicole Perlroth, Ana Swanson and Ronen Bergman, "U.S. Blacklists Israeli Firm NSO Group Over Spyware," *The New York Times* (November 3, 2021).

[38] "A Year After Lockdown: Stalkerware on the Rise," *NortonLifeLock.com* (June 24, 2021).

[40] Hal Varian, "Beyond Big Data," Paper presented at Presented at the NABE (National Association for Business Economics) Annual Meeting, September 10, 2013, San Francisco, CA..

[41] Zuboff.

[42] Sarah R. Blenner, JD, MPH, Melanie Köllmer, PhD, Adam J. Rouse, JD, LLM, et al., "Privacy Policies of Android Diabetes Apps and Sharing of Health Information," *Journal of the American Medical Association (JAMA)* (March 8, 2016).

[43] "Deceived by Design: How tech companies use dark patterns to discourage us from exercising our rights to privacy," *Forbrukerrådet-The Norwegian Consumer Agency* (June 27, 2018)..

[44] Natasha Singer and Aaron Krolik, "Grindr and OkCupid Spread Personal Details, Study Says," *The New York Times* (January 13, 2020).

[45] *Carpenter v. United States*, 2018.

[46] Byron Tau and Michelle Hackman, "Federal Agencies Use Cellphone Location Data for Immigration Enforcement: Commercial database that maps movements of millions of cellphones is deployed by immigration and border authorities," *The Wall Street Journal* (February 7, 2020).

[47] Zuboff, 300.

[48] Ibid.

[49] "Upstream's Secure-D detects malware spike in Q1 2020 with 29,000 malicious Android apps at play, double 2019 figures," *Upstream Systems.com* (June 2020).

50 Lachlan Keller, "What decentralization can offer Web 3.0 and social media," *Forkasyt.com* (November 22, 2021).

51 Ryan Mac, Charlie Warzel, and Alex Kantrowitz, "Growth At Any Cost: Top Facebook Executive Defended Data Collection In 2016 Memo — And Warned That Facebook Could Get People Killed," *BuzzFeed* (March 29, 2018).

52 Ben Ray Redman, *The Portable Voltaire* (New York: Penguin, 1977).

53 Will Durant and Ariel Durant, *The Age of Reason Begins* (New York: Simon and Schuster, 1961), 19.

54 Jean-Jacques Rousseau, trans. G. D. H. Cole, *The Social Contract and Discourses by Jean-Jacques Rousseau* (London: J. M. Dent and Sons, 1923).

55 Will Durant and Ariel Durant, *Rousseau and Revolution* (New York: Simon & Schuster, 1967).

56 Jean-Jacques Rousseau, "A Discourse on Inequality," Peter Gay, *The Basic Political Writings of Jean-Jacques Rousseau* (Cambridge, M A: Hackett Press, 1987), 25.

57 Rousseau, "On the Origin of the Inequality of Mankind, the Second Part," (1754), *A Dissertation on the Origin and Foundation of the Inequality of Mankind* (CreateSpace Independent Publishing Platform, 2014).

58 Thomas Ricks, *First Principles: What America's Founders Learned from the Greeks and Romans and How That Shaped Our Country* (New York: Harper, 2020).

59 Alexander Hamilton, "Draft of a Resolution for the Legislature of New York for the Amendment of the Constitution of the United States," January 29, 1802.

60 James Parton, *Life of Voltaire* (Boston: Houghton Mifflin, 1881), 620.

61 This first-hand account is disputed by the officials of the great Pantheon cemetery. In 1898, the *Sidney Morning Herald* reported that French officials, concerned by the rumors that their two great heroes had been so dishonored, had Voltaire's tomb opened so they could confirm his identity. Which they proudly did. "The Bones of Voltaire and Rousseau," The *Sydney Morning Herald* (February 2, 1898).

62 Part of a speech Durkheim gave in Paris in the early thirties, quoted by friends and others who attended.

63 Émile Durkheim, *The Elementary Forms of Religious Life (1912)* (Oxford, UK: Oxford University Press, 2001), 295.

64 Steven Lukes, *Émile Durkheim: His Life and Work* (Stanford, CA: Stanford University Press, 1973), 65.

65 Grant Wacker, *America's Pastor, Billy Graham and the Shaping of a Nation* (Cambridge, MA, Harvard University Press, 2014), 70.

[66] Émile Durkheim, *Division of Labor* (New York: Free Press 1964), 41.

[67] Jared Keller, "The U.S. Suicide Rate Is at Its Highest in a Half-Century: New CDC data suggests suicide is becoming more commonplace in America," *Pacific Standard* (Dec 4, 2018).

[68] Cora Peterson et al., "Suicide Rates by Industry and Occupation — National Violent Death Reporting System, 32 States, 2016," *Centers for Disease Control and Prevention* (2020).

[69] "Suicide," National Institute of Mental Health (February, 2021).

[71] Edward Burnett Tylor, *Primitive Culture: Researches into the Development of Mythology* (London: John Murray, 1871).

[72] Herbert Simon, *Administrative Behavior* (New York: Macmillan, 1957).

[73] Christopher Burns, *Deadly Decisions*: *How False Knowledge Sank the Titanic, Blew Up the Shuttle, and Led America into War* (New York, Prometheus Books, 2008).

[74] Lukes, 135.

[75] Ibid., 128.

[76] Durkheim, *Division of Labor,* 129.

[77] Ibid., 554.

[78] Wells was nominated four times.

[79] "Victorians, Religion," *English Heritage.org.*.

[80] More recent studies have concluded that Prince Albert died of Crohn's disease, not typhoid.

[81] Alfred Lord Tennyson, "Ulysses."

[82] Adam Roberts, *H. G. Wells: A Literary Life*, (London: Palgrave Macmillan, 2019), 55.

[83] Mark Strauss, "H.G. Wells' Remarkable Scientific Article About Evolution On Mars," *Gizmodo.com* (May 2014)..

[84] Angela Saini, "In the twisted story of eugenics, the bad guy is all of us," *The Guardian* (October 3, 2019).

[85] Vincent Brome, *H.G. Wells: A Biography* (London: Longmans, Green, 1951), 96.

[86] Graham Ball, "The sordid secret life of HG Wells," *The (UK) Express* (March 30, 2010).

[87] H. G. Wells, *World Brain*, (H. G. Wells Library, 2016. Originally published in 1938.).

[88] Wells, "The Brain Organization of the Modern World, Lecture delivered in America, October and November, 1937," from *World Brain.*

[89] Vannevar Bush.

[90] Lord Sankey, "A Declaration of the Rights of Man," 1940.

[91] Michael Sherbourne, *H. G. Wells: Another Kind of Life* (London: Peter Owen, 1988), 327-329.

[92] Wells, *World Brain*.

[93] Sherbourne, 343.

[94] Sankey.

[95] Sherbourne, 331.

[96] Friedrich Nietzsche, *Ecce Homo (1888)* (New York: Penguin, 1992).

[97] Friedrich Nietzsche, *Zarathustra:* Part I, Goals, *(1883)*. (Cambridge, UK: Cambridge University Press, 2011).

[98] Widely attributed to Nietzsche, but not found in his major works. There are many quotes attributed to the man that cannot be accurately sourced, and to make matters worse, when his sister published his books after his death, she often modified them in order to bring his thoughts into line with the anti-Semitic, pro-Nazi sentiments of the time, changes that have since been discredited.

[99] Friedrich Nietzsche, *Zarathustra, Prologue,* 5.

[100] Jean-Paul Sartre, *Existentialism is Humanism* (New Haven, CT: Yale University Press, 2007). I have edited this text very slightly to remove any unintended confusion. All further quotes are from this source.

[101] United States Delegation to the General Assembly and Staff, January 17, 1946, US Department of State, Office of the Historian..

[102] Richard Kreitner, "January 10, 1946: The General Assembly of the United Nations Convenes for the First Time," *The Nation* (January 10, 2015)..

[103] Dan Eshet, F*undamental Freedoms: Eleanor Roosevelt and the Universal Declaration of Human Rights* (Brookline, MA: Facing History and Ourselves National Foundation, 2010).

[104] Blanche Wiesen Cook, *Eleanor Roosevelt, Volume 3: The War Years and After, 1939-1962* (New York: Penguin, 2017), 492.

[105] Joseph P. Lash, *Eleanor: The Years Alone* (New York: W.W. Norton, 1972), 117.

[106] Hazel Rowley, *Franklin and Eleanor: An Extraordinary Marriage* (New York: Farrar, Straus & Giroux, 2010).

[107] Lash, 39.

[108] Ibid., 47.

[109] Ibid., 48.

[110] "Resolution 1, Establishment of a Commission to Deal with the Problems Raised by the Discovery of Atomic Energy." United Nations, January 24, 1946.

[111] Lash, 54.

[112] Eshet.

[113] Lash, 53.

[114] Eshet.

[115] Lash, 57

[116] Lu Hong and Scott E. Page, "Groups of diverse problem solvers can outperform groups of high-ability problem solvers," *Proceedings of the National Academy of Sciences* (November 16, 2004).

[117] Thomas W. Malone and Michael S. Bernstein, eds., *Handbook of Collective Intelligence* (Cambridge, MA: The MIT Press, 2015), 159.

[118] Allida M. Black, editor, *The Eleanor Roosevelt Papers, Volume 1: The Human Rights Years, 1945–1948* (Farmington Hills, MI: Thomson Gale), 849.

[119] Allida M. Black, editor, *The Eleanor Roosevelt Papers*, "Commission on Humans Rights verbatim record, fourteenth meeting February 4, 1947" (Farmington Hills, MI: Thomson Gale) 508–09.

[120] *Universal Declaration of Human Rights*, United Nations, 1946.

[121] Lash, 69.

[122] Ibid., 74.

[123] Eleanor Roosevelt, *On My Own: The Years Since the White House* (New York: Harper, 1958).

[124] "Final UHDR Speech", *Eleanor Roosevelt Papers Project*, Columbian College of Arts and Sciences.

[125] Peter Danchin, "The Universal Declaration of Human Rights, Drafting History, 1948," Columbia University,.

[126] Eleanor Roosevelt was nominated for the Nobel Peace Prize three times during her life, but the award went first to René Cassin, the French jurist, citing his work on the Declaration for Human Rights. When she was nominated again for an unprecedented posthumous award, Henry Kissinger wrote: "Mrs. Roosevelt was one of the great human beings of our time. She stood for peace and international understanding not only as intellectual propositions but as a way of life... a symbol of compassion in a world of increasing righteousness." (Lash, 337).

[127] US House of Representatives, *Life and Ideals of Anna Eleanor Roosevelt* (San Francisco: University Press of the Pacific, 2001).

[128] Woodrow Wilson, "Address of the President of the United States to the Senate," January 22, 1917.

[129] Stanley Meisler, *United Nations, a History* (New York: Grove Press, 1995), 2.

[130] Meisler, 16.

[131] John Cavanagh, Phyllis Bennis, and Sarah Anderson, "Coalition of the Willing or Coalition of the Coerced?" *Institute for Policy Studies* (February 26, 2003), 23.

[132] Martin Bright, Ed Vulliamy, and Peter Beaumont, "Revealed: US dirty tricks to win vote on Iraq war," *The Guardian* (March 1, 2003).

[133] In 2007, the US Congressional Budget Office estimated that the total long-term cost of the Iraq war would be $2.4 trillion, including $700 billion in interest alone. See "U.S. CBO estimates $2.4 trillion long-term war costs," *Reuters* (October 24, 2007).

[134] Based on its own survey of nearly 10,000 households in 2006-2007, the Iraq Family Health Survey estimated that there were 151,000 violent deaths in Iraq related to the war, from 2002 to 2006. See Phil Lewis, "Violence-related mortality in Iraq from 2002 to 2006," *The New England Journal of Medicine* (January 10, 2008).

[135] Steven M. Rosenthal, "Slashing Corporate Taxes: Foreign Investors Are Surprise Winners," *Washington: Tax Policy Center* (2017).

[136] Kathryn Kranhold, "You paid taxes. These corporations didn't," *The Center for Public Integrity* (April 11, 2019).

[137] Kenny Stancil, "Amazon, Facebook and other tech giants paid almost $100B less in taxes than they claimed: analysis," *Salon*, (June 1, 2021).

[138] Mary Hanbury, "11 American companies that are no longer American," *Business Insider* (August 2, 2018).

[139] Gabriel Zucman and Gus Wezerek, "This is Tax Evasion, Plain and Simple," *The New York Times* (July 7, 2021).

[140] *The Yearbook of International Organizations*, Union of International Associations (2019).

[141] Kirsten Matthews and Vivian Ho, "The grand impact of the Gates Foundation. Sixty billion dollars and one famous person can affect the spending and research focus of public agencies," *EMBO Report,* National Center for Biotechnology Information, U. S. National Library of Medicine (May 2008).

[142] Danielle Zach, D. Conor Seyle, and Jens Vestergaard Madsen, "Burden-Sharing Multi-level Governance: A Study of the Contact Group on Piracy Off the Coast of Somalia," *One Earth Future Foundation* (2013).

[143] Rephael Harel Ben-Ari, *The Legal Status of International Non-Governmental Organizations: Analysis of Past and Present Initiatives (1912-2012)* (Leiden, Netherlands: Martinus Nijhoff, 2013).

[144] Deborah D. Avant, Martha Finnemore, and Susan K. Sell, eds., *Who Governs the Globe?* (Cambridge, UK: Cambridge University Press, 2010), 5.

[145] "Gangs Beyond Borders; California and the Fight Against Transnational Organized Crime," State of California, March 2014.

[146] Thomas G. Weiss, D. Conor Seyle, and Kelsey Coolidge, "The Rise of Non-State Actors in Global Governance: Opportunities and Limitations," *The One Earth Future Foundation* (2013).

[147] Matthew Teague, "Childhood's End: A too-brief encounter with Arthur C. Clarke, the grand old man of science-fiction visionaries," *Popular Science* (August, 2004).

[148] Arthur C. Clarke, "Credo," first appearing in Clifton Fadiman, *Living Philosophies* (New York: Doubleday, 1991).

[149] Arthur C. Clarke, *Childhood's End* (New York: Random House, 1953), 67.

[150] Ibid., 172.

[151] Ibid., 177.

[152] Ibid., 178.

[153] Gary Westfahl, *William Gibson* (Champaign, IL: University of Illinois Press, 2013), 11.

[154] Westfahl, 18.

[155] Martin Walker, "Blade Runner on electro-steroids," *[Johannesburg, South Africa] Mail & Guardian* (September 1996).

[156] William Gibson, *Neuromancer* (New York: Ace Science Fiction, 1984), 51.

[157] Ibid.

[158] Robert A. Heinlein, *Stranger in a Strange Land* (New York: Putnam, 1961).

[159] Frank Herbert, *Dune* (Philadelphia: Chilton Books, 1965).

[160] Arthur C. Clarke, "The Final Goodbye," *Youtube.com* (2008).

[161] Carl Sagan, Stephen Hawking, and Arthur C. Clarke, "God, The Universe and Everything Else," *Youtube.com* (1988).

[162] Mark Farinas, "Doing Away With the Conference Room," *TrekComic.com* (October 24, 2018).

[163] Marilyn Ferguson, *The Aquarian Conspiracy* (Los Angeles: J. P. Tarcher, 1980), 98.

[164] Ferguson, 110.

[165] *The New York Times* (September 28, 1986).

[166] Marilyn Ferguson, "A Conversation with Marilyn Ferguson," *Youtube.com* (1992),.

[167] Ibid., 383-84.

[168] Ibid., 63.

[169] Ibid., 215.

[170] Ibid., 214.

[171] Ibid., 233.

[172] Ibid., 214.

[173] Ibid., 158.

[174] Ibid., 382.

[175] Elaine Woo, "Marilyn Ferguson, 70, dies; writer's 'The Aquarian Conspiracy' was pivotal in New Age movement," *The Los Angeles Times* (November 2, 2008).

[176] Paul Marks, "Interview [with Jimmy Wales]: Knowledge to the people," *New Scientist, Technology* (January 31, 2007).

[177] Marshall Poe, "The Hive: Can thousands of Wikipedians be wrong? How an attempt to build an online encyclopedia touched off history's biggest experiment in collaborative knowledge," *The Atlantic Monthly* (September 2006).

[178] F. A. Hayek, "The Use of Knowledge in Society," *The American Economic Review* No.4. Vol. XXXV (September 1945) 519–30.

[179] Michael Foucault, *Beyond structuralism and Hermeneutics* (San Francisco: Harvester Wheatsheaf, 1982).

[180] To see this in action, choose a topic on Wikipedia and click on the "talk" tab at the top of the page. Now you are behind the scenes, looking at the contributions, debates, changes and corrections that go on constantly as editors and contributors from around the world work to make the article better.

[181] Dariusz Jemielniak, *Common Knowledge, An Ethnography of Wikipedia* (Stanford, CA: Stanford University Press, 2014), 88. Jemielniak is head of the Center for Organizations and Workplaces at Kozminski University in Warsaw. He is a trustee of the Wiki Foundation and a Wikipedia Steward.

[182] "Jimbo Wales testifies before U.S. Senate Committee on Homeland Security and Government Operations," S. HRG. 110-894. E-government 2.0: improving innovation, collaboration, and access. Hearing before the Committee on Homeland Security and Governmental Affairs. United States Senate. One Hundred Tenth Congress, first session. December 11, 2007.

[183] "Jimmy Wales Responds," *Slashdot.com*, posted by Roblimo (July 28, 2004).

[184] Katherine Mangu-Ward, "Wikipedia and Beyond: Jimmy Wales' sprawling vision," *Reason* (June 2007).

[185] Jemielniak, 16.

[186] Daniel Oberhaus, "Nearly All of Wikipedia Is Written by Just 1 Percent of Its Editors," *Motherboard* (November 7, 2017)..

[187] Tom Simonite, "The Decline of Wikipedia," *MIT Technology Review* (October 22, 2013).

[188] Jemielniak, 160.

[189] Ibid., 33-35.

[190] Wikipedia: Editorial oversight and control. Wikipedia..

[191] Jemielniak, 36.

[192] Monica Anderson, Paul Hitlin, and Michelle Atkinson, "Wikipedia at 15: Millions of readers in scores of languages," *Pew Research Center* (January 14, 2016).

[193] "The top 500 sites on the web," *Alexa.com.*.

[194] "Wikipedia survives research test," *BBC.com* (December 15, 2005).

[195] Jimmy Wales, "Wikipedia is an encyclopedia," *Wikimedia* (March 8, 2005).

[196] Jemielniak, 121.

[197] Ibid., 161.

[198] Ibid., 130.

[199] Ibid., 20.

[200] Ibid., 18.

[201] Ibid., 169.

[202] Tom Simonite, "The Decline of Wikipedia," *MIT Technology Review* (July 2, 2013).

[203] Francis Fukuyama, "Friedrich A. Hayek, Big-Government Skeptic," *The New York Times* (May 6, 2012)..

[205] Robert McCrum, "The Masterpiece that Killed George Orwell," *The Guardian* (May 9, 2009).

[206] "Early History of Confucianism*,"* *Facts and Details.com* (2020).

[207] Inga Clendinnen, *Ambivalent Conquests: Maya and Spaniard in Yucatan, 1517-1570, 2nd. Ed.* (Cambridge, UK: Cambridge University Press, 1987), 70.

[208] Raymond Zhong, Paul Mozur, Jeff Kao and Aaron Krolik, "No 'Negative' News: How China Censored the Coronavirus," *The New York Times* (Jan. 13, 2021).

[209] Rachel Botsman, "Big data meets Big Brother as China moves to rate its citizens," *Wired* (October 21, 2017).

[210] Simina Mistreanu, "Life Inside China's Social Credit Laboratory," *Foreign Policy* (April 3, 2018).

[211] Muyi Xiao and Paul Mozur, "A Digital Manhunt: How Chinese Police Track Critics on Twitter and Facebook," *The New York Times* (December 31, 2021).

[212] Chris Buckley, Vivian Wang, and Keith Bradsher, "Living by the Code: In China, Covid-Era Controls May Outlast the Virus," *The New York Times* (January 30, 2022).

[213] Matt Pottinger and David Feith, "The Most Powerful Data Broker in the World Is Winning the War Against the U.S.," *The New York Times* (November 30, 2021).

[214] "Vladimir Putin calls for 'reliable' Russian version of Wikipedia", *The Guardian* (November 5, 2019).

[215] "Russia: New Law Expands Government Control Online," *Human Rights Watch* (October 31, 2019).

[216] Merrit Kennedy, "New Russian Law Gives Government Sweeping Power Over Internet," *NPR* (November 1, 2019).

[217] Tom Barned, "Saudi Arabia prosecutor says people who post satire on social media can be jailed," *The (UK) Independent* (September 5, 2018).

[218] Chris Morris, "Facebook Is Rating How Trustworthy You Are," *Fortune* (August 21, 2018).

[219] Sam Schechner and Mark Secada, "You Give Apps Sensitive Personal Information. Then They Tell Facebook: Wall Street Journal testing reveals how the social-media giant collects a wide range of private data from developers; This is a big mess," *The Wall Street Journal* (February 22, 2019).

[220] Kashmir Hill, "I Got Access to My Secret Consumer Score. Now You Can Get Yours, Too," *The New York Times* (November 4, 2019).

[221] Rachel Levinson-Waldman and Mary Pat Dwyer, "LAPD Documents Show What One Social Media Surveillance Firm Promises Police," *The Brennan Center* (November 17, 2021).

[222] Dorian Lynskey, *The Ministry of Truth; the Biography of George Orwell's 1984,* (New York: Doubleday, 2019).

[223] Ibid., 124.

[224] Big Brother's slogan in George Orwell's *1984*.

225 According to Tech Kabahren, a techie blog from India, many of the functions imagined by Orwell are now in place. Several sources cited in the blog report that the FBI has the ability from a remote location to activate any cell phone and turn its microphone into a listening device that transmits collected signals to an FBI listening post. In the last several years other governments have implemented intelligence gathering networks able to secretly intercept and analyze internet traffic passing through Skype, Google Talk, and similar message systems. They can intercept messages with keywords such as 'attack,' 'bomb,' 'blast,' or 'kill' in real time from the enormous number of tweets, status updates, emails, instant messaging transcripts, internet calls, blogs, forums, and even images exchanged on the world's networks. ("30 years of 1984: 8 Tech predictions of George Orwell that have come true," *Tech Kabahren,* (October, 2016).

226 Burns, *Deadly Decisions.*

227 Kevin Brown, "What went down (and up) in 2020 U.S. ad spending, *Advertising Age* (March 15, 2021).

228 Guy DeBord, *Society of the Spectacle* (Detroit: Black & Red, 2002). First published by Editions Buchet-Chastel in 1967 as La Société du Spectacle. The first English translation was published by Black & Red in 1970 and revised in 1977 incorporating numerous improvements suggested by friends and critics of the first translation.

229 Edward Rothstein, "Philosophers Draw On a Film Drawing On Philosophers," *The New York Times* (May 24, 2003).

230 Jean Baudrillard, *Simulations* (Cambridge, MA: SimiotextI, The MIT Press 1983).

231 Zuboff.

232 Alex Pentland, "Society's Nervous System: Building Effective Government, Energy, and Public Health Systems," *MIT Media Lab* (October, 2011).

233 Ibid.

234 Nicholas Confessore et al., "The Follower Factory," *The New York Times* (January 27, 2018).

235 Oliver Milman, "Revealed: quarter of all tweets about climate crisis produced by bots," *The Guardian* (February 21, 2020).

236 Allen Kim, "Nearly half of the Twitter accounts discussing 'reopening America' may be bots, researchers say," *CNN* (May 22, 2020).

237 Erum Salam, "Majority of misinformation came from 12 people, report finds," *The Guardian* (July 12, 2021).

238 David McCabe, "Opposition to Net Neutrality Was Faked, New York Says," *The New York Times* (May 6, 2021).

[239] Mike Elgan, "The future of 3D holograms comes into focus," *Computerworld* (January 20, 2018).

[240] Dean Nelson, "Modi: 'Magic' Modi uses hologram to address dozens of rallies at once," *The (UK) Telegraph* (May 2, 2014).

[241] Phil Gallo, "Michael Jackson Hologram Rocks Billboard Music Awards: Watch & Go Behind the Scenes," *Billboard* (May 18, 2014).

[242] Andrea Murad and Will Smale, "How hologram tech may soon replace video calls," *BBC* (December 12, 2021).

[243] Press Release: "Greg Cross wants your next employee to be an AI-powered digital human," *Soul Machines.com* (October 4, 2018).

[244] Jordan Teicher, "Could your next employee be an AI-powered digital human?" *IBM.com* (July 9, 2018).

[245] Sophie J. Nightingale and Hany Farid, "AI-synthesized faces are indistinguishable from real faces and more trustworthy," *PNAS* (February 22, 2022).

[246] J. D. Maddox, "The Day I Realized I Would Never Find Weapons of Mass Destruction in Iraq," *The New York Times* (January 29, 2020).

[247] Burns, *Deadly Decisions.*

[248] In 1967, Albert Mehrabian and his colleagues advanced the thesis that communications of feelings and attitudes rely 55 percent on body language, particularly facial expressions. 38 percent of the message relies on inflection and the tone of voice, and only 7 percent is conveyed in the words we use. This interesting but flawed insight has been broadly misinterpreted to claim that 93 percent of our human communications is nonverbal. See Albert Mehrabian, *Silent Messages: Implicit Communication of Emotions and Attitudes,* 2nd ed.), 1981,

[249] Vanessa K. Bohns, "A Face-to-Face Request Is 34 Times More Successful Than an Email," *Harvard Business Review* (April 11, 2017).

[250] Michael D. Shear and David E. Sanger, "Cameras Off: G7 Summit Heralds the Return of In-Person Diplomacy," *The New York Times* (June 1, 2021).

[251] David Gelles, "What Bosses Really Think About the Future of the Office," *The New York Times* (November 12, 2021).

[252] Recent studies have suggested that these functions may occur more in both areas than originally thought, and may actually migrate to other parts of the brain if the original area is damaged.

[253] Thomas Lewis et al., *A General Theory of Love* (New York: Vintage, 2001).

[254] "Emotional Contagion: Why Emotions Are Contagious," *Healthline.com* (2019).

[255] R. W. Picard, "Affective Computing," *M.I.T Media Laboratory* (November 26, 1995)..

[256] "Share of children owning tablets and smartphones in the United Kingdom from 2018, by age," *Statistica.com.*.

[257] Sonia Livingstone, "Reading the runes to anticipate children's digital futures," *London School of Economics and Political Science* (January 6th, 2016).

[258] Sean Coughlan, "Most children sleep with mobile phone beside bed," *BBC*, (January, 2020).

[259] Donna Hermawati et al., "Early electronic screen exposure and autistic-like symptoms," *Intractable & Rare Diseases Research (IRDR)*, (Bethesda, MD: U.S. National Library of Medicine, February, 2018).

[260] "Community Life Survey 2018-19", *UK Department for Digital Culture, Media & Sport* (July 2019)..

[261] Brian A, Primack et al., "Social Media Use and Perceived Social Isolation Among Young Adults in the U.S.," *American Journal of Preventive Medicine* (July 2017).

[262] Ajit Shah, "The Relationship between General Population Suicide Rates and the Internet: A Cross-National Study," *Suicide and Life-Threatening Behavior* Vol. 40, No. 2, (2010), 146-150..

[263] Patent Number US9427185B2, issued 2016, "User behavior monitoring on a computerized device."

[264] Lora Kolodny, "Affectiva raises $14 million to bring apps, robots emotional intelligence," *Techcrunch.com* (May 25, 2016).

[265] Darren Davidson, "Facebook targets 'insecure' young people," *The Australian Business Review* (May 1, 2017)..

[266] Curtis Silver, "Patents Reveal How Facebook Wants To Capture Your Emotions, Facial Expressions And Mood," *Forbes* (June 8, 2017)..

[267] Matt Day, "Amazon Is Working on a Device That Can Read Human Emotions," *Bloomberg* (May 23, 2019).

[268] Charles Duhigg, "What Google Learned From Its Quest to Build the Perfect Team," *The New York Times* (February 25, 2016).

[269] Anita Woolley, Christopher F. Chabris, Alex Pentland, Nada Hashmi, and Thomas Malone, "Evidence from a Collective Intelligence Factor in the Performance of Human Groups," *Science* Vol. 330, Issue 6004, (October 2010), 686-688.

[270] James Wallace, "Aerospace Notebook: Machismo Cockpit Culture Puts Safety in Jeopardy," *Seattle Post-Intelligencer* (November 20, 2007).

271 Dr. Gerald B Healy, "Ending Medical Errors with Airline Industry's Help," *Boston Globe* (January 8, 2008).

272 Jürgen Habermas, *The Structural Transformation of the Public Sphere: An Inquiry into a Category of Bourgeois Society*, (Cambridge, MA, The MIT Press, 1991), 30, translation from the original German, published 1962.

273 "The Flagellants Attempt to Repel the Black Death, 1349," EyeWitness to History, (2010). /

274 Stephen Greenberg, "The Dreadful Visitation: Public Health and Public Awareness in Seventeenth-century London," *Bulletin of the Medical Library Association*, National Library of Medicine (October, 1997).

275 "Spanish flu: The deadliest pandemic in history," *Live Science.com* (March, 2020).

276 William J. Broad, and Dan Levin, "Trump Muses About Light as Remedy, but Also Disinfectant, Which Is Dangerous," *The New York Times* (April 24, 2020).

277 David Clarissa, et al, "Reliance on Facebook for news and its influence on political engagement," *PLOS One* (March, 2019).

278 Andrey Simonov et al, "The Persuasive Effect of Fox News: Non-Compliance With Social Distancing During The COVID-19 Pandemic," *NBER Working Paper Series*, National Bureau of Economic Research (May, 2020).

279 Matt Laslo, "The Fight Over Section 230 — and the Internet as We Know It," *Wired Magazine* (August 2019).

280 Hilary Brueck, "Brazil's tragic ivermectin frenzy is a warning to the US, experts say," *Insider.com* (October 4, 2021).

281 Jake Horton, "Covid Brazil: Why could Bolsonaro face charges?," *BBC* (October 27, 2021).

282 Vanessa Barbara, "Miracle Cures and Magnetic People. Brazil's Fake News Is Utterly Bizarre," *The New York Times* (July 5, 2021).

283 Mark Scott, "Facebook did little to moderate posts in the world's most violent countries," *Politico* (October 25, 2021).

284 Michelle Nichols and Giulia Paravicini, "About 350,000 people in Ethiopia's Tigray in famine -U.N. analysis," Reuters (June 11, 2021).

285 Nick Robins-Early, "How Facebook Is Stoking a Civil War in Ethiopia," *Vice World News* (November 8, 2021).

[286] Sam McNeil and Victoria Milko, "Hate speech in Myanmar continues to thrive on Facebook," *Associated Press* (November 18, 2021).

[287] Max Fisher, "Belonging Is Stronger Than Facts: The Age of Misinformation," *The New York Times* (May 13, 2021).

[288] Zeynep Tufekci, "How social media took us from Tahrir Square to Donald Trump," *MIT Technology Review* (August 14, 2018).

[289] Fran Parkin, *Max Weber* (Abbington, UK: Routledge, 2002), 34.

[290] Don Tapscott, "How the blockchain is changing money and business," *TED Talks* (September 16, 2016).

[291] Lawrence Mishel and Julia Wolfe, "CEO compensation has grown 940% since 1978: Typical worker compensation has risen only 12% during that time," *Economic Policy Institute* (August 2019).

[292] "Global Wealth Report 2020," *Credit Suisse* (2020).

[293] "Hunger in America is Growing," *Feeding America.com* (2020).

[294] Jesse Eisinger, Jeff Ernsthausen and Paul Kiel, "The Secret IRS Files: Trove of Never-Before-Seen Records Reveal How the Wealthiest Avoid Income Tax," *ProPublica.com* (June 8, 2021).

[295] "Public trust in federal government near historic lows for more than a decade," *Pew Research Center* (September 14, 2020).

[296] Daily Kos/National Politics Survey, October 2021.

[297] Jennifer Agiesta and Ariel Edwards-Levy, "CNN Poll: Most Americans feel democracy is under attack in the US," *CNN* (September 15, 2021).

[298] Julie Bosman, Jan Hoffman, Margot Sanger-Katz and Tim Arango, "Who Are the Unvaccinated in America? There's No One Answer," *The New York Times* (July 31, 2021).

[299] 21st Annual Edelman Trust Barometer, *Edelman.com*, 2021.

[300] Wael Ghonim, "Let's design social media that drives real change", *TED Talks* (2016).

[301] Ibid.

[302] Nancy Scola, "Ghonim: Our Revolution Is Like Wikipedia," *Personal Democracy Forum: Tech President* (February 14, 2011).

[303] Nesrine Malik, "The Arab spring wasn't in vain. Next time will be different," *The Guardian* (December 21, 2020).

[304] Louis Rosenberg, "Human Swarming and the Future of Collective Intelligence," *Singularity.com* (July, 2015).

[305] Adam B. Ellick, and Irfan Ashraf, "Class Dismissed: Malala's Story," *The New York Times* (October 9, 2012).

[306] Damian Carrington, "Our leaders are like children, school strike founder tells climate summit," *The Guardian* (December 4, 2018).

[307] "Transcript: Greta Thunberg's Speech at the U.N. Climate Action Summit," *NPR* (September 23, 2019).

[308] Trevor Marshallsea, "Greta's story," *Ecologist* (February 28, 2020).

[309] Abraham Lincoln, First Inaugural Address, March 4, 1861.

[310] Martin Pengelly, "Drunken Giuliani urged Trump to 'just say we won' on election night, book says," *The Guardian* (July 13, 2021).

[311] Tierney Sneed and Matt Shuham, "The Capitol Mob Was Only the Finale of Trump's Conspiracy to Overturn the Election," *Talking Points Memo* (January 25, 2021).

[312] Katie Benner, "Trump Pressed Justice Dept. to Declare Election Results Corrupt, Notes Show," *The New York Times* (July 30, 2021).

[313] Josh Kovensky, "Notes from Top DOJ Official on Trump's Conspiracy to Overturn 2020 Election," *Talking Points Memo* (July 30, 2021).

[314] "American Oversight Obtains Seven Phony Certificates of Pro-Trump Electors," *American Oversight* (March 2, 2021).

[315] Jeffrey Clarke Draft Letter, Dept of Justice, (December 28, 2020).

[316] Kyle Cheney, "Trump calls on GOP state legislatures to overturn election results," *Politico* (November 21, 2020).

[317] Bob Woodward and Robert Costa, *Peril*, (New York: Simon and Schuster, 2021).

[318] Jane Lytvyenko and Molly Hensley-Clancy, "The Rioters Who Took Over the Capitol Have Been Planning Online in the Open For Weeks," *BuzzFeed News* (January 6, 2021).

[319] Sheera Frenkel, "The storming of Capitol Hill was organized on social media," *The New York Times* (January 6, 2021).

[320] Dan Mihalopoulos, "Chicago-Area Billionaire Gave Millions To 'Patriots' Group That Backed Pro-Trump Rally," *WBEZ Chicago* (January 12, 2021).

[321] Celine Castronuovo, "Officials determined troubling posts did not indicate threat ahead of Capitol riot," *The Hill* (April 4, 2021).

[322] Michael S. Schmidt, "Trump Says Pence Can Overturn His Loss in Congress. That's Not How It Works," *The New York Times* (January 5, 2021).

[323] Joseph Tanfani, Michael Berens, and Ned Parker, "How Trump's pied pipers rallied a faithful mob to the Capitol," *Reuters* (January 11, 2021).

[324] Jemima McEvoy, "Trump Raised $250 Million Since Election to Challenge Outcome — Here's Where Most Of the Money Will Actually Go," *Forbes* (January 31, 2021).

[325] Luke Broadwater, "Republican lawmakers are accused of giving Capitol tours to insurrectionists before the riot as new inquiries are opened," *The New York Times* (January 13, 2021).

[326] Betsy Woodruff Swan and Nicholas Wu, "Secret Service warned Capitol Police about violent threats 1 day before Jan. 6," *Politico* (August 25, 2021).

[327] Luke Broadwater and Mark Mazzetti, *"*At the Willard and the White House, the Jan. 6 Panel Widens Its Net," *The New York Times* (Nov. 9, 2021).

[328] Robert Farley, Lori Robertson, Eugene Kiely, and D'Angelo Gore, "Debunking Trump's Latest Arizona Election Claims," *FactCheck.org - Annenberg Public Policy Center* (July 20, 2021).

[329] Clara Hendrickson, "Trump repeated lies about Michigan's election before pro-Trump supporters stormed Capitol," *The Detroit Free Press* (January 6, 2021).

[330] Maggie Haberman, "Trump Told Crowd 'You Will Never Take Back Our Country With Weakness,'" *The New York Times* (January 6, 2021).

[331] Associated Press, "The 'Oath Keepers': U.S. charges against Capitol riot suspects detail paramilitary tactics, violent rhetoric," *AZ Central* (January 19, 2021).

[332] Sunlen Serfaty, Devan Cole and Alex Rogers, "As riot raged at Capitol, Trump tried to call senators to overturn election," *CNN* (January 8, 2021).

[333] Hunter, "Jim Jordan, Matt Gaetz begged Trump to call off violent crowd during Jan. 6 insurrection," *Daily Kos* (August 30, 2021).

[334] Christina Zhao, "Jan. 6 panel has 'firsthand testimony' that Ivanka asked Trump to intervene during riot, Cheney says," *NBC News* (January 2, 2022).

[335] Kaitlan Collins, Zachary Cohen, Barbara Starr, and Jennifer Hansler, "Pence took lead as Trump initially resisted sending National Guard to Capitol," *CNN* (January 7, 2021).

[336] In an extraordinary example of multimedia journalism, *The New York Times* created a 40-minute video record of the January 6 attack which should be required watching for anyone interested in understanding the real nature of the insurrection. "Inside the Capitol Riot: An Exclusive Video Investigation," *The New York Times* (June 30, 2021).

[337] Robert A. Pape and Keven Ruby, "The Capitol Rioters Aren't Like Other Extremists," *The Atlantic Monthly* (February 2, 2021).

[338] Ibid.

[339] *The Insurrection Index* (PublicWise, January 2022).

[340] Jane Mayer, "The Big Money Behind the Big Lie," *The New Yorker* (August 2, 2021).

[341] Milton Friedman, *Capitalism and Freedom* (Chicago: University of Chicago Press, 1962).

[342] George Steiner, *After Babel*: *Aspects of Language and Translation* (Oxford, UK: Oxford University Press, 1998).

[343] Ibid.

[344] Charles Darwin, *The Descent of Man, and Selection in Relation to Sex* (New York: D. Appleton, 1878), 98.

[345] Edward O. Wilson, *On Human Nature* (Cambridge, MA: Harvard University Press, 1979), 153.

[346] Wilson, 207.

[347] Wendy C. King, et al, "Time trends and factors related to COVID-19 vaccine hesitancy from January-May 2021 among US adults: Findings from a large-scale national survey," *MedRxiv* (July 23, 2021).

[348] "COVID-19 vaccine is associated with fewer asymptomatic SARS-CoV-2 infections," *St. Jude Children's Research Hospital* (May 6, 2021).

[349] Robin I. M. Dunbar, "The Social Brain Hypothesis and Human Evolution," *Oxford Research Encyclopedia, Psychology* (March 2016).

[350] John Hawks, "How Has the Human Brain Evolved?," *Scientific American* (July 2013).

[351] Eze, M. O. *Intellectual History in Contemporary South Africa* (London, Palgrave Macmillan, 2010) 190–191.

[352] "Hunhu/Ubuntu in the Traditional Thought of Southern Africa," *Internet Encyclopedia of Philosophy*.

[353] K. Gyekye, *Tradition and Modernity: Reflections on the African Experience* (New York: Oxford University Press, 1997).

[354] Eric K. Yamamoto, E.K. 1997. "Race Apologies," *Journal of Gender, Race and Justice (1998*, Vol. 1) 47-88.

[355] Desmond Tutu, *No Future without Forgiveness.* (New York: Doubleday, 1999).

[356] Barack Obama, "Memorial Address for Nelson Mandela," *American Rhetoric, Online Speech Bank* (December 10, 2013).

[357] Jessica Heron-Langton, "Central Saint Martins students are making scrubs for NHS workers," *Dazed Digital.com* (April 6, 2020).

[358] Barbara Mack, "Florida Woman Inadvertently Starts Revolution Inside Convenience Store," *Sunny Skyz.com* (August 6, 2021).

[359] Orwell, George, *1984* (London, Secker and Warburg, 1949).

[361] Rachel Caspari, "The Evolution of Grandparents," *Scientific American* (August, 2011).

[362] Robin McKee, "Wisdom of grandparents helped rise of prehistoric man," *The Guardian* (July 23, 2011).

[363] Pallab Ghosh, "Neanderthal extinction not caused by brutal wipe out," *BBC* (February 9, 2022).

[364] Caspari.

[365] Adrian F. Ward, "Scientists Probe Human Nature--and Discover We Are Good, After All: Recent studies find our first impulses are selfless," *Scientific American* (November 20, 2012).

[366] Rutger Bregman, "The real Lord of the Flies: what happened when six boys were shipwrecked for 15 months," *The Guardian* (May 9, 2020).

[367] Elyse Wanshel, "Teen Girls Organized A 10,000-Person Black Lives Matter Protest in Nashville: Six teenagers pulled off the region's largest protest against racism and police brutality in recent memory, local news reported," *Huffington Post* (June 5, 2020).

[368] Caitlin Oprysko, "There is something different here: Obama says he's encouraged by mass protests of George Floyd killing," *Politico* (June 3, 2020).

[369] Pierre Teilhard de Chardin, *Phenomenon* (in King, 66.).

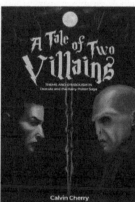

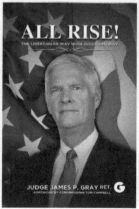